FAITHFULNESS AND HOLINESS

FAITHFULNESS & HOLINESS

THE WITNESS OF J. C. RYLE

AN APPRECIATION BY

J. I. PACKER

Including the full text of the first edition of Ryle's classic book, *Holiness*

WHEATON, ILLINOIS

Faithfulness and Holiness: The Witness of J. C. Ryle

Copyright © 2002 by J. I. Packer

Published by Crossway
         1300 Crescent Street
         Wheaton, Illinois 60187

Cover design: Studio Gearbox

Cover photo: Getty Images

First printing, 2002

Reprinted in Trade Paperback, 2011

Unless otherwise noted, Scripture quotations are from the King James Version of the Bible.

Scripture quotations marked ESV are from the ESV® Bible (*The Holy Bible, English Standard Version®*), copyright © 2001 by Crossway. All rights reserved.

ISBN 13: 978-1-4335-1582-8

Library of Congress Cataloging-in-Publication Data
Packer, J. I. (James Innell)
   Faithfulness and Holiness : the witness of J.C. Ryle : an appreciation / J.I. Packer ;
including the full text of the first edition of J.C. Ryle's classic book Holiness.
     p.   cm.
   Includes bibliographical references and index.
   ISBN 1-58134-358-2 (alk. paper)
   1. Ryle, J. C. (John Charles), 1816-1900. 2. Holiness. I. Ryle J. C. (John
Charles), 1816-1900. Holiness. II. Title.
BX5199.R9 P33   2002
283'.092—dc21   2001006920

Crossway is a publishing ministry of Good News Publishers.

VP   22   21   20   19   18
15   14   13   12   11   10   9   8   7   6   5   4   3   2

CONTENTS

FAITHFULNESS AND HOLINESS
J. I. Packer

HOLINESS
J. C. Ryle

Author's Note

The following pages contain an expanded version of material used in addresses commemorating Bishop John Charles Ryle in London (Great St. Helen's, Bishopsgate), Hove, Guildford, and Liverpool (All Saints, Childwall) in September 2000. Special thanks are due to the Rev. Eric Bramhall (Vicar of Childwall), whose invitation initiated the tour; to the St. Antholin Trustees, who sponsored the London lecture; and to a number of friends who gave hospitality to a wandering scholar on his travels. And as an old-fashioned geek wedded to his typewriter, I must also thank Naomi Packer for her sterling work on my behalf.

FOREWORD

The present volume, devoted to Bishop John Charles Ryle, who died in 1900, just over a century ago, is really two books in one.

The first is a survey of Ryle's life and work, highlighting his quality and stature as an English evangelical leader.

The second is a reprint of the first edition of his book *Holiness*, published in 1877.

Why have these items been put together?

The short answer is: each is needed if Ryle's strength as a mentor both for his own contemporaries and for ourselves is to be properly appreciated.

Ryle, who came to faith in the year of Queen Victoria's accession and died one year before she did, was, from start to finish, three things together—an evangelical believer; an Anglican Churchman; and a pastoral instructor. As an evangelical, he maintained the style and substance of those clergy who gathered first around George Whitefield and then around John Newton in the eighteenth century. As a Churchman, he vigorously upheld the Reformed, anti-Roman Catholic theology of the Thirty-nine Articles, along with the Protestant catholicity embodied in the Book of Common Prayer. And as a pastor he taught Christian conduct, devotion, and character transformed by the Holy Spirit in the way that the great seventeenth-century Puritans had done before him. All the best elements of the Church of England's evangelical heritage were embodied in him, arguably in the best way. He was a big man both physically and spiritually, and his brains, energy, vision, drive, independence, clear head, kind heart, fair mind, salty speech, good sense, impatience with stupidity, firmness of principle, and freedom from inhibitions would have made him a leader in any field. As it was, insofar as Anglican evangelicals had one acknowledged leader for the last third of the nineteenth century, Ryle was that man.

Ryle honed his skills, but never changed his tune. While industrial, commercial, and educational development brought a new coolness and sophistication to England's national culture, and while the Church of England struggled with a plethora of new emphases, visions, tasks, and cross-currents of debate, Ryle remained the man he had been before 1850. Thus, though thought of as a mover and shaker when he was young, he was widely written off as a dinosaur in his last years, and that undervaluing of him continues still. The essay that makes up the first part of the present book seeks to correct this.

The aim of the second part is that today's readers should see the wisdom and feel the force of Ryle as a spiritual guide. To this end, reprinting the first edition of *Holiness* in its entirety seemed the best way to go, for several reasons.

First, the alternative—reprinting selected snippets from Ryle on a number of different topics—has against it the fact that Ryle's public utterances (which most chapters in his topical books evidently are) do not excerpt or abbreviate well. Ryle was a clear, strong, discursive thinker who enforced his points by cumulative effect, using his quick-fire drumbeat rhetoric to work each up to a climax that is at once a hammer blow and a release of mental tension. Clearly, this was his pulpit style, and it goes far to explain his effectiveness as a preacher. Also, each section of his discourses gains strength of impact from its place in the overall formal structure, of which excerpting inevitably loses sight. Fairness to Ryle, therefore, seemed to demand that whole chapters—that is, entire messages—be reproduced.

Second, while many of Ryle's books, including even the second edition of *Holiness* (1879, often reprinted), impress the reader as a set of some twenty coordinate yet separate messages on a single multi-faceted theme, rather than as a series of stages in a single line of thought, these seven chapters were meant to be read as a set, restoring biblical breadth and depth to evangelical minds that had been swept away by fashionable holiness teaching that was actually extreme, shallow, biblically incorrect, and a hindrance to growth in grace. Ryle's response was not to cross swords with its exponents, but to lay out afresh, biblically, systematically, and in practical terms, the true fundamentals of Christian sanctity, with constant appeal to Puritan and other pundits who had trodden this path before him. Earlier versions of the chapters on Sanctification, Holiness, the Fight, and Assurance had already been published as tracts, but the rest was new, called forth by the corrective strategy the author was fulfilling. These seven chapters are the nearest thing to a treatise that Ryle ever composed, and they enable one to assess the range and balance of his mind, and the shrewdness of his judgment on spiritual things, better than any alternative selection of items would do.

Third, while much of Ryle seems dated, culturally and situationally, what he has to say on the interior aspects of personal holiness in Christianity is of perennial importance. Though Ryle's rhetoric retains its Victorian tinge, his points, biblical and Puritan as they are, are uniformly relevant to Christian living here and now, and indeed speak as pungently to our own shallownesses and superficialities as they did to the counterparts of these lapses a century and a quarter ago.

Lampooning Bishop Ryle as a ham-fisted, Bible-punching caveman, a heavy-handed primitive, a bull in a china shop, and a faded old clown, has been a popular sport among non-evangelicals from Ryle's day to our own. But I see him as a single-minded Christian communicator of profound biblical, theological, and pastoral wisdom, a man and minister of giant personal stature and electric force of utterance that sympathetic readers still feel ("unction" was the old name for it), and I aim to present him as such. I think this added material will both confirm my estimate and enrich my readers.

What is offered, then, in the second part of this book is simply the best of Ryle the Puritan-type pastor. Real Christians will find it a gold mine, a feast, a spur and a heart-warmer, food, drink, medicine, and a course of vitamins, all in one. Reading it will, I trust, confirm to you the estimate of Ryle in my essay as a great man and—more important!—fill your heart with the realism, wisdom, energy, lowliness, sensitivity, love, and joy that come from Christ. So may Ryle truly come into his own in all our lives.

—*J. I. Packer*

1

A Great Man

Three days before I sat down to write these pages I told a Canadian clergy friend that I had been in England giving commemorative lectures on Bishop Ryle, who died just a century ago. "Ryle!" said he: "Isn't he wonderful? I read a chapter of Ryle as a devotional every morning. I'm just finishing *Holiness* and then I'll start on *Practical Religion*." There was one man to whom Ryle was still speaking, a hundred years after his death. The ongoing sales of Ryle's books around the world show that there are many others who value him as my friend does. Here, then, it seems, is a pastor, teacher, and bishop worth knowing about, and it is both a privilege and a pleasure to endeavor to introduce a new generation to him.

Who was Ryle? Born in 1816, the son of a Macclesfield silk manufacturer and banker who went bankrupt in 1841, he was a long-time country clergyman who over a generation established himself as a foremost spokesman for evangelical concerns. Then in 1880, at the age of 64, he was made the first bishop of the city and diocese of Liverpool, where he worked tirelessly and fruitfully till he retired and died twenty years later. Preaching in the procathedral three days after Ryle's burial, Canon Richard Hobson, a senior clergyman who had been in the diocese from its foundation, declared: "A great man has just now fallen in Israel, in the decease of the dear Bishop. Yes, he was great through the abounding grace of God. He was great in stature; great in mental power; great in spirituality; great as a preacher and expositor of God's most holy Word; great in hospitality; great as a writer of Gospel tracts; great as an author of works that will long live; great as a Bishop of the Reformed Evangelical Protestant Church of England, of which he was a noble defender; great as first Bishop of Liverpool. I am bold to say, that perhaps few men in the nineteenth century did as much for God, for truth, and for righteousness, among the English speaking race, and in the world, as our late Bishop."[1] This was, I think, a just estimate, which the following pages will confirm.

I like to call Ryle "the Puritan Bishop," not just because it is factually and historically warranted (though indeed it is, as we shall see), but to make a point—more exactly, two points, both basic if we are to understand this man.

First: When I call Ryle the Puritan bishop, I am identifying the version of Christianity that he stood for. I am using the word as he himself used it, as a label for a type of evangelical believer that emerged in the Church of England in the sixteenth century and reached its high peak of development in the seventeenth century in men like Richard Baxter, John Owen, Richard Sibbes, John Flavel, Thomas Brooks, Thomas Manton, Thomas Watson, Robert Traill, William Bridge, Thomas Goodwin, Stephen Charnock, Jeremiah Burroughs, John Bunyan, William Gurnall, and others of similar outlook. This type was in Ryle's view, as in mine, the best type of evangelical that the world has seen, and for Ryle that meant, quite simply, the best type of Christian. Here, too, I agree with him. As a matter of history, this evangelical ideal was standard in England for at least three centuries, from 1600 to 1900, and among Anglicans—certainly among Anglican bishops!—Ryle was the last outstanding representative of it in its pure form. To be sure, he would think it tragic that such a thing should be said of him a hundred years after his death, for he believed that maintaining the Puritan ideal and grooming clergy in it is a permanent necessity for Anglican spiritual health; and who am I to disagree with him on that? The fact remains, however, that his embodiment of the Puritan outlook has not been matched in ability or influence by anyone in the Church of England since his day.

Second: When I call Ryle the Puritan bishop, I am not distinguishing him from some other Ryle who was not a Puritan bishop, but I am claiming him as a Puritan bishop par excellence, preeminent, above any other bishop, before or since, who might have attracted the adjective "Puritan" to himself. As a matter of fact, from the eighteenth to the twentieth century, none did. There were Puritan bishops in the seventeenth century: Hall, Davenant, Usher, Reynolds, Leighton, and Hopkins, for instance—and Hooper and Grindal at least were sixteenth-century representatives of the type—but Ryle seems to me to excel them all. A worthy appreciation of Ryle's greatness requires, as it seems to me, that I enter this claim at the outset, and then spend my strength making it good.

With Hobson, therefore, I designate the Puritan bishop, John Charles Ryle, a great man. But what is meant when we say that? What makes a man great? What warrants us in so describing him? Not everyone who can fairly be called good, worthy, bold, wise, forceful, thrustful, principled, unbudging, down-to-earth, clear-headed, large-hearted, and well-balanced (all of which adjectives fit Ryle) deserves to be called great; what makes the difference? What are the further qualities that distinguish a great man from other good men? There are, I think, three.

First, there is his *achievement*. Great persons make their mark in their own sphere, whatever that is. (Think of Martin Luther and Albert Einstein.) Second, there is his *impact*. Great persons become inspirers and energizers of others, benchmark figures whose personal ideals and ways of behaving set standards for others that were not set, or at least not taken seriously, before. (Think of John Wesley and Winston Churchill.) Third, there is his *universality*. Great persons transcend the limits of their own age, and embody insight and wisdom for all who come after them. (Think of Augustine and John Calvin.) By these criteria Ryle was most certainly a great man. He made his mark in his own day as a leader who had a fine brain; an effective, in-your-face way with words; a clear and compelling vision of spiritual reality; outstanding pastoral power deployed on paper in more than a dozen large books and over two hundred tracts of various sizes, with a total circulation of twelve million in at least a dozen languages; and impressive organizing skills, as his twenty years in Liverpool most fully showed. His ministry had a life-changing impact on many in his own time, as his writings have had since. And though he was a Victorian of the Victorians, when you read him today you hardly notice his Victorianism; what grabs you is the vividness, vigor, and cumulative clarity with which he sets forth truth about God, the human heart, Jesus Christ our Savior, the Holy Spirit our Sanctifier, the Holy Scriptures as the sole source of our knowledge of divine things, the disciplines and duties of godliness to which gospel grace calls us, and the constitutional commitment of the Church of England to all this. Ryle was a popular communicator with solid learning and great flair, and his books on Christian basics, with his expositions of the four Gospels and his two stunning studies of Anglican evangelical heroes, belong among the all-time Christian classics; their quality becomes ever more apparent as the years go by. Great books have been described as the lifeblood of master spirits. This description most surely applies to the works of J. C. Ryle. Judged by his achievements, impact, and universality, therefore, this man was outstanding, and it is high time he was appreciated at his true worth.

2

A GREAT VICTORIAN

Ryle, as I said, was a dyed-in-the-wool Victorian—actually, an early Victorian, who became a Christian in the year that Victoria became queen, whose views on everything were basically settled by 1850, and who throughout his episcopate seemed to his non-evangelical peers like a dinosaur. (The same was often said of the Anglican evangelical constituency as a whole, but that is another story.) Ryle's Victorianism has sometimes hindered full appreciation of his stature; so it is as well to come to terms with it now, before our profiling of him as a man of God goes any further.

Today, a century on since Queen Victoria died, we find it hard to tune in to any of the great Victorians—Dickens, Gladstone, Newman, Tennyson, Spurgeon, Florence Nightingale, Ryle, or whoever—because English-speaking culture is still somewhat in reaction against the value-system which they all embodied. It is not just that they were idealists who took life seriously, whereas we today are disillusioned debunkers who don't; it is, quite precisely, that they shared a whole series of specific assumptions about community life that our alienated age finds both comic and repellent, so that the people themselves strike us as remote and slightly weird. That makes it harder to grasp the greatness of a leader like Ryle than it is to measure the genius of great men further from us—Athanasius and Augustine and Anselm and Bernard and Luther and Calvin and Cranmer and Cromwell and Whitefield and Edwards and Wesley and Wilberforce, for example. Ryle transcended the limits of his time, as did all the men just mentioned, but he was cast in the early Victorian mould, and unless we take account of this we shall not properly understand him.

Think back for a moment, then, into the Victorian world. In that world society was stratified by privilege. At the top were the aristocracy, the "good" families with titles, long pedigrees, fine country estates, and relatively old money. Next came the learned professions—scholars, lawyers, physicians, and clergy, plus those army officers, bankers, engineers, gentlemen farmers, and factory owners whose lineage showed them to be "quality." In these two classes males were "gentlemen" and females were "ladies"; others were not so called.[1] Next in line down were the tenant farmers, the newly rich, and the commercial classes, who practiced "trade," the vulgar business of making things, supplying goods and services, and so turning a profit. Then at the bottom of the heap was the servant class from which domestics, laborers, and factory hands were drawn, persons who were taught to look up to their "betters" and never to act "above their station." These were the poor. As a hymn from that era, "All Things Bright and Beautiful," expresses it:

> The rich man in his castle, the poor man at his gate,
> God made them high and lowly, and ordered their estate.

So the first Victorians as a body assumed, and Ryle with them,[2] though, as we shall see, his circumstances burned out of him any temptation to snobbery and paternalism that might have been there before.

Then the overall Victorian mood was upbeat to the point of complacency. England was leading the world commercially; England had an empire on which the sun never set; England, unlike so much of Europe, had peace at home; being English was something to be proud of. Everyone's duty was to maintain, develop, and adorn the existing order of things, and not rock the British boat. Gravity and pomposity, social conservatism and stylized philanthropy, doing one's duty and setting a good example, were the prime virtues of the "haves"; honesty, reliability, hard work, and self-help were the prime virtues of the "have-nots." Most Victorians thought of Protestant Christianity, institutionalized in the national Church, as England's religion, and (most would have added) a good thing too; for Roman Catholicism, in addition to being wrong on basics, was essentially foreign, majored in superstitious priestcraft, abused the conscience, and damped down all forms of individual and corporate enterprise. As writers such as Anthony Trollope show, the Church of England, like Parliament, was felt to benefit English people less by what it did or failed to do than simply by being there, and so keeping worse things away. Such was the mind-set of the world to which Ryle belonged, and within which he did his own Christian thinking.

Yet Ryle's early Victorianism is, as was said, remarkably unobtrusive in his published writings. There are several reasons for this.

First, his brisk, spare, punchy style on paper, with its cultivated forcefulness, its use of the simplest words, its fusillades of short, one-clause sentences under weighty parallel headings, its rib-jabbing drumbeat rhetoric, its easy logical flow, its total lack of sentimentality, and its resolve to call a spade a spade—a style that he achieved, so he said, by crucifying the style he had before—owed nothing to the sluggish longwindedness of most Victorian literary models.

Second, Ryle's avowed concern was to revivify the English evangelical heritage of the three centuries before his time, without involving himself too deeply in the detailed debates of his own day that, however they turned out, would not have had this enlivening effect. When he expressed his mind on controverted Church questions, it was always to clear the way for what occupied his heart, namely, making God's grace in Christ effectively known nationwide. His well-informed urging that the way forward here was to go back to the old paths (*Old Paths* is actually the title of one of his books) set him apart from most Victorian thought.

Third, the things Ryle opposed in a direct way—half-heartedness and self-deception in religion, and the Roman Catholic system, and the conceit, skepticism, and indefiniteness of Anglican liberal theology and formal ritualistic worship—are still with us, so that it is not hard to read Ryle as if he wrote directly for us of the twenty-first century. On all these matters Ryle is blunt and plain, and hits nails on the head with prophetic power that readers feel today.

Fourth, Ryle's method was always to expound Scripture with didactic application to real human needs, or else to narrate heroic history with a biblical assessment and contrast with his own times at every turn of the road, and never to claim, concede, or imply that the nineteenth century was in any way wiser than earlier eras had been.

These features of his work raised him above the typical Victorian limitations and established him as a mentor for would-be biblical Christians in every age.

To write Ryle off simply because he was a Victorian, therefore, would be the height of folly. Wisdom prompts us, rather, to recognize him as a gifted exponent of the everlasting gospel of Jesus Christ, and to listen to him accordingly.

3

A GREAT SUFFERER

Ryle was a big man (six feet three and a half inches tall, large-boned, 220 pounds in weight), and had a big voice: stentorian, some called it. Always strong-minded and energetic, he never let the grass grow under his feet, but behaved in public as a mover and shaker, speaking and acting in a brusque, leaderlike, no-nonsense manner. He had been a sportsman, captaining first Eton and then Oxford at cricket, and when he was fifty-seven he declared that captaincy had given him "power of commanding, of managing, organizing and directing, of seeing through men's capacities and using every man in the post to which he was best suited, of bearing and forbearing, of keeping men around me in good temper, which I have found of infinite use."[1] His brilliant mind, powerful memory, and ready tongue had gained him an outstanding first class in his Oxford degree, and he was ever a practical, forthright, down-to-earth realist, impatient with evasion and inaction, and unable to suffer fools or frivolity gladly. So he was admired; but the other side of this, as one might expect, was that many people found him formidable, and in the early years of his ministry especially he was felt to be cool and standoffish in ordinary social relationships. No doubt his emotional and relational reserve was largely natural, but other factors operated. For several years, for instance, he cut down on socializing because he was dodging young women who wanted to marry him. And his sense of distance from other people whom he met was enormously intensified by his experience of the riches-to-rags event of his father's bankruptcy, which scarred him for life and left him in his Victorian milieu a fish out of water. The shame of finding himself cut off from his titled and moneyed friends in Cheshire and elsewhere, and reduced to "such thorough poverty, that I have often hardly known how to get on,"[2] and having to start a new life in a new place in a different social bracket, left him permanently raw inside. By Victorian standards this was the ultimate disgrace, and it was all the more painful in view of Ryle's rosy prospects before the crash. In his Autobiography of 1873 he lifts the veil on this.

Suffering, says the New Testament, is par for the Christian course. The original Puritans had been great sufferers,[3] and in 1646 John Geree, a Puritan ejected from his pastorate for being a Royalist, wrote (in his tract, *The Character of an Old English Puritan*) that *Vincit qui patitur* (he who suffers conquers) was in practice the Puritan's motto.[4] Ryle, the Puritan bishop, had suffered too, and this was part of the making of him, as we shall soon see.

Ryle's very frank and painfully honest Autobiography[5] was not written for publication but for his family. It starts thus: "I dictate this autobiography of myself at the age of fifty-seven [i.e., in 1873] in order that my children may possess some accurate account of my history of life, after I am dead."[6] Questions arise at once. First, to whom did he dictate it? That is not known, nor knowable, since the original manuscript has not survived. The story stops at 1860, with the death of Ryle's second wife and he himself longing to move from Helmingham, where he had been vicar since 1844, and where relations with John Tollemache, dictatorial lord of the manor, had broken down. A tempting guess is that he dictated it to Henrietta, the third Mrs. Ryle, whom he married in 1861 following his move to Stradbroke. By then he was something of an evangelical celebrity, and Henrietta, who speedily became a great success as stepmother to his five children and a great help to him in the Sunday school and as personal secretary and parish photographer as well as in other ways, would naturally have wished to know all about her husband's earlier years, and to have pressed the point that his children needed to know it all too. Second, why did he stop at 1860, thirteen years before the dictating was actually done? The tempting guess here is that he viewed his story up to 1860 as essentially one of divine guidance and refining through pain and grief, and that he saw 1861 as a watershed year, starting a period of public acceptance and inner happiness such as he had never known before. His stipend at Stradbroke was twice that of Helmingham, enabling him to employ a curate all the time (he had seven altogether); there was no lord of the manor to contend with; and his twelve good years with robust, middle-aged, mature, organ-playing, outgoing Henrietta had contrasted totally with the incessant troubles and anxieties that had beset him in his two previous marriages due to his wives' sicknesses. So, one supposes, he judged that it was precisely about the pre-1860 events that his children needed to know, because of the lessons they contained with regard to the saving power and providence of God, who leads sinners to faith in Christ and overrules circumstantial evil for their spiritual good. In this Ryle was showing himself a true Puritan parent, conscientiously seeking to pass on to his children such knowledge of God and such wisdom for living as had come to him during his own pilgrimage.

The first half of the Autobiography gives full accounts of Ryle's family, first and second home, education, conversion, and entry into the pastoral ministry as an indirect result of the family bankruptcy in 1841. In telling the story he gives poignant testimony to the trauma of that event; an extended quote is warranted:

> It would perhaps be impossible to give any correct idea of the stunning violence of the blow, which the ruin inflicted upon all. We got up one summer's morning with all the world before us as usual, and went to bed that same night completely and entirely ruined. The immediate consequences were bitter and painful in the extreme, and humiliating to the utmost degree. The creditors naturally rightly and justly seized everything and we children were left with nothing but our own personal property and our clothes.

As captain of the Macclesfield troop of the Cheshire Yeomanry (a semi-military, semi-police force that might be called out to quell riots), Ryle had two horses and a uniform that he sold for one hundred pounds, and he ended up with about two hundred and fifty pounds all told:

> This for a young man of twenty-five, about to go into Parliament, a county magistrate, and commonly reckoned to be son and heir, with 15,000 pounds p.a., was rather a fall. The whole circumstances of that time were just about as painful as could be conceived, and, at the end of 32 years, are as vividly before my mind as if they were yesterday. Our household was of course immediately broken up—menservants, butler, underbutler, footman, coachman, groom, housekeeper, housemaids . . .

Henbury, the thousand-acre family home since 1837, which Ryle loved, was sold, and Ryle himself stayed on for "the most trying and miserable six weeks I ever passed in my life" to help his father wind up his affairs:

> . . . I was going to leave my father's house without the least idea what was going to happen, where I was going to live, or what I was going to do. No one, in fact, but God has the least idea what I suffered in those times. . . . The plain fact was that there was no one of the family whom it touched more than it did me. . . . I . . . as the eldest son, twenty-five, with all the world before me, lost everything . . . if

I had not been a Christian at that time, I do not know if I should not have committed suicide. As it was, everybody said how beautifully I behaved, how resigned I was, what an example of contentment I was. Never was there a more complete mistake. God alone knows how the iron entered into my soul and how my whole frame, body, mind and spirit reeled and were shaken to the foundation under the blow of my father's ruin. Of course I know it was all right [i.e., God had planned it, as its outcome showed], but I am quite certain it inflicted a wound on my body and mind of which I feel the effects most heavily at this day and shall feel it if I live to be a hundred. To suppose that people do not feel things because they do not scream and yell and fill the air with their cries, is simple nonsense.

My children and those who read these lines [i.e., other members of the family] may be surprised at the strength of this language. But . . . I do not believe I met with any person who appeared to realize or understand what I went through in 1841. . . . Unthinking people, I repeat, did not see much in it, and fancied it was no trial to me at all. For myself I can only say that the wound it inflicted in me in both body and mind was nearly mortal, and I do not think there has been a single day in my life for thirty-two years, that I have not remembered the faint [i.e., courage-draining] humiliation of having to leave Henbury. . . .

Taking a moral and spiritual view of it, I have not the least doubt *it was all for the best*. If my father's affairs had prospered and I had never been ruined, my life of course would have been a very different one. I should probably have gone into Parliament very soon. . . . I should never have been a clergyman, never have preached, written a tract or a book. Perhaps I might have made shipwreck in spiritual things. So I do not mean to say at all, that I wish it to have been different from what it was. All I mean to say is that I was deeply wounded . . . suffered deeply . . . and I do not think I have ever recovered in body and mind from the effect. . . . ever since I left Cheshire, I have never felt at home, but a *sojourner* and a *dweller* in a lodging, and I never expect to feel anything else as long as I live.[7]

What Ryle reveals to his children here is that the memory of the bankruptcy crisis had become a permanent running sore inside him. Sourness, isolationism, and despair now threatened, and had constantly to be kept at bay. Hard work serving others proved able to alleviate the sourness and keep him cheerful as he fought the Lord's battles in parishes, from platforms, and in print: hence, though, may have derived the occasional touch of drivenness and defiance that to some minds mars the rhetorical style of his books. And hence must have derived some of the personal reserve and gruff abruptness that people sensed in him, in that stiff-upper-lip Victorian culture. Nobody in Ryle's time idealized pastoral ministry as the work of the wounded healer, in the manner so common today,[8] and Ryle himself would have dismissed the idea as improperly shifting interest from the message to the messenger. Nonetheless, one may guess that Ryle's expositions of Christ-centered, cross-focused, covenant-oriented comfort and encouragement in the face of trouble and disappointment would have been less solid and strong had Ryle's own heart not needed to taste the power of this message so often, and at so deep a level.[9]

The Autobiography goes on to tell how, very reluctantly, for compelling financial reasons, Ryle, having left Cheshire behind him, accepted the offer of an assistant curate's post in Hampshire and was ordained by the evangelical Bishop of Winchester, Charles Sumner, in December 1841, six months after the collapse of the bank. "I never had any particular desire to become a clergyman, and those who fancied that my self will and natural tastes were gratified by it were totally and entirely mistaken. . . . I particularly disliked the idea of becoming a clergyman, having a strong feeling that God did not intend all Christian men to become clergymen. . . . I could see nothing whatever before me but to become a clergyman because that brought me in some income at once. . . . My mother and father, neither of them, liked it at all, though they were quite unable to suggest to me anything better."[10] So pastoring became his profession from that point on.

After two rather grotesque years in the rural backwater Exbury in the New Forest as curate to the bishop's son-in-law, who spent most of the time in Malta, Ryle resigned for health reasons.[11] "Constant headache, indigestion, and disturbances of the heart then began and have been my plagues, and have disturbed me ever since that time, and will probably be my end at last."[12] With his salary of 84 pounds a year (16 pounds of the nominal 100 pounds being preempted as rent for the furniture of his house), poverty had been a further plague. "I never felt [before] what a miserable thing it is for a man to be first rich and then poor. . . . Those only who have been rich till they were twenty-five, and then become poor can comprehend what endless mortification your circumstances entail upon you."[13]

Following five months' ministry in St. Thomas's Church, Winchester where, again, the salary was insufficient, Ryle was offered in 1844 the living of Helmingham, a rural parish in Suffolk with a population of 300, where the stipend was 500 pounds a year. The burden of poverty thus seemed to be lifted, and he could afford to marry, which he did.[14] But then we are told how the bad health of both his first and second wives drained his resources and increased his troubles over a period of fifteen years, and the Autobiography ends at the point where "I was once more left a widower, with five children . . . and altogether more disconsolable and helpless than ever." The final paragraph, running on from the sentence just quoted, is as follows:

> Few can have any idea how much wear and tear and anxiety of mind and body I had to go through for at least five years before my wife died. I very rarely slept out of our own house in order that I might be in the way [i.e., present to help] if my wife wanted anything. I have frequently in the depth of winter driven distances of twelve, fifteen, twenty or even thirty miles in an open carriage to speak or preach, and then returned home the same distance immediately afterwards, rather than sleep away from my own house. As to holidays, rest, and relaxation in the year, I never had any at all; while the whole business of entertaining and amusing the three little boys in an evening devolved entirely upon me. In fact the whole state of things was a heavy strain upon me, both in body and mind, and I often wonder how I lived through it.[15]

Here, abruptly, the record stops; Ryle lets this paragraph stand as its conclusion. Evidently, then, what he wanted his children to realize, when they read the story after his death, was, first, the intensity of the distresses he endured and, second, the divine overruling of them all for long-term good. In closing his chapter on the bank crash he wrote:

> God never expects us to feel no suffering or pain when it pleases him to visit us with affliction. There are great mistakes upon this point. Submission to God's will is perfectly compatible with intense and keen suffering under the chastisement of his will. Troubles in fact not felt are not troubles at all. To feel trouble deeply and yet submit to it patiently is what is required of a Christian. . . . I ask my children and everyone who may read this autobiography to remember that I felt most acutely my father's ruin, my exile from Cheshire with the destruction of all my worldly property and I have never ceased to feel them from that day to this; but I would have them know that I was submissive to God's will and had a firm and deep conviction that all was right, though I could not see it or feel it at the time.[16]

The sense that all was right sustained him constantly, whatever the pressures. "His life was like Nehemiah's, in many ways," comments Guthrie Clark, "and he could testify that at every crisis it was the good Hand of God upon him which brought him through."[17] Well and truly said! More of God's hand on Ryle's life will be seen shortly.

4

A GREAT CHANGE

The faith that enabled Ryle to cope with the circumstances described so far, and which he now sought to spread, was not something he was born with or learned at home. It crystallized within him in 1837, during his last year at Oxford and the six months following his brilliantly successful degree examination.[1] As he himself puts it, "About the end of 1837, my character underwent a thorough and entire change, in consequence of a complete alteration in my view of religion, both as to my belief and practice. This change was . . . exceedingly great. . . ."[2] "It was not a sudden immediate change but very gradual. I cannot trace it to any one person, or any one event or thing, but to a singular variety of persons and things. In all of them I believe now the Holy Ghost was working though I did not know it at the time."[3] Ryle is speaking of the reality of his conversion, regeneration, and becoming a Christian.

The way was paved by evangelical preaching in a new church in Macclesfield, under which both his sister Susan and an ordinand friend were converted; by the outcry against this preaching, in the face of which "my natural independence, combativeness, and love of minorities, and hearty dislike of swimming with the stream, combined to make me think that these new evangelical preachers who were so sneered at and disliked were probably right";[4] by hearing Ephesians 2:8 read one time in church with significant pauses, thus achieving great emphasis ("By grace—are ye saved—through faith—and that not of yourselves—it is the gift of God"); by starting to read his Bible and to pray regularly during an illness just before his finals; and by remembering the teaching of the Anglican Thirty-nine Articles, which he had previously studied both for the Newcastle scholarship at Eton and for his degree. Out of this step-by-step process came a convictional clarity that merits a further extended quote from the Autobiography:

It may interest my children to know what were the points in religion by which my opinions at this period of my life became strongly marked . . . when this great change came over me. . . . The leading things which seemed to flash out before my mind, as clearly and sharply as the picture on a photographic plate when the developing liquid is poured over it, were such as these:

The extreme sinfulness of sin, and my own personal sinfulness, helplessness, and spiritual need; the entire suitableness of the Lord Jesus Christ by His sacrifice, substitution and intercession to be the Saviour of a sinner's soul; the absolute necessity of anybody who would be saved being born again or converted by the Holy Ghost; the indispensable necessity of holiness of life, being the only evidence of a true Christian; the absolute need of coming out from the world and being separate from its vain customs, recreation, and standards of what is right, as well as from its sins; the supremacy of the Bible as the only rule of what is true in faith, or right in practice, and the need of regular study and reading it; the absolute necessity of daily private prayer and communion with God if anyone intends to live the life of a true Christian; the enormous values of what are called Protestant principles as compared to Romanism; the unspeakable excellence and beauty of the doctrine of the Second Advent of our Lord and Saviour Jesus Christ; the unutterable folly of supposing that baptism is regeneration or formal going to Church Christianity or taking the sacrament a means of wiping away sins, or clergymen to know more of the Bible than other people or to be mediators between God and men by virtue of their office. I say that all these principles seemed to grow upon my mind about the winter after I was twenty-one. I am quite certain I knew nothing of them at all before, and I am as certain as I am of my own existence that they rose up within my mind in a distinct though mysterious manner, without the instrumentality of any particular person. Nothing I can remember to this day appeared to me so clear and distinct, as my own sinfulness, Christ's preciousness, the value of the Bible, the absolute necessity of coming out of the world, the need of being born again, and the enormous folly of the whole doctrine of baptismal regeneration. All these things, I repeat, seemed to flash on me like a sunbeam in the winter of 1837. . . . Before that time I was dead in sins and on the high road to hell, and from that time I have become alive and had a hope of heaven. And nothing to my mind can account for it, but the free sovereign grace of God.[5]

Ryle should be understood here as saying, not that he had never previously met these evangelical notions in any form, but that they had not made sense to him, nor seemed true to him, nor coalesced in his mind as a life-system taught by God, until now. Once formed, however, these convictions never left him, and he began to witness to them and argue for them at home and in wider society. He goes on to tell how his conversion brought painful estrangement from his family and former friends, but led him "by a kind of immediate free-masonry" to new friends, people of his own social class who "I gratefully record were great helps to me in one way and another; strengthened me in my principles, encouraged me in my practice, solved my difficulties, assisted me by their advice, counseled me in many of my perplexities, and cheered me generally by showing me that I was not quite alone in the world." Then he rounds off the account of his conversion year as follows:

> . . . the three and one-half years following the winter of 1837 [i.e., until the bankruptcy] . . . were a season of very great trial to me . . . but I have no doubt it was all for good. I believe it gave a decision and thoroughness to my Christianity, with all its defects, for which I shall always have reason to thank God.[6]

5

A GREAT EVANGELICAL

What Ryle's account of the "great change" shows us is that in 1837 he became a mainstream Anglican evangelical, as Anglican evangelicalism had been understood for a century prior to his time. As the evangelicals, with the Reformers and Puritans, had done before him, he denied baptismal regeneration from the start, and always correlated regeneration with conversion. This was central to his evangelical identity. He continued as he had begun, and forty years later, in 1877, he published *Knots Untied*, a classic volume in which, drawing on material he had already put out in tract form, he covered the then current disputes about authentic Anglican identity and development, vindicating an evangelical stance at every turn. It was his most popular book in his own lifetime, going through ten printings before 1900, and it still has a great deal to say to struggling Anglicans in the increasingly post-Christian West. The opening chapter is titled "Evangelical Religion," and is, in effect, Ryle explaining and defining in an Anglican frame what he takes the gospel of Jesus Christ to be. There are no surprises here, but Ryle's flavor is richest when he speaks for himself, so a further extended quote seems to be called for:

> Has Evangelical Religion any distinctive principles? I answer, it has. Are they worth contending for? I answer, they are. . . . To the question "what Evangelical Religion is?" the simplest answer I can give is to point out what appear to be its leading features. These I consider to be five in number.
>
> (i) The first leading feature in Evangelical Religion is the *absolute supremacy it assigns to Holy Scripture,* as the only rule of faith and practice. . . . Show us anything plainly written in that Book, and, however trying to flesh and blood, we will receive it, believe it, and submit to it. Show us anything, as religion, which is contrary to that Book,

and, however specious, plausible, beautiful, and apparently desirable, we will not have it at any price. . . . Here is rock: all else is sand.

(ii) The second leading feature in Evangelical Religion is *the depth and prominence it assigns to the doctrine of human sinfulness and corruption.* . . . All men . . . are not only in a miserable, pitiable, and bankrupt condition, but in a state of guilt, imminent danger, and condemnation before God. They are not only at enmity with their Maker, and have no title to heaven, but they have no will to serve their Maker, no love to their Maker, and no meetness for heaven. . . . Hence we protest with all our heart against formalism, sacramentalism, and every species of mere external or vicarious Christianity. We maintain that all such religion is founded on an inadequate view of man's spiritual need. It requires far more than this to save, or satisfy, or sanctify a soul. It requires nothing less than the blood of God the Son applied to the conscience, and the grace of God the Holy Ghost entirely renewing the heart. . . . Next to the Bible, as its foundation, it [i.e., evangelical religion] is based on a clear view of original sin.

(iii) The third leading feature of Evangelical Religion is *the paramount importance it attaches to the work and office of our Lord Jesus Christ,* and to the nature of the salvation which He has wrought out for man. . . . All who believe on Him are, even while they live, completely forgiven and justified from all things—are reckoned completely righteous before God. . . . We hold that an experimental [i.e., experiential] knowledge of Christ crucified and interceding, is the very essence of Christianity, and that in teaching men the Christian religion we can never dwell too much on Christ himself, and can never speak too strongly of the fullness, freeness, presentness, and simplicity of the salvation there is in him for every one that believes. . . . We say that life eternal is to know Christ, believe in Christ, abide in Christ, have daily heart communion with Christ, by simple personal faith, and that everything in religion is useful so far as it helps forward that life of faith, but no further.

(iv) The fourth leading feature in Evangelical Religion is the *high place which it assigns to the inward work of the Holy Spirit in the heart of man.* . . . We maintain that the things which need most to be pressed on men's attention are those mighty works of the Holy Spirit, inward repentance, inward faith, inward hope, inward hatred of sin, and inward love to God's law. . . . We hold that, as an inward work of the Holy Ghost is a necessary thing to a man's salvation, so also it is a thing that must be inwardly felt. . . . there can be no real conversion to God, no new creation in Christ, no new birth of the Spirit, where there is nothing felt and experienced within. . . . We insist that where there is nothing felt within the heart of a man, there is nothing really possessed.

(v) The fifth and last leading feature in Evangelical Religion is the importance which it attaches to the outward and visible work of the Holy Ghost in the life of man. . . . The true grace of God is a thing that will always make itself manifest in the conduct, behaviour, tastes, ways, choices and habits of him who has it. It is not a dormant thing. . . . To tell a man he is "born of God," or regenerated, while he is living in carelessness or sin, is a dangerous delusion. . . . Where there is the grace of the Spirit there will always be more or less fruit of the Spirit. . . . where there is nothing seen, there is nothing possessed.[1]

Ryle goes on in this chapter to counter suspicions that evangelicalism despises scholarship and "the wisdom of days gone by," or that it under-values the Church, or its ministry, or the dominical sacraments, or the Prayer Book, or bishops, or beauty, or Christian unity, or spiritual disci-plines. Gems from these pages include: "We protest against the modern practice of first personifying the Church, then deifying it, and finally idol-izing it." "We steadily refuse to admit that Christ's Sacraments convey grace *ex opere operato,* and that . . . they are the grand media between Christ and the soul, above faith, above preaching, and above prayer."[2] Finally Ryle shows how the evangelical message can be obscured by persons who actually hold to its constituent elements but do not suffi-ciently highlight Christ crucified, risen, and mighty to save, and he calls for firmness in holding fast to pure, clear evangelical faith. Elsewhere he begs his readers to study the Thirty-nine Articles, where evangelicalism as defined is made beautifully plain.[3] His supreme concern, as is obvious, is that all Anglicans should know the gospel conceptually, know Jesus Christ experientially, and be able to diagnose the spiritual slippage of all who, for whatever reason and in whatever way, are retreating from the gospel in order to peddle something else.

Ryle's basic position as a Christian instructor can be stated thus: 1) The Bible is the Word of God, and its teaching has decisive authority. 2) Evangelicalism, both as a doctrine leading to a particular form of devo-tion and as a form of devotion founded on a particular doctrine, is a fully coherent and demonstrably correct understanding of what is central in the Bible. 3) Evangelicalism comes to us as a fully developed legacy from the past—from the Reformers of the sixteenth century, the Puritans of the seventeenth, and the Revival leaders of the eighteenth, who were all at one on the five leading features of evangelical religion. 4) The Thirty-nine Articles are the Anglican confession of faith, under the supreme author-ity of the Scriptures, and, historically interpreted, they will be found to embody Protestant evangelicalism in an unambiguous way. 5) The Book of Common Prayer, which is authoritative only for liturgical usage, not for doctrine, is to be interpreted by the Bible and the Articles, and not invoked as a key for interpreting either, as the exponents of baptismal regeneration were constantly doing. 6) Protestant evangelicalism should thus be seen as mainstream, normative Anglicanism, in relation to which Anglican comprehensiveness ought to be defined and the limits of tolerance be set and maintained.[4] 7) These principles should be clearly taught and upheld in all congregations, and it is in terms of them that the nature of the reality of the Church should be understood and its public life of worship and witness lived.

Such was Ryle's Anglican evangelicalism: biblical, historical, constitutional, spiritual. His presentation of it stands out, not because it differs substantially from what other evangelicals might say, but because he sets it forth so clearly, so brilliantly, and so compellingly—in a word, so very, very well. No Anglican to my knowledge has ever expounded this position more fully, fairly, or masterfully than did Ryle. In this, as in so much else, his work retains benchmark status; for surely in principle his evangelicalism is neither more nor less than New Testament Christianity.

6

A GREAT PURITAN

As was said, Ryle looked back to the seventeenth-century Puritans as classic evangelicals, and made no secret of being "a thorough lover of Puritan theology."[1] So, in the Introduction to *Light from Old Times* (1890), an enlargement of what was previously published as *Protestant Facts and Men* (1882), which was itself an enlargement of *Bishops and Clergy of Other Days* (1868), he wrote a vigorous apologia for these men:

> With regard to the Puritans, of whom I have brought forward three specimens in this volume,[2] I believe that they deserve almost as much attention in the present day as the Reformers. I want to promote acquaintance with them. . . . Never, I believe, were men so little understood and so absurdly maligned as the Puritans. . . .
>
> The common impression . . . is that they were ignorant, fanatical dissenters, who troubled England in the seventeenth century—that they hated the Monarchical form of government, and cut off Charles the First's head—that they hated the Church of England, and caused its destruction—and that they were unlearned enthusiasts who despised knowledge and study, and regarded all set forms of worship as Popery. There are some . . . who are never weary of flinging the epithet "Puritanical" at Evangelical Churchmen, as the hardest word of scorn that they can employ. Let no Churchman's heart fail when he hears himself stigmatized as "a Puritan." The man who tells the world that there is any disgrace in being "a Puritan" is only exposing his own ignorance.
>
> 1. The Puritans were *not enemies to the monarchy*. . . . The great majority of them protested strongly against the execution of Charles I, and were active agents in bringing back Charles II to England, and placing the crown on his head after Oliver Cromwell's death.
>
> 2. The Puritans were *not enemies to the Church of England*. They would gladly have seen her government and ceremonial improved,

and more liberty allowed to her ministers in the conduct of public worship. And they were quite right! But the bulk of them were originally ordained by Bishops, and had no special objection either to Episcopacy or a Liturgy. Baxter . . . testifies that a very few concessions in 1662 would have retained in the Church of England sixteen hundred out of the two thousand who were driven out by the Act of Uniformity on St. Bartholomew's day.

3. The Puritans were *not unlearned and ignorant men.* The great majority of them were Oxford and Cambridge graduates. . . . Their works still speak for them on the shelves of every well-furnished theological library . . . The Puritans, as a body, have done more to elevate the national character than any class of Englishman that ever lived.

For myself, I can only say, that the very reason why many in this day dislike the Puritans is the very reason why I love them. . . . They deserve honour, in my opinion, on account of their bold and outspoken *Protestantism.* They deserve honour on account of their clear, sharply-cut, distinct *Evangelicalism.* I want to see their writings more widely read, and their conduct more fairly judged and duly appreciated by English Churchmen. . . . As long as I live, I hope I shall never be ashamed to stand up for them.[3]

On questions of spiritual life and godliness, Ryle regularly cited Puritan writings as "the product of an age when . . . experimental religion was more deeply studied, and far better understood, than it is now."[4] In all matters relating to communion with God, the Puritans were the weightiest human authority that he recognized.

It is clear, then, that Ryle may as truly and justifiably be called a Puritan as he is called an evangelical.

7

A Great Agenda

A further point must now be made about Ryle's Puritanism: namely, that he worked to an entirely Puritan agenda. The purposes, priorities, and principles of action in Ryle's ministry over more than half a century corresponded directly to those of the historic Puritan clergy two centuries and more before him. Ryle aimed at four things: the evangelizing of English people; the purging of the English national Church; the uniting of English Christians; and the holiness of English believers. These objectives match what the Puritans sought in their day. Let me spell this out.

First, Ryle pursued the goal of evangelism, understood in terms of directing people toward the thorough convictional, attitudinal, and fiducial change that he himself had undergone (conversion and regeneration, that is, according to the Puritan formula). He did this through his preaching and his tracts, both of which were constantly evangelistic in this broad sense. (The decision-centered herding that counts as evangelism today was not Ryle's concept.) Though he supported with goodwill ventures like the visit to Liverpool of Moody and Sankey in 1883, and the Liverpool General Christian Mission in 1895, his basic strategy for evangelism was institutional rather than spasmodic—the regular Sunday pulpit; the Sunday school; preparation for confirmation; home visitation with prayer on a regular basis; plus personal and domestic reading of the Bible, tracts, and good (that is, spiritually helpful) books. It was a permanent priority with him to recruit layfolk who would work with clergy to fulfill this pattern of ministry. The pattern itself corresponds almost exactly to what the Puritan Richard Baxter had set up in Kidderminster, and many more Puritan clergy in other places, two centuries before Ryle's time. In evangelism, Ryle was not only Christ-centered; he was Puritan-minded.

Second, Ryle pursued the goal of purging the Church by combining with his positive evangelical teaching opposition to Romanizing and

liberal tendencies, that is, to the externalism and medievalism of the ritualists, and the skepticism about biblical and evangelical supernaturalism
that marked the *Essays and Reviews* school, as we may call it. He saw
these two constituencies as latter-day Pharisees and Sadducees, thus:

> The doctrine of the Pharisees may be summed up in three words: they
> were formalists, tradition-worshippers, and self-righteous. . . .
>
> The doctrine of the Sadducees . . . may be summed up in three
> words: free-thinking, skepticism, and rationalism. . . .
>
> We have among us, on the one side, a school of men who, wit-
> tingly or unwittingly, are paving the way into the Church of Rome—a
> school that professes to draw its principles from primitive tradition,
> the writings of the Fathers, and the voice of the Church—a school
> that talks and writes so much about the Church, the ministry, and the
> sacraments, that it makes them, like Aaron's rod, swallow up every-
> thing else in Christianity—a school that attaches vast importance to
> the outward form and ceremonial of religion—to gestures, postures,
> bowings, crosses, piscinas, sedilia, credence-tables, rood-screens, albs,
> tunicles, copes, chasubles, altar-cloths, incense, images, banners, pro-
> cessions, floral decorations, and many other like things. . . . I refer . . .
> to the school of Churchmen called Ritualists . . . upon them has fallen
> the mantle of the Pharisees.
>
> We have, on the other hand, a school of men who, wittingly or
> unwittingly, appear to pave the way to Socinianism[1]—a school which
> holds strange views about the plenary inspiration of Holy Scripture—
> strange views about the doctrine of sacrifice, and the Atonement of
> our Lord and Saviour Jesus Christ—strange views about the eternity
> of punishment, and God's love to man—a school strong in negatives
> but very weak in positives—skilful in raising doubts, but impotent
> in laying them—clever in unsettling and unscrewing men's faith, but
> powerless to offer any firm rest for the sole of our foot . . . on them
> has fallen the mantle of the Sadducees.
>
> I believe the most powerful champion of the Pharisees is not the
> man who bids you honestly and openly come out and join the Church
> of Rome: it is the man who says that he agrees on all points with you
> in *doctrine* . . . all he asks you to do is to *add* a little more to your
> belief, in order to make your Christianity perfect. . . .
>
> I consider the most dangerous champion of the Sadducee school
> is not the man who tells you openly that he wants you . . . to become
> a free-thinker and a skeptic. It is the man who begins with quietly
> insinuating doubts . . . whether we ought to be so positive in saying
> "This is the truth, and that falsehood," doubts whether we ought to
> think men wrong who differ from us on religious opinions, since they
> may after all be as much right as we are. . . . It is the man who always

begins talking in a vague way about God being a God of love, and hints that we ought to believe perhaps that all men, whatever doctrine they profess, will be saved.[2]

Ryle could not and did not expect to gain popularity by such utterances, nor did he. But he believed his polemics were necessary because the gospel was at stake, and the true glory and knowledge of Jesus Christ were being overshadowed, indeed, largely taken away. It is not hard to see this in his squaring off against the liberals, for with uncanny prescience he verbalizes the way liberal views present themselves to evangelicals still. As for the ritualists, we must remember that in those pre-Vatican II days their usages were meant not simply to express overall reverence for God and to celebrate overall continuity in the Church; their avowed purpose was to inculcate the Tridentine doctrine of the Mass in an Anglican form—the doctrine, that is, of Christ's "real" presence in a unique way in consecrated bread and wine, and of the celebrant offering these elements to God to link the Church with Christ's offering of himself to his Father in sacrifice—and with that the doctrine of the unique role of the priest as mediator between the sinner and the Savior, both at the Lord's Table and in the confessional. Ryle saw all this not only as unbiblical and ruled out by the Thirty-nine Articles and as an ominous lurch Rome-ward, but as impoverishing believers, making it harder for them to realize the love for them, the accessibility to them, and the abiding presence with them of Jesus Christ the Church's Lord. We cannot but admire the acumen with which Ryle detects the thin ends of the ideological wedges, and the passion for the truth of Christ according to the Bible that leads him to do so. And we should not overlook the remarkable correspondence between what Ryle writes against these two forms of error and what the Puritan John Owen was writing for the last twenty years of his life, after 1662, about the bad influence in England of Roman Catholic persuasions on the one hand and Anglican latitudinarian persuasions on the other. In seeking to preserve the gospel and flush anti-evangelical error out of the Church, Ryle was decidedly Puritan-minded.

Third, Ryle sought unity among Christians, both within and outside the Church of England. Within Anglicanism, especially during his years as a bishop, he constantly called for what he described in his first Pastoral Letter to his Liverpool diocese as "a spirit of brotherly love, charity, and forbearance among Churchmen." We may think some of each other's ideas wrong, and think ourselves bound to say so, but love and goodwill at the personal level must not perish on that account. The Pastoral continues:

In a fallen world like ours, and in a free country like England, it is vain to expect all men to see things alike and to interpret the language of the formularies precisely in the same way. Let us on no account be colourless Churchmen destitute of any distinct opinions. But so long as any brother walks loyally within the limits of the Articles and the Prayer Book, let us respect him and treat him courteously, even when we do not altogether agree with him. I entreat every clergyman in my diocese, for Christ's sake, to abhor and avoid all needless divisions, and to follow after peace as well as truth.[3]

That was the word of a veteran unity-seeker. Ryle's failure during the Stradbroke years to bring evangelical clergy together on questions of policy was not for want of trying.[4] His attendance at Church Congresses (annual gatherings in different centers from 1861 on to discuss Church affairs, which gave ritualists a platform) brought criticism, but he defended it as a gesture of goodwill through which mutual understanding might be advanced, and evangelicalism gain more respect.[5] And at the 1870 Congress, speaking on Home Reunion, he brought the house down when he argued for repeal of the 1662 Act of Uniformity, the authorizing of shorter services, and the mobilizing of the laity for ministry, and expressed regret that John Wesley was not made Archbishop of Canterbury.[6]

As regards Anglican rapprochement with the Free Churches, Ryle recognized that "our own internal divisions place an insuperable barrier in the way of reunion. . . . So long as our own beloved Church of England is infected with semi-Romanism on the extreme right, and semi-unbelief on the extreme left, and cannot cure or expel these diseases, so long, we may depend on it, our Nonconformist brethren will never embark in our ship."[7] However, courtesy and consideration to non-Anglican Protestants, so he maintained, were always possible, and therefore were always a duty.

In all of this Ryle reminds one of Richard Baxter, the seventeenth-century evangelist, pastor, author, and Puritan leader whose quest for Christian unity in England, in one form or another, occupied him for the last half-century of his long life.

Ryle's fourth objective was the holiness of English believers. This was supremely a Puritan purpose. Sanctification, we may fairly say, was the focus of all Puritan ministry, both in the pulpit and on paper, for in Puritan thought, conversion was always viewed in relation to the entire Christian life of which it was the beginning. One need look no further than Bunyan's *Pilgrim's Progress* to see this. Charles Simeon had once said that his ministry had a threefold aim—to humble the sinner, to exalt the Savior, and to promote holiness—and such was Ryle's perspective too, as his publications from the start amply show. His tracts labor constantly to make plain "that union with Christ is the root of holiness," and "what immense encouragement Jesus Christ holds out to all who strive to be holy."[8] But the subject gave him added concern after 1870, when what seemed to him a skewed version of these themes suddenly became all the rage among evangelical people of all denominations. This was the doctrine that some called "Pearsall Smithism," after the magnetic American layman who spread it; it declared that immediate sanctification and holiness are achieved, just as instantaneous justification and conversion are achieved, by one decisive act of faith and commitment to Christ. On this view, sanctification means simply deliverance from the practice of known sin, a perfection of behavior rather than of heart. Pearsall Smith's message, set out in his book *Holiness Through Faith* (1870) and proclaimed at major English conferences on holiness at Oxford in 1874 and Brighton in 1875, could be put thus:

> You received a finished salvation through a crucified Savior by simple faith in him, did you not? You did nothing except take the gift; works, effort, exertion did not enter into it. So with sanctification: you must stop striving and trust Christ to do everything in you as he has already done all for you. Just believe this, and abide in him, as a branch in the vine, living by the sap, the life-energy, that flows from the parent stem. Let Christ live in you, filling you with his Spirit and expressing his life through you. How easy it is, once you know the secret! How peaceful! How joyful and triumphant! Instability and sinful stumbling become things of the past; it is like a second conversion, a total renewing of your life. Open yourself to it, and it will be yours—right now!

Ryle thought this teaching unbalanced, shallow, unrealistic, and dangerous to spiritual well-being. It seemed to him alarmingly neglectful, for it shrugged off the biblical stress on the necessary exertions of self-discipline and spiritual warfare (which means battling to say no when world, flesh, and devil urge you to say yes; and to say yes when weariness, apathy, and unbelief prompt you to say no). By harping on consecration as a complete recipe for holiness, this teaching diverted attention from the detailed guidance on Christian relationships of which Paul's letters (for instance) are packed full. Its idea of victory and peace obliged it to evade the natural sense of Romans 7:14-25 as a cross-section of normal mature Christian experience, in which reach constantly exceeds grasp, and to read these verses as relating either to unconverted persons or to

Christians who are weak and sick because their life is all self-effort and they do not yet know the secret of sanctification; thus, in effect, it treated Paul's display of good spiritual health as one of bad spiritual health, while idealizing a conflict-free life which would itself be one of bad spiritual health, because it would rest on deep self-ignorance.

And there would be other unhappy effects. Inevitably, Ryle thought, "Smithism" would betray shallow people into self-deluded pride because of what, in their stirred-up state, they are led to think they have attained, while at the same time it would dismay and discourage sensitive souls, who fight hard but know that nothing like Smithic perfection ever comes their way. Also, its incautious rhapsodizing about being yielded (passively, by the renouncing of personal exertion) to the indwelling Christ would tend to practical antinomianism (lawlessness); for such thoughts, as history has shown, lead excited devotees to think that every strong impulse within them is Christ indicating his present will, and that when they act it is not they but Christ, who has so taken them over that they are no longer to be held accountable for the things they do. The safeguard would have been to show that, in Scripture, "yielding" and "abiding" are matters not of mystical passivity but of resolute habitual obedience, in which you pray as hard as you work and work as hard as you pray, because you know that God works in you to make you will and do his pleasure as set forth in his Word; but this Smith did not point out, nor seem to see.

Finally, the highlighting of consecration as the neglected secret of holiness seemed to Ryle to show a shocking cluelessness about repentance in conversion. For how can there be conversion without repentance? And what is consecration if not just the sustaining of that repentance, that turning from self-will to God, that every true believer should be practicing from the start of his or her Christian life? So what is new?

Ryle's direct response to all this was the masterly book *Holiness: Its Nature, Hindrances, Difficulties, and Roots* (1877; 2nd ed., enlarged, 1879). This is a book that, so he tells us elsewhere,[9] should be read in conjunction with his *Practical Religion* (1878), which is a kind of *vade-mecum* on living the Christian life. All the chapters in both books are based on biblical texts, and appear to have started life as sermons. The first seven chapters in *Holiness* are titled: 1) Sin; 2) Sanctification; 3) Holiness; 4) The Fight; 5) The Cost; 6) Growth; 7) Assurance. Much Puritan material is quoted to enforce their teaching. Then, in the 1879 enlarged edition, the messages that make up the rest of the book present Christ calling, warning, encouraging, enabling, and upholding those committed to the struggle for a truly holy life. The twenty-one chapters of *Practical Religion* are titled: 1) Self-Inquiry; 2) Self-Exertion; 3) Reality; 4) Prayer; 5) Bible-Reading; 6) Going to the Table; 7) Charity; 8) Zeal; 9) Freedom; 10) Happiness; 11) Formality; 12) The World; 13) Riches and Poverty; 14) The Best Friend; 15) Sickness; 16) The Family of God; 17) Our Home; 18) Heirs of God; 19) The Great Gathering; 20) The Great Separation; 21) Eternity. From the themes that these titles announce, one can gauge at once the range, emphases, weight, and richness of Ryle's own positive holiness teaching. Ryle is authentically Puritan both in the importance he gives to the topic and in the specific instruction he offers regarding it.

Anglicans' eyebrows still sometimes rise, as they did in Ryle's day, when any of their number are said to be Puritan in any sense at all; but to point out that Ryle's fourfold ministerial agenda matches what we may call the Puritan quadrilateral is not to say anything that should cause surprise. It is only to say that Ryle lined up with Calvin, and Augustine, and the apostle Paul, all of whom fulfilled their ministries in terms of the same set of pastoral priorities. It is only to say that Ryle kept in mind the Ordinal of the Book of Common Prayer, which commissions Anglican clergy precisely to this fourfold task. Far from being eccentric or unbalanced, therefore, the Puritan quadrilateral constitutes the proper agenda for all Christian leaders anywhere in any age, and the eccentrics, if any, will be those who fail to give equal emphasis to the practice of evangelism, the preserving of truth, the promotion of unity, and the pursuit of holy maturity among believers, in the way that the Puritans did before them. Paradoxical as it sounds to say it, Ryle's practical endorsement of the Puritan quadrilateral is the clearest possible proof of his being a mainstream Anglican minister, catholic through being Protestant, evangelical through being Reformed, and Pauline through being Puritan. What nobler pedigree, I ask, could anyone have?

8

A Great Anglican

The shape and substance of Ryle's Anglicanism are now clear. Scotland's "Rabbi" Duncan famously identified himself as "first a Christian, then a Protestant, then a Calvinist, then a paedobaptist, then a Presbyterian." Put "Anglican" for "Presbyterian," and there you have Ryle's view of himself (though he always said "evangelical" rather then "Calvinist"; but Calvinistic evangelicalism was what he had in mind). His claim for Anglicanism, like Duncan's for Presbyterianism, was that it is mainstream biblical religion. His own Anglicanism, as we have seen, stemmed neither from cultural inertia nor from shallow sentimentality, but from sober rational reflection and critical scriptural assessment. Brought up to attend Anglican Sunday services as a matter of respectable habit, he became convinced in the process of his conversion that the definitions, declarations, and denials of the Thirty-nine Articles, the Anglican confession of faith, were biblically correct. We noted this earlier. In due course he became equally convinced that the Church of England's other foundation documents, the Book of Common Prayer and the Homilies, were fully acceptable and edifying; and also, that there was no better organizational system for the Church on earth, at least in England, than the liturgical, ministerial, parochial, and diocesan structures that were already in place. "I am satisfied that, *well administered,* the Church of England is more calculated to help souls to heaven than any Church on earth."[1] We find him constantly defending Anglican arrangements in principle while seeking to improve them in practice. The system, he thought, had the potential to secure more good and avoid more evil than any alternative; all that was needed was clergy who would work it properly.

The conviction that the Anglican parochial system was adequate not only for rural communities but also for large industrial towns was basic to Ryle's strategy when Bishop of Liverpool. Speaking at the Derby

Church Congress in 1882 on "Can the Church Reach the Masses?" he first called for Christ-centered preaching "with fiery liveliness and directness of style,"[2] as modeled by Whitefield and Moody, and then developed the proposition: "if we want to bring the working classes to Church, *there needs, throughout the land, a great increase of sympathy and friendly personal dealing with them on the part of the clergy.*" To help make his point, he cited,

> a parish of 5000 people in Liverpool with not a rich man in it, but only small shopkeepers, artisans and poor. There are only thirty families in it which keep a servant. . . . There are 195 houses with more than one family in each. There are 133 families living in cellars. . . . What does the Church of England do in this parish?
>
> In a plain brick Church, holding 1000, built thirteen years ago, there is a simple, hearty service, and an average attendance of 700 on Sunday morning, 350 in the afternoon, and 950 in the evening. . . . In three mission rooms there is an average attendance of about 350 in the morning, and 450 in the evening. The communicants are almost all of the working classes, and nearly half men. . . .
>
> The worthy minister of this parish began his work alone about fourteen years ago, with four people in a cellar. After his Church was built, he had only eight communicants at his first administration of the Lord's Supper. He now has 800 communicants and is aided by two paid curates, one paid Scripture reader, one paid Bible-woman, and one paid organist. But he has besides, 82 voluntary Sunday School teachers, 120 Church workers, 18 Bible classes, with 600 adults on the register, and 1700 Sunday scholars. There are six services in Church every week and four services in mission rooms throughout the year, besides two prayer meetings every month. . . . The congregation raises 800 pounds a year for the cause of God. There is not a single house of ill fame . . . in the parish. . . .
>
> The incumbent . . . is a man who tries to preach Christ in the pulpit, and to visit his people in a Christ-like, sympathizing way as a pastor, at the rate of 75 families a week, and to these two things I attribute his success.[3]

> Conclusion:

> . . . with a proper supply of clergy and lay-helpers of the right sort, and a reasonable subdivision of our large parishes, we have no reason to despair about the working classes.[4]

Such was Ryle's idea of the pastoral potential of the Church of England—provided only that it gained, and retained, the fully evangelical character that its title deeds required. On this, Ryle's discourse, "The Lessons of English Church History," revealed his mind in a very striking way. Well-read in history as in theology, and pastorally focused as always, he offered an analysis that remains hard to forget.

The first lesson, drawn from the three centuries before the Reformation, was: *English religion was never in so dark and bad a condition as it was in the days when Romanism had everything its own way in England.* "Practically, the religion of most Englishmen was Mary-worship, saint-worship, and slavery to priests. The true doctrine of Scripture concerning Christ and the Holy Ghost were almost unknown. The truth about repentance, faith, conversion, and justification, was nearly as much lost sight of as if it had never existed."

The second lesson, drawn from the period 1530–1600, was: *The change of these seventy years is a cause for unmixed thankfulness, and . . . the greatest blessing God had ever bestowed on this country was the Protestant Reformation.* Biblical and evangelical standards of faith, holiness, and worship were established at that time.

The third lesson, drawn from the 150 years from the beginning of the seventeenth century to the middle of the eighteenth, was: *Departure from the principles of the Reformation inflicted irreparable injury on the Church of England.* The Laudian attempt to un-protestantize the Church alienated ordinary Englishmen from the Church and led to the banning of the entire Anglican order during the time of the Civil War and the Commonwealth, the vengeful ejecting of Puritan clergy under the Act of Uniformity in 1662, and the creating of organized Dissent, hostile to the Church of England then and since.

The fourth lesson, drawn from the hundred years 1730–1830, was: *The revival of Reformation principles in the eighteenth century was the salvation of the Church of England.* Into a situation of almost unrelieved unspirituality God sent the evangelical awakening, whereby through the work of a handful of heroes—hardly more—he brought the Church of England back from the dead. For substance, the awakening was neither more nor less than "the revival of Reformation doctrines." Ryle gives a footnote reference to his 1869 book titled *Christian Leaders of the Last Century* (current printings have *Eighteenth* for *Last,* of course), where the heroes' stories are told in full, and the Anglican resurrection is more largely described.

Then, drawn from the year 1830 to the time of writing, came the final—not lesson, but utterance of "conclusions that I have arrived at in my own mind," namely: *Ritualism is a fresh departure from the prin-*

ciples of the Reformation and a movement toward Rome, and . . . as such it endangers the very existence of the Church of England. How so? The conclusion is one that Ryle lived with for a generation and often voiced, so we will let him answer the question at some length in his own words:

> Once and for all, I must honestly avow that my chief fears of Ritualism arise from the effect which it has on the minds of the lower and middle classes. They do not like it. They will not have it. They call it Popery.
>
> Shallow-minded members of the aristocracy, ill-taught ascetics, self-willed and half-instructed members of evangelical families, who want to mix ball-going and worldliness with religious formalism, and to compound for the one by supporting the other, idle young ladies and thoughtless young men, who love anything gaudy, sensational, and theatrical in worship, all these may stick to Ritualism and stoutly support it. They are like . . . babies who care for toys more than food. But Ritualism does not meet the wants of the hard-working, the hard-headed, the hard-handed masses of the middle classes, and intelligent artisans, the brain and muscle of England. These men want food for their souls. . . . If the Church can only offer them Ritualism, they will turn away from her in disgust. . . . Disestablishment will come. . . . The Church of a minority will not be spared in England any more than in Ireland. . . . The Church of England, once disestablished, will split into pieces, or become a mere sect, like the Scotch Episcopal Church; and the pages of history will then record that she made shipwreck of all her greatness by the suicidal attempt to recede from Protestantism and re-introduce Popery.
>
> Such are my reasons for regarding Ritualism with unmixed dislike. . . . The leaders of the ritualists, I willingly allow, may be zealous, earnest, able, well-meaning men. They may conscientiously believe, like many of Laud's school, that they are helping the Church of England. . . . But it is my belief that, like Laud's school, they are ruining the Church.[5]

As is perhaps already clear, Ryle's Anglicanism had come to be a matter of love. Sometimes he said so. "I love the Church of which I am a minister."[6] "I am deeply convinced of the excellency of my own Church—I would even say, if it were not a proud boast, its superiority over any other Church upon earth."[7] However one assesses Ryle's belief that the ritualists of his day were either purposefully trekking or unwittingly backing into Rome, and that the focus on formal correctness in ritualistic worship made it necessarily shallow and barren, there cannot be much doubt that he was right to think ordinary Englishmen would never appreciate it, and so it would always alienate the great majority rather than attract them. Ryle's longing, therefore, to see the Church of England's evangelizing influence in the nation maximized was quite sufficient to justify his hostility to ritualism without regard for the other arguments. Ryle's assertions of Anglicanism are not just advocacy; they express affection too. Ryle speaks of the Church of England as a lover, proud of the excellences yet distressed at the waywardness of his beloved and her failures to make the best of herself. This needs to be seen.

The Victorian era saw institutional development everywhere, and cries for the structural overhaul of the Church of England were constant. In discussions on Church Reform, as the field of debate was labeled, Ryle the theological conservative showed himself commonsensically pragmatic and pastorally progressive, in a statesmanlike way that left many of his evangelical contemporaries behind. He called for a new code of canon law and "a National Church Council, composed of bishops, presbyters and laymen."[8] Greater lay involvement seemed to him the key to the Church's future across the board. In the spirit of Richard Hooker and in opposition to the ideology of clergy control, he urged that laypeople be given an executive role, with veto, in "everything that the Church says and does, except ordaining and ministering in the congregation."[9] This would include clergy appointments. And there was more, as the excerpt last quoted shows. Following Gladstone's disestablishing of the Irish Church in 1871 (a move that Ryle deeply disapproved, as he disapproved of most of Gladstone's policies), Ryle feared that without the changes he called for—and with them, too, perhaps—pressure for the disestablishing and disendowing of the Church of England would soon become irresistible, to nobody's benefit and with much more harm to the country.[10] So, for pastoral rather than political reasons, he became a doughty performer in what was then called Church Defense. As he always made plain, he valued the Church's established status not as a bastion of privilege but as a springboard for service, a help toward the fulfilling of the Church's national mission, namely, the discipling of all the English people. The Church's bad track record here must be frankly faced, so Ryle argued, but that is no reason to marginalize the institution as such, and so put at risk future hopes of doing better.

In all this to-ing and fro-ing about the Church's institutional structures, what we see still is the lover seeking to encourage and enable his beloved to make the best of herself, moving beyond past lapses and gearing up for future ministry in a realistic adult way.

It was the Church's failures, more than anything else, that had produced England's non-Anglican evangelical Protestantism. In the face of general Anglican elitism and unconcern with regard to Nonconformists, Ryle was refreshingly blunt about this:

> I believe that the first seeds of Dissent were sown by the narrow intolerance of the Church in the days of the Stuarts. The wretched attempt to produce uniformity by fines and penalties and imprisonment "drove wise men almost mad" . . . the utter deadness and apathy of the Church in the last [eighteenth] century did even more to drive men and women out of our pale. . . . Bishops who scandalously neglected their dioceses, and were everything that bishops ought not to be—parochial clergymen who did nothing for souls, preached no Gospel, and lived terribly worldly lives—these . . . fitted the country; these were the real founders of Dissent. We reap what our forefathers sowed, and it is no use to complain. . . . English Church apathy has created English nonconformity. . . . That old saying is too much forgotten: *"Schismaticus est qui separationem causat, non qui separat"* [The schismatic is the one who causes the separation, not the one who separates].[11]

Humble goodwill toward non-Anglican evangelicals, therefore, is proper, even if we think some of their beliefs and attitudes mistaken. Ryle was a good deal more positive at this point than many of his contemporaries. "I admire their gifts, their graces, and their zeal. . . . I never forget that English Dissent was mainly created by the abominable bigotry or shameful neglect of English bishops and clergymen. I always steadily refuse to unChurch Dissenters, to deny the validity of their orders, to ignore their sacraments, or to hand them over to the 'uncovenanted mercies' of God. I am always glad . . . to co-operate with them whenever I can."[12] But for all that, Ryle's head and heart remained fixed. He was a member and minister of the Church of England; there God had set him to live and serve; the Anglican way was good; and that was that.

9

A GREAT BISHOP

The story of Ryle's elevation to become the first Bishop of Liverpool has a certain charm. He was hardly the most natural choice, for since his five months in Winchester he had only been a village clergyman in the depths of East Anglia (Helmingham, with 300 inhabitants, 1844–1861; Stradbroke, with 1,300, thereafter), he was now in his mid-sixties, and he was already about to move to another appointment. Having been evangelicalism's best-known and most respected writer and spokesman through the 1870s and a canon of Norwich Cathedral since 1872, Ryle had been offered the Deanery of Salisbury in March 1880, presumably as a relatively light though honorific job for his old age. He had told his congregation that, little as he wanted to move from Stradbroke, he had accepted the offer "as a soldier of Christ, fighting for the preservation of the Gospel within the Church," and believing that the evangelical cause would profit by his promotion.[1]

But on April 16, before he could be installed as Dean, the Prime Minister, Benjamin Disraeli, summoned him to London. Lord Sandon, M.P. for Liverpool, met him off the train at Liverpool Street station.

Ryle asked why he had been required to come. "We have sent for you for one purpose," said Lord Sandon, "to ask you to accept the Bishopric of Liverpool." One guesses there was a short pause; then Ryle replied, "Well, you strike me all of a heap. I don't know what to say." Sandon explained that, having just lost the election to Gladstone's Liberals, the Tories would "go out of office next Monday"; Gladstone would then come in, so "you must give us your answer as soon as you possibly can. You see if you don't make up your mind we will lose the Bishopric of Liverpool." Ryle pointed out that he was sixty-four and not wealthy, as bishops needed to be. "We know all that," said Sandon; "we made up our minds about that. Now will you be Bishop of Liverpool or not?" Ryle decided. "My Lord," he said, "I will go." Sandon jumped for joy and took him to meet Disraeli. In conversation Ryle stressed that, not being a younger man, he would find it hard going in a newly created diocese. (Up to this point Liverpool had been part of the diocese of Chester, and so had no financial or administrative structure of its own for Ryle to inherit.) "I think you have a pretty good constitution," said Disraeli affably, "and I think you will live a few years yet." So the matter was settled. "On 19 April letters patent were issued appointing the new Bishop, just three days before Gladstone took office as Prime Minister."[2]

Naturally, reactions to the appointment varied. Sandon was certainly overjoyed, for he had expected to lose his seat if the Tory government did not appoint a strong Protestant bishop. Disraeli's first thought for Liverpool had been the younger and less forthright E. H. Bickersteth, Dean of Lichfield, but he was content with Ryle; after all, Gladstone came from Liverpool's leading High Church family, and the High Church vote had contributed to Gladstone's electoral victory, and Ryle would be a powerful counterweight to Gladstone on his home turf. Sophisticated *Vanity Fair* said that "the unregenerate" would call Ryle a tub-thumper and itself described him, dismissively enough, as "a good man, not at all large-minded, but very much in earnest."[3] Richard Hobson wrote that the appointment "was hailed with delight by every evangelical Churchman throughout the world."[4] By contrast, Lord Halifax, president of the English Church Union, a body committed to Anglo-Catholic faith and practice, wrote to H. P. Liddon: "I must relieve my feelings. Canon Ryle Bishop of Liverpool! . . . I rejoice beyond the expression of words that we have got rid of Lord Beaconsfield [Disraeli]."[5] Earlier, *The Times* had wondered publicly how "the eager and restless temperament of the controversialist" would adjust to Salisbury;[6] now the question was, how would Ryle adjust to being a bishop?

The question cut deep. Up to this point Ryle's public stance had been that of an advocate—dogmatic, outspoken, and masterful—projecting the gospel of personal conversion to Christ through a life-transforming regeneration by the Holy Spirit, and arguing against Roman Catholicism and ritualism, doctrinal indifferentism and liberal skepticism, baptismal regeneration and all forms of the notion that the unregenerate might yet be spiritually on safe ground. His ministry had thus been divisive in the way that faithful gospel preaching regularly is. There are always Church people who resent being told that they need to be born again. Then, too, at Church Congresses Ryle had defended the Church-state connection, including the place of the Judicial Committee of the Privy Council as the highest ecclesiastical court of appeal; called for a reform of Convocation that would bring in layfolk to share with clergy in decision-making; and urged that large urban parishes be subdivided into working units in which no clergyman would have more than 3,500 people to look after. These had been controversial ideas at the time. Now the calling of an Anglican bishop was (and is), over and above his ongoing presbyteral ministry of word and sacrament and his work of confirming and ordaining, to manage the personnel, projects, and internal discipline of his diocese as its leader, unifier, point man for strategy, and anchor-man for stability. Liverpool's strong anti-Roman and anti-ritualist constituency, long tutored by the formidable Irishman Hugh McNeile, looked to Ryle to enforce Protestant standards; the few ritualist clergy in the diocese braced themselves for bruising conflict. Ryle, however, handled this difficult situation in an admirably wise and peaceful way.

His opinions did not change or weaken. "The views which I held as a presbyter I still hold as a Bishop."[7] But, though an unashamed party man, he refused to be a party bishop. He positioned himself from the start as an evangelical committed to maintain a constitutional comprehensiveness, as we saw earlier. To the Bishopric Committee, at his first meeting with them, he declared: "You know my opinions; I am a committed man. I come among you as a Protestant and Evangelical; but I come with a desire to hold out the right hand to all loyal Churchmen, holding at the same time my own opinions determinedly."[8] He chose evangelicals as his archdeacons, whom he regarded as his right-hand men, but included Broad Church clergy among his twenty-four appointed canons. (Ritualists seemed to him disloyal Churchmen, so he did not promote them.) At his annual diocesan conferences and his triennial visitations he delivered to the diocese's leaders ninety-minute addresses dealing with local and national Church affairs; these were statesmanlike and forward-looking, and not in any way party utterances.[9]

His stated permanent priorities were to increase the number of clergy, lay workers, and church buildings, so that no clergyman should have more than 5,000 souls to care for (thus he adjusted his ideal figure of 3,500) and everyone in Liverpool should have an Anglican place of worship at hand and an Anglican pastoral agent in regular touch with them. So, over the years, he ordained 553 deacons and 541 priests; licensed at least 45 salaried lay Scripture readers and 31 Bible women; founded the Lay Helpers Association, whose 580 members worked in Sunday schools and Bible classes, helped in mission services, cared for the sick, and visited as tract distributors from house to house; created

36 new parishes and built 90 new churches and mission halls; started a Sustentation Fund to ensure that clergy salaries were never less than 200 pounds per annum (raised to 295 pounds in 1899); and instituted a Diocesan Incumbents' Pension Fund to enable sick and aged clergy to retire. Overall, it was a remarkable achievement, the more so in view of what he had found when he arrived. "There is not a Diocese in England or Wales," he told his clergy in his second triennial Charge to them, in 1884, "in which the Established Church has to work under such *disadvantages and difficulties*, as the new Diocese of Liverpool. . . . Our Diocese is thoroughly undermanned and imperfectly equipped, and its first Protestant Bishop [Liverpool already had a Roman Catholic bishop] is in the position of a captain of some huge steamship who is suddenly called upon to start a voyage across the Atlantic with half the crew, and half the engineers, and half the coals that the ship requires."[10] By 1900, however, Liverpool diocese was an impressive going concern, a transformation for which the credit must go principally to the prime planner, director, organizer, encourager, and cajoler—Ryle himself.

In the days before the General Ordination Examination was even a twinkle in anyone's eye, bishops had complete discretion as to whom they ordained, and it is worth noting that Ryle, anxious as he was to attract young men to minister in Liverpool, maintained exacting educational standards. "I have not the least desire to lower the standard of requirements for the office of a deacon, and I cannot sympathize," he said in the same Charge of 1884, "with those who press Bishops to bring into the ministry men who know little or nothing about Latin, Greek, Church History, the English Reformation, the Prayer Book, Church Catechism, or Evidences of Christianity, and are only godly men who know the Bible and can talk about the Gospel. I think the office of the ministry demands men of a higher standard than this."[11] His examining chaplains included H. C. G. Moule, first principal of Ridley Hall, Cambridge; C. H. Waller, tutor and second principal in due course of the London College of Divinity (St. John's Hall, Highbury); and his own son, Herbert Ryle, principal of St. David's College, Lampeter (though this brilliant young man's embrace of higher criticism brought an end to his chaplaincy in 1887); and both deacon's and priest's examinations were treated very seriously. Candidates were sometimes refused ordination on grounds of incompetence, and clergy employing deacons as curates were told they must give them time to study. "It is a painful fact . . . that when a deacon comes up for priest's orders he seldom does so well and passes so good an examination as he did when he was ordained deacon, and has evidently not had

time to keep up his reading."[12] Whatever truth there may have been during the last hundred and more years in the idea that Anglican evangelical
clergy are educational lightweights, Ryle at least should be acquitted from
any responsibility for such a state of affairs.

Maintaining Sunday schools was never easy, and in many places
today has become very hard. In light of this, it is striking to see what
importance Ryle attached to Sunday schools in this his programmatic
Charge of 1884:

> There never was a time when it was so important to provide definite,
> thorough, dogmatic religious teaching for the children of the Church
> at least one day in the week. . . . I solemnly charge every incumbent in
> my Diocese to bestow as much care as he possibly can upon his Sunday
> school, to do his utmost to procure efficient teachers, and to take care
> that the time at the Sunday school is well spent, and not frittered away
> by those well-meaning persons who are content to read weak little
> story-books, and make children smile. Bible and Prayer-book instruc-
> tion should always come to the front, and clear teaching about the
> doctrines necessary to salvation should never be lost sight of.[13]

Some hold it against Ryle that he did not give priority to building a cathedral for the diocese. The facts are that at first he sought to implement this
project, but disagreements about site and design, followed by withdrawal
of the architect, failure to raise money, and finally, the lapsing of the
Liverpool Cathedral Act of Parliament in 1888, put an end to the plan.
Sir William Forwood, a member of the Cathedral Committee, was disap-
pointed, and wrote afterwards, somewhat sourly, that "the bishop did
not help the cause for though in a way he was anxious that a cathedral
should be built, he freely expressed his opinion both in public and private,
that additional Churches and mission halls would be more useful."[14]
At this distance, however, one can only applaud Ryle's sentiment.[15] St.
Peter's, a parish church near the city center, served as the procathedral
throughout Ryle's episcopate.

Censuring Ryle was in his day a constant habit, and both then and
since he has been made to bear blame, quite unjustly, for what happened
in the case of James Bell Cox, a ritualist priest who ignored Ryle's request
that he abandon the twelve illegal worship practices about which Dr. James
Hakes, chairman of the Liverpool branch of the Church Association, had
formally complained. When in 1885 Hakes began legal proceedings
against Cox, Ryle could have vetoed them but did not, on the grounds that
"every British subject has a right to bring his complaint before those who

administer the laws of the country" (a principle enshrined, as he pointed out, in the Magna Carta). On these grounds he had hitherto backed and justified the Church Association policy of taking lawless ritualists to court, while acknowledging that the need to do so highlighted the breakdown of ordinary church discipline and thus was extremely bad news;[16] and he saw no reason to switch principles now, though two petitions from within the diocese begged him to use the veto in order to maintain peace and avoid scandal. If Ryle was at fault in this, as many thought he was, his error lay precisely in being a conscientious constitutionalist who would not deprive anyone of their legal rights for the sake of a quiet life. So litigation went ahead, winding its way through various courts, none of which would Bell Cox recognize as having any authority to control his ministry; and at the end of three years the House of Lords gave judgment in Bell Cox's favor, so that he went back to doing all that he had been doing before. Ryle was damned by his foes because he had not vetoed the prosecution; he would have been damned by his friends had he vetoed it. It was for him a no-win situation, brought about by the cool defiance of a single clergyman, acting on conviction, and the fierce pertinacity of a single layman, also acting on conviction, against the background of twenty years' disputing as to what the Ornaments Rubric in the Book of Common Prayer did and did not allow in public worship. Hindsight prompts sympathy; the bishop was caught in the neatest trap imaginable. It is interesting to note what Ryle said in his 1889 diocesan conference address, after "three years of cease-less anxiety" (while the case dragged on),[17] with regard to the "primary causes of our 'unhappy divisions'":

> I believe the *Ornaments Rubric* . . . is an obscure and clumsy state-ment, which ought to be . . . replaced by an intelligible rule.
>
> I believe that imprisonment of *clergymen for contumacy* [i.e., contempt of court: Bell Cox had undergone this for seventeen days, and a certain Sidney Green of Manchester diocese for eighteen months] is a disgrace. . . . However mistaken a clergyman may be, imprisonment makes him a martyr. . . . If the sentence of a competent Church Court in a question of doctrine or ritual is not obeyed, the only punishment should be suspension or deprivation.
>
> I believe that the continuance of the *Episcopal Veto* does great mischief. . . . It is a most invidious power, which no Bishop can exercise without offending one party or another in his own diocese, and without risking flat contradiction to the decisions of his brother Bishops. . . . Among the laity, I am convinced that the veto is a fertile source of grave dissatisfaction.
>
> Last, but not least, I believe we shall never have peace until there

is some reform of our *Ecclesiastical Courts*. . . . More than five years
ago a Royal Commission reported that they were defective, and made
suggestions for the creation of better tribunals. But . . . nothing whatever has been done . . . and the result is that for doctrinal and ritual
disputes the Church has practically no law at all! This must be wrong.[18]

What Ryle sought was a workable system of doctrinal and ceremonial discipline for the maintaining of the Church of England's defined standards and
character. This should be noted as a further Puritan trait in his Christian
makeup, for insistence on such discipline as a mark of a properly function-
ing, God-honoring Church was always central to the Puritan platform.

One gets the sense that toward the end of his episcopate Ryle was felt
by some at least to be somewhat of an embarrassment. This was partly
because of his age (he was England's oldest bishop); partly because he
continued forthrightly to voice what was heard as old-fashioned doctrine
that paid no deference to—indeed, ordinarily took no notice of—England's
academic theological elite; partly because the text-based expository style of
preaching that he practiced and modeled so pungently had become alien to
much of the rest of the Church; partly because England's growing mood of
doctrinal indifference and skepticism about the Bible and its teaching made
definite beliefs like Ryle's seem primitive and uncouth; partly because the
outlook and style of most younger evangelicals was much less craggy than
his own; and partly because he had schooled the diocese and its clergy in so
simple, even simplistic, an evangelistic and discipling mode, thereby putting
Liverpool substantially out of step with the rest of the Church of England.
His own ideals were vividly reflected in his farewell letter to the diocese at
the time of his resignation. As the following extract shows, over more than
fifty years nothing had changed for John Charles Ryle:

Let me . . . charge all the clergy . . . never to neglect their preaching. . . . Your people . . . will not be content with dull, tame sermons.
They want life, and light, and fire, and love in the pulpit as well as
in the parish. Let them have plenty of it. Never forget that a lively,
Christ-exalting minister will always have a Churchgoing people.

Last, but not least, cultivate and study the habit of being at peace
with all your brother ministers. . . .

Cling to the old Church of England, my lay brethren, cling to its
Bible, its Prayer-book, and its Articles. Let no charitable institution
suffer. Consider the many poor and needy. Support missionary work
at home and abroad. Help the underpaid clergy. Never forget that the
principles of the Protestant Reformation made this country what she
is, and let nothing ever tempt you to forsake them.[19]

No, Ryle had not changed; here were the goals and guidelines that had shaped his ministry from the start. But England had changed. In the so-called "naughty nineties," the impact of secular skepticism, evolutionism, and materialism in the wider world of thought began at last to be felt, and the spirit of religious indifference that we have learned to call "post-Christian" set in. At that time, as is clear in hindsight, the Church of England also changed, not just by seeking in a general way to accommodate the cultural drift, but by quite specifically taking "higher criticism" on board (*Lux Mundi*, Charles Gore's liberal catholic manifesto of 1889, was the watershed here). This diluted and weakened the Church's corporate commitment to the truth of biblical doctrines as such in a way that has never yet been remedied. Creedal and confessional supernaturalism gave way to a cool, cloudy immanentism; Protestant passion for offsetting the Church of England against Roman Catholicism faded away; a revulsion against the thought of hell for anyone took place; and a groundswell of universal and undiscriminating tolerance appeared, wanting the leadership "to declare the Church a kind of Noah's ark, within which every kind of opinion and creed shall dwell safe and undisturbed, and the only terms of communion shall be willingness to come inside and let your neighbour alone,"[20] as Ryle acidly put it. This change was relatively sudden; Ryle noted it, commented sadly on it, and argued vigorously against it, but without effect. Culture and Church in England continue still along these same general lines. One result is an ongoing failure to do justice to Ryle as the leader and pioneer that he was.

Cool assessments of Ryle's episcopate have been common. It is true that he was elderly and intellectually set in his ways when appointed; that having only worked in village and market-town communities he was without experience of industrial cities when he came to Liverpool; that his romantic desire to die in harness arguably led him to postpone retirement too long (though the quality of his leadership to 1898 prompts an argument the other way); that bishops' meetings did not excite him and he did not bother to attend the 1888 Lambeth Conference, afterwards dissociating himself from its Encyclical Letter; and that, for all his labor in setting up buildings and mobilizing manpower (womanpower too) to evangelize working people, it was only in one or two parishes like Hobson's that this enterprise had noteworthy success. Yet that is not the whole story, nor its main part. A better estimate of Ryle's episcopate is gained by observing what he left behind him.

Ryle had been a devoted, hardworking, stern yet genial and empathetic bishop throughout,[21] and as we saw, he left the diocese which he had organized and built up a going, indeed a flourishing, concern. In his last triennial visitation address he expressed the hope that "my clergy will believe that the first Bishop of the new See of Liverpool loved his Diocese, and tried to promote its spiritual prosperity according to the light which God gave him."[22] Similarly, in the farewell letter cited above, he wrote: "I only ask you to remember that I was sixty-four, and not a young man, when I came here, and to believe that, amid many difficulties, I have tried to do my duty."[23] Ryle's modesty left no room for making grandiose claims, but by all relevant standards of reckoning, bearing in mind that he started entirely from scratch, his episcopate must be rated outstandingly successful in raising funds and maintaining morale, in rationalizing parochial structures and maximizing lay ministry, and in establishing Liverpool as a diocese of significant evangelical cast, quality, and strength—probably, during his time, the most markedly evangelical and most energetically evangelizing diocese that the Church of England has ever seen. The statesmanlike clear-headedness, common sense, and pastoral realism with which, in the sixteen public utterances between 1881 and 1898 that are contained in *Charges and Addresses,* Ryle set goals, nailed evils, specified needed changes, and vindicated what should not be changed merit highest praise, as does the tireless way he worked into his eighties to make the good things happen. His achievements called for a big biography; why did no one at once take in hand to write one?[24] Because, so I suspect, the people who both knew him well and had ability for the task felt they would embarrass themselves by paying major attention to this embattled old Protestant, who had been so remote from England's dominant religious trends and had indeed skewered them so trenchantly every time he took notice of them. "Ryle was a good bishop," wrote Michael Smout in 1975. "Not outstanding perhaps, but very able."[25] Damned with faint praise? Hobson, as we saw, went further, declaring Ryle "great as first Bishop of Liverpool," and that seems to me the truer estimate.

10

A GREAT PREACHER

Toward the end of his life the famous conductor Toscanini developed a distinctive all-purpose style of orchestral performance that made his work instantly recognizable, whatever music he was playing. At the start of his ministry, as was indicated earlier, Ryle developed a distinctive prose style that served him equally well as preacher, debater, speechmaker, counselor, and writer. It was a brisk, blunt style, pungent and persuasive, made up of short, abrupt, in-your-face sentences, rarely with more than one subordinate clause, all regularly piled together to produce cumulative and drumbeat effects. It was a personal, conversational style, aiming to make the hearer or reader feel individually addressed, and involving much use of the first person singular pronoun. The title of Ryle's first tract, a summary of his first sermon at Helmingham printed as *I Have Somewhat to Say unto Thee,* mirrors this perfectly. His style was fulsome in the sense that the thought unfolded slowly and steadily through the lively barrage of verbal gunfire, and it was also economical in the sense that the thought kept moving, no word was wasted. Ryle never just marked time, and again and again, to use his own phrases, he was able to focus his points in a few "picked and packed" words that would "strike and stick." His divisions were always clear ("for one thing . . . for another thing"), his headings stuck out, his down-to-earth illustrations and rhetorical emphases gave a sense of the drama, the dangers, the challenges, glories, and joys of life under the eye and hand of the God of the gospel; and thus, in a word, he communicated brilliantly at popular level. Didactic energy, honest humility, warm-hearted fellow-feeling, and courage to tell the truth as he saw it were equally expressed in everything he wrote and, so far as the evidence allows a generalization, everything he said, whether in private or in public.[1] If, from an evangelical Christian standpoint, Charles Haddon Spurgeon was the greatest Victorian preacher, John Charles Ryle was certainly the greatest Victorian tract writer, and his tremendous vitality in expounding the Bible, declaring the gospel, defending the faith, assessing people and periods, analyzing the Church's problems, and arguing for needed reforms, is still felt by all who read his work.

How Ryle's style was formed is an open secret. At Exbury, in the first months of his ministry, he had realized the need for an arresting simplicity of speech that would keep countryfolk listening to him, and in his 1887 lecture to clergy, "Simplicity in Preaching," he spelled out what he had found to be the path to it—a clear head; everyday words; short sentences; direct address; illustrations (analogies, anecdotes, and so on); "brains"; and prayer. Stressing that being simple is hard, he gave seekers after simplicity this advice:

> Read good models. . . . take the English Bible. . . . read John Bunyan's immortal . . . *Pilgrim's Progress*. Read it again and again. . . . Do not be above reading the Puritans . . . Baxter, and Watson, and Traill, and Flavel, and Charnock, and Hall, and Henry. . . . Read beside them the best models of modern English that you can get at . . . William Cobbett . . . John Bright . . . the speeches of Lord Chatham and Patrick Henry. Last, but not least, never forget . . . Shakespeare. Models of this sort must really be studied, and studied "with brains," too, if you wish to attain a good style of composition in preaching. On the other hand, do not be above talking to the poor. . . . Sit down with your people by the fireside, and exchange thoughts with them on all subjects. Find out how they think and how they express themselves.[2]

You, too, Ryle is saying, can become a didactic preacher (and writer, too) who grabs and holds people, if you are prepared to work at it in this way. Rather sweetly, he declares: "I am not a bit ashamed to say that I often read the sermons of Mr. Spurgeon. I like to gather hints about preaching from all quarters. . . . Now when you read Mr. Spurgeon's sermons, note how clearly and perspicuously he divides a sermon, and fills each division with beautiful and simple ideas. How easily you grasp his meaning! . . . great truths, that hang to you like hooks of steel, and which . . . you never forget!"[3] Spurgeon once called Ryle the best man in the Church of England; here Ryle in effect hails Spurgeon as the best preacher anywhere in the country.

But now, given Ryle's uncommon preaching and teaching skills, what was to be taught? The short answer was (and still is) the Bible and the gospel. At the close of "Simplicity in Preaching," Ryle had warned:

All the simplicity in the world can do no good, unless you preach the simple gospel of Jesus Christ so fully and clearly that everybody can understand it. If Christ crucified has not his rightful place in your sermons, and sin is not exposed as it should be, and your people are not plainly told what they ought to believe, and be, and do, your preaching is of no use.[4]

Through all Ryle's tracts and printed sermons the themes of sin and grace, the lostness of fallen humans, and the all-sufficiency of Jesus Christ, the crucified and risen Savior given to us to trust, are focal. Ryle followed the Reformers in treating these truths as the hermeneutical key to the Scriptures, and did not think he understood any biblical passage till he saw how it bore on the unfolding of them.

This becomes clear on the grandest scale in Ryle's seven-volume series of *Expository Thoughts* on the four Gospels. Ryle hoped that the bite-size units into which he divided his material would be useful for family prayers in Christian homes, for private devotional meditations, and for pastoral visitors reading to the poor and sick. *Matthew* (1858) and *Mark* (1857) are totally non-technical; *Luke* (1858) and *John* (1865, 1869, 1873), in two and three volumes respectively, have shrewd exegetical notes appended to the expositions, and Ryle gives lists of the eighty-odd commentaries he had consulted; but his style remains simple and popular from start to finish. An extended extract from Ryle's treatment of John 6:28-34 will illustrate the sin-and-grace focus and the heart-searching application that marks these precious expositions throughout:

We should observe, for one thing, in these verses, *the spiritual igno-rance and unbelief of the natural man.* Twice over we see this brought out and exemplified. When our Lord bade his hearers "labor for the meat which endureth to eternal life," they immediately began to think of works to be done, and a goodness of their own to be established. "What shall we do, that we might work the works of God?" Doing, doing, doing, was their only idea of the way to heaven. Again, when our Lord spoke of himself as one sent of God, and the need of believ-ing on him at once, they turn round with the question, "What sign showest thou? What dost thou work?" Fresh from the mighty miracle of the loaves and fishes, one might have thought they had had a sign sufficient to convince them. Taught by our Lord Jesus Christ himself, one might have expected a greater readiness to believe. But alas! There are no limits to man's dullness, prejudice, and unbelief in spiritual mat-ters. It is a striking fact that the only thing which our Lord is said to have "marvelled" at during his earthly ministry, was man's "unbelief" (Mark 6:6).

We shall do well to remember this, if we ever try to do good to others in the matter of religion. We must not be cast down because our words are not believed, and our efforts seem thrown away. We must not complain of it as a strange thing, and suppose that the people we have to deal with are peculiarly stubborn and hard. We must recollect that this is the very cup of which our Lord had to drink, and like him we must patiently work on. If even he, so perfect and so plain a Teacher, was not believed, what right have we to wonder if men do not believe us? Happy are the ministers, and missionaries, and teachers who keep these things in mind! It will save them much bitter disappointment. In working for God, it is of first importance to understand what we must expect in man. Few things are so little realized as the extent of human unbelief.

We should observe, for another thing, in these verses *the high honour Christ puts on faith in himself*. The Jews had asked him, "What shall we do, that we might work the works of God?" In reply he says, "This is the work of God, that ye believe on him whom he hath sent." A truly striking and remarkable expression! If any two things are put in strong contrast, in the New Testament, they are faith and works. Not working, but believing,—not of works but through faith,—are words familiar to all careful Bible-readers. Yet here the great Head of the Church declares that believing on him is the highest and greatest of all "works!" It is the "work of God."

Doubtless our Lord did not mean that there is anything meritorious in believing. Man's faith, at the very best, is feeble and defective. Regarded as a "work," it cannot stand the severity of God's judgment, deserve pardon, or purchase heaven. But our Lord did mean that faith in himself, as the only Saviour, is the first act of the soul which God requires at a sinner's hands. Till a man believes on Jesus, and rests on Jesus as a lost sinner, he is nothing. Our Lord did mean that faith in himself is that act of the soul which specially pleases God. When the Father sees a sinner casting aside his own righteousness, and simply trusting in his dear Son, he is well pleased. Without such faith it is impossible to please God. Our Lord did mean that faith in himself is the root of all saving religion. There is no life in a man till he believes. Above all, our Lord did mean that faith in himself is the hardest of all spiritual acts to the natural man. Did the Jews want something to do in religion? Let them know that the greatest thing they had to do was to cast aside their pride, confess their guilt and need, and humbly believe.

Let all who know anything of true faith thank God and rejoice. Blessed are they that believe! It is an attainment which many of the wise of this world have never yet reached. We may feel ourselves poor, weak sinners. But do we believe? We may fail and come short in many things. But do we believe? He that has learned to feel his sins, and to trust Christ as a Saviour, has learned the two hardest and greatest lessons in Christianity. He has been in the best of schools. He has been taught by the Holy Ghost. . . .

And now let us take heed to ourselves, and make sure that we are among those who eat the bread of God and live. Let us not be content with lazy waiting, but let us actually come to Christ, and eat the bread of life, and believe to the saving of our souls. The Jews could say, "Evermore give us this bread." But it may be feared they went no further. Let us never rest till, by faith we have eaten this bread, and can say, "Christ is mine. I have tasted that the Lord is gracious. I know and feel that I am his."[5]

Ryle's gifts as a preacher and teacher with a fiery, weighty, emphatic delivery in a loud, commanding voice made him a popular speaker among evangelicals within a very few years of his ordination. In his own view, however, he did not reach his pulpit prime till long after. "Why I was popular [in London, in the 1850s] I really do not know, for I am certain that my preaching was very inferior to what it was after I turned fifty. But it was always bold and aggressive and downright, and I suppose was very unlike what London congregations generally heard."[6] In the year of Ryle's death T. J. Maddon, Archdeacon of Warrington, obtained Ryle's permission to edit a selection of twenty-four of his sermons (published by Hodder and Stoughton as *The Christian Race and Other Sermons*); Ryle, having handed him all the sermon scripts still in his possession, wrote him the following letter:

It is a great relief to me that you have carried off my old sermons. You have my full permission to do what you will with these. Not a few were written long ago before I was 35! And now I am an old sinner of 83. Not a few were written in my first living in Helmingham and the earliest of all in my first curacy at Exbury in the New Forest and are *very raw*. Not one was written after I became a Bishop. Some of them are very unfinished and only fit to be burned. . . . show them no mercy. My first was preached in 1842 and now it is 1900. They are all my own and I never copied any one's.[7]

What Ryle wrote of the Puritan Samuel Ward, once Town Preacher of Ipswich, Suffolk, expresses perfectly what his own sermons and tracts aimed at and, indeed, achieved:

He is always to the point, always about the main things in Divinity. To exalt the Lord Jesus Christ as high as possible, to cast down man's pride, to expose the sinfulness of sin, to spread out broadly and fully the remedy of the Gospel, to awaken the unconverted sinner and alarm him, to build up the true Christian and comfort him—these seem to have been objects Ward proposed to himself in every sermon. And was he not right? Well would it be for the Churches if we had more preachers like him.[8]

To the last two sentences the Christian heart is still constrained to say *yes*.

11

A GREAT LEGACY

The true greatness of great men is not always discerned in their own lifetime. Surely John Charles Ryle is a case in point. No one can, or ever did, deny that he was strong, clear-headed, well-informed, hard-working, forthright, courageous, practical, and commonsensical, a man of integrity devoted to the glory of Christ, the saving of sinners, and the evangelical renewal of England's national Church; but beyond this, imperfect sympathy with his outlook has led to his being rated among Anglicans generally as, all in all, nothing special, and among non-Anglicans as an international Calvinist who really should not have invested himself so thoroughly in the Church of England. Both categories of assessment seem to me to miss much of Ryle's greatness; for of that greatness Ryle's vision of Anglican spiritual renewal through ministry to the whole community, and his loyalty to the Anglican system as a means of effecting renewal, is a significant part. It is in hope of setting the record straight here, and showing Ryle's full stature, that I now round off my survey by focusing on six stellar excellences that I see in this great Puritan bishop.

First comes Ryle's enduring of evangelical disfavor.

Nineteenth-century Anglican evangelicals were always a minority and were consistently marginalized and mocked, more or less, in both the Church and society. Their constant insistence that all are sinners needing new birth, and that worship, fellowship, witness, and Samaritanship are life's true priorities condemned both the dignified dullness of the clergy and the routine churchgoing of the laity, and so gave offense, to which the mockery was a defensive response. Ryle experienced this at home as a young convert,[1] and the forthrightness of his ministry during his years as a country parson, while filling the buildings where he preached, meant that many of his peers resented him and kept him at arm's length. When he became a bishop, the story was similar; reading between the lines, it is clear that he was always something of a speckled bird among his episcopal colleagues, much as he was respected for his zeal, ability, and achievements. Then in addition, over and above the general coolness toward him as an evangelical, some of his published opinions earned him active, belittling dislike from at least two powerful quarters.

High Church sacramentalists, who were labeled Tractarians during the dizzy decade before their leader, John Henry Newman, became a Roman Catholic in 1845, and whom Ryle called ritualists by reason of the baroque and medieval ceremonial that they brought in about 1860, and who later named themselves Anglo-Catholics, had several reasons for hostility to Ryle. First, appealing to the Gorham Judgment of 1850[2] as well as to the New Testament, Ryle censured their cherished belief in baptismal regeneration and their consequent failure to seek the conversion of adult Churchpeople and to highlight the inward realities of the new heart expressing itself in a new life. Second, as we saw earlier, he insisted that, whether they perceived this or not, their ritualizing of Holy Communion to express their ideas of Christ's real presence and the clergyman's sacrificing priesthood was a major move away from the Bible down the road to Rome. Third, he knowledgeably rehabilitated the English Reformers and John Foxe the martyrologist in the face of High Church accusations that these men were liars, fools, and bigots. Fourth, he constantly supported the London Church Association, founded in 1865, in its strategy of enforcing the legal limits on ritual by prosecutions of ritualists.[3] Fifth, he made no bones about declaring, "I believe that the Roman Catholic Church is the great predicted apostasy from the faith, and is Babylon and anti-Christ,"[4] thus reinforcing traditional English hostility to any convergence Romewards at any level. But ritualist clergy grew in numbers, and Ryle's anti-sacerdotal anti-sacramentalism marginalized him increasingly.

Broad Church advocates of a rationality that sought to assimilate new intellectual developments wrote Ryle off because he held to the old paths of evangelical faith as marked out through the revival a century before. He resisted the de-supernaturalizing of the Bible that the higher criticism brought[5] and, as we saw, tagged as modern Sadducees the revisionists who produced *Essays and Reviews* in 1860, and who with their followers called in question the finality of the Christian gospel in the world of religions and the certainty that pagans perish, which did so much to fuel the evangelical missionary movement. But these views made headway as the nineteenth century wore on, and Ryle's persistent opposition to them marginalized him as intellectually antediluvian.

Ryle's writings over the half-century of their production give no hint of hurt, doubt, or discouragement from any of this, nor during his episcopate does the sometimes scurrilous criticism directed at him by Liverpool's local papers, the *Mercury, Courier, Daily Post,* and *Echo,* and especially the *Porcupine* and *Liberal Review,* seem to have bothered him. (Then as now, Liverpool was a lively place, and then as now, evangelicals were often singled out for lampooning.) The reasons are not far to seek. First, as we have seen from his account of the bank crash, he could hide any deep personal feelings that he had. The stiff upper lip was part of the culture of the Victorian gentleman, and, as Ryle's son Herbert later said to his own son Edward, "We Ryles are very reserved in some ways."[6] But, second, it is possible that there were no feelings of deep hurt at all, for Ryle was sure of his ground, was confident he was right, and had learned to take opposition in stride as he worked for God, while his very strong belief in God's guiding hand assured him that everything in his life was making ultimate sense, whether at the moment he could see and feel that or not.[7] As some Canadians live cheerfully with mosquitoes, so Bishop Ryle seems to have lived cheerfully with his sniping critics. So he never grew bitter or disillusioned, nor did the warmth of his geniality toward his friends and loved ones ever decline, and though some thought him combative, conceited, and even cross-grained because of the vigor with which he pressed his views, he stands before us still as a striking example of humble, equable, unflinching, and unyielding steadiness in the many-sided work of the Lord. If we ask after Ryle's legacy, surely his example in this is a major part of it: for in both the modern world and the Church of England, evangelicals are far from being the flavor of the month, and the marginalizing of them continues.

Second comes Ryle's practice of evangelical family life.

The seventeenth-century Puritans saw the family as the first and fundamental social unit, and made much of the need for father to rule, teach, and take family prayers daily; for mother to support father, backing him up in everything; and for the children to be obedient, to be given primary education by their parents, and to experience home as a joyful place. The nineteenth-century evangelicals embraced the same ideal. We saw earlier how during the Helmingham years, when his wife was chronically ill, Ryle took responsibility for looking after their three boys; out of this a very close and warm relationship developed. Here is Herbert Ryle reminiscing about it: "In the country life of Suffolk he was everything to us— taught us games, natural history, astronomy, and insisted on our never being idle, and carefully fostered our love of books. To us boys he was extraordinarily indulgent. And he was tolerant to a degree little known or recognized. The High Church writers deliberately sought to destroy his position by detraction. Much as he differed from me in many points, he never suffered the shadow of a difference to come between us in the intimacy of our affection. And since the time I went to school at the age of nine and a half I never received from him a harsh word."[8] A teenager, afterwards an archdeacon, S. R. James, visited Stradbroke when the two elder Ryle boys were also in their teens, and wrote of it thus: "Mr. Ryle, with his gigantic figure and stentorian voice, was perhaps rather formidable to a youthful visitor, but he was very kind and hearty, and I soon felt at home. The atmosphere of the house was . . . devotional: daily Bible readings, somewhat lengthy family prayers, and a good deal of religious talk. But all was quite wholesome and unpretentious, and I don't think any of us were bored."[9] Beyond question, Ryle was a fine father.

He was a fine husband too. His care for his first two wives was exemplary, and his bonding with his third wife seems to have been very deep indeed. Her death in 1889, by his own confession, hit him very hard; nothing, he said, was the same afterwards. The words he wrote for her headstone in Childwall churchyard are revealing. "Here rests in hope waiting for the coming of our Lord Jesus Christ and our gathering together unto him Henrietta Amelia Ryle . . . for 27 years wife of J. C. Ryle, D.D., Bishop of Liverpool. . . ." Then follow three texts: first, "Christ is all" (Col. 3:11); third, "The blood of Jesus Christ . . . cleanseth us from all sin" (1 John 1:7); and in between these part of 2 Kings 4:26: "Say unto her, Is it well with thee? Is it well with thy husband? And she answered, It is well." He visited her grave weekly for the rest of his life, meditating often, one supposes, on and around the wording of that text. Ryle, we see, stands before us not only as a champion of Puritan faith, but as a striking specimen of the Puritan husband and family man.

Many have urged that no family is complete without a dog. No information exists as to whether the Ryles kept a dog at Helmingham, Stradbroke, or Liverpool, but we know that he had one at Exbury,[10] and that when he was a boy in Macclesfield he was given "a Lyme mastiff puppy . . . which afterwards grew to a huge dog, and I have his brass collar now [1873]. I hope it will always be kept in my family."[11] Dog lovers will feel the poignancy of Ryle's account of the final parting in August 1841 when he left Henbury for the last time:

> Nothing I think touched me that morning so much as the face of my old Lyme mastiff, Caesar, who was especially fond of me. I remember he looked at me as if he did not understand it, and could not see why he could not go with me too. Poor dog, for a whole month afterwards he

made his way into the house every morning as soon as the doors were opened, and went up to my room; there he lay at the door from morning till night and nothing would induce him to stir. When . . . it became dark he used to get up, smell at the bottom of the door, whine piteously and walk downstairs. This he repeated every day for a month.

Finally Caesar was given away to one of Ryle's Christian friends; but,

there he was not understood, was treated as a dog and not as a friend, became soured in temper, was always chained up and did not live long.[12]

Ryle was habitually factual and unsentimental in his account of things, but a good deal of his capacity for friendship and for love and pain within the family shine through in the above narrative. This side of Ryle, though rarely on show, was always part of him, balancing the sometimes elephantine humor and seeming offhandedness that made some think he had no finer or gentler feelings. It was a sad irony that all his sons drifted, more or less, from his faith, and only his daughter Jessie Isabella maintained it intact. Whatever caused this, it was certainly not a failure of fatherhood on Ryle's part. Ryle's robust humanity and warmth at home is a further sphere in which he is an example to us.

Third comes Ryle's declaration of evangelical belief. About this several things need to be said.

First, Ryle was always a reader, a scholar, and a thinker. His skill as a tract-writer and pamphleteer must not make us forget that he took a brilliant first class in his Oxford degree, and that he collected a large theological library, probably the single possession that he valued most,[13] and that he read theology all his life. He was not an academic;[14] he was a pastor, and as he read, alongside the question "Is this true?" the question "What effect will this have on ordinary people?" was always in his mind; yet he was as far as possible from the popular image of an evangelical as a largely uneducated man whose beliefs would bend and break if he knew more. After commending the Puritan William Gurnall's *The Christian in Complete Armour* as one of the "books in which Scripture is reverently regarded as the only rule of faith and practice—books in which Christ and the Holy Ghost have their rightful office—books in which justification, and sanctification, and regeneration, and faith, and grace, and holiness are clearly, distinctly, and accurately delineated, and exhibited . . . books which do real good," Ryle revealingly adds:

For my own part, I can only say that I read everything I can get hold of which professes to throw light on my Master's business, and the work of Christ among men. But the more I read, the less I admire modern theology. [He was writing in 1864.] The more I study the productions of the new schools of theological teachers, the more I marvel that men and women can be satisfied with such writing. There is a vagueness, a mistiness, a shallowness, an indistinctness, a superficiality, an aimlessness, a hollowness about the literature of the Catholic or broader [i.e., "Broad Church"] systems, as they are called, which to my mind stamps their origin on their face. They are of the earth, earthy. . . . In matters of theology the old is better.[15]

It was knowledge, not ignorance, that kept Ryle true to Reformational, Puritan, and evangelical theology and made him unwilling to endorse any of the theological and critical novelties of his time.

Second, Ryle had a passion for truth. He believed that the human mind was made for truth, and that God in Scripture has set truth before us, and that we owe it to both him and ourselves to have definite opinions about religious questions. In *Principles for Churchmen* he made his point here by mocking what he called the "jellyfish" mentality. Dislike of dogma, he wrote,

is an epidemic which is just now doing great harm, and specially among young people. . . . It produces what I must venture to call . . . a "jelly-fish" Christianity in the land: that is, a Christianity without bone, or muscle, or power. A jelly-fish . . . is a pretty and graceful object when it floats in the sea, contracting and expanding like a little, delicate, transparent umbrella. Yet the same jelly-fish, when cast on the shore, is a mere helpless lump, without capacity for movement, self-defense, or self-preservation. Alas! It is a vivid type of much of the religion of this day, of which the leading principle is, "No dogma, no distinct tenets, no positive doctrine." We have hundreds of "jelly-fish" clergymen, who seem not to have a single bone in their body of divinity. They have no definite opinions; they belong to no school or party; they are so afraid of "extreme views" that they have no views at all. We have thousands of "jelly-fish" sermons preached every year, sermons without an edge, or a point, or a corner, smooth as billiard balls, awakening no sinner, and edifying no saint. We have Legions of "jelly-fish" young men annually turned out from our Universities, armed with a few scraps of second-hand philosophy, who think it a mark of cleverness and intellect to have no decided opinions about anything in religion, and to be utterly unable to make up their minds as to what is Christian truth. They live apparently in a state of suspense, like Mahomet's fabled coffin, hanging between heaven and earth. . . . And last, and worst of all, we have myriads of "jelly-fish" worshippers—respectable Church-going people, who have no distinct and definite views about any point in theology. They cannot discern things that differ, any more than color-blind people can distinguish colors. They think everybody is right and nobody wrong, everything is true and nothing is false, all sermons are good and none are bad, every clergyman is sound and no clergyman unsound. They are "tossed to and fro, like children, by every wind of doctrine"; often carried away by any new excitement and sensational movement; ever ready for new things, because they have no firm grasp on the old; and utterly unable to "render a reason of the hope that is in them." . . . Never was it so important for laymen to hold systematic views of truth, and for ordained ministers to "enunciate dogma" very clearly and distinctly in their teaching.[16]

Ryle himself set an example of doing this throughout his ministry, as has already become clear, and as his published tracts and "papers" (we would say, chapters) unite to show.

Third, all of Ryle's printed material has the rhetorical style of a spoken address or preached sermon, in which Ryle invites his readers into an intimacy of communication that is at once bluff, heart-searching, didactic, masterful, and passionately committed to the glory of God through the welfare of sinners who seriously believe, repent, and obey, and who maintain spiritual honesty and humility as they do so. Most of the publications originated, as has already been pointed out, in actual sermons and addresses of this kind. It is easy to overlook the learning behind the wisdom in this kind of popular communication, and to treat the end product as ephemeral rather than definitive; when scholarly people want to be definitive, we expect them to write whole books. But Ryle's books were regularly just collections of these separate speech-like compositions, topically connected but not part of a cumulative argument—sermons and tracts bound together, in fact, as their full titles often in effect proclaimed.[17] So their theological weight has regularly been undervalued. It is, in fact, considerable and indeed crushing.

Full-scale exposition of Ryle's grand surveys of evangelical belief is not possible here; but Guthrie Clark felicitously focused Ryle's seven peak themes, as stated in the bishop's own words, and I cannot do better than quote the lengthy passage in which he does this. The ground covered will by now be familiar, and some of the quoted sentences we have met before, but there is a Ryle-like force in Clark's restatement that makes it fully worthy of our attention.

1. *The sufficiency and supremacy of Holy Scripture.* "Prove all things by the Word of God—all ministers, all teaching, all doctrines, all sermons, all writings, all opinions, all practices—prove all by the Word of God. Measure all by the measure of the Bible. . . . That which can abide the fire of the Bible, receive, hold, believe and obey. That which cannot abide the fire of the Bible, reject, refuse, repudiate and cast away."

2. *The total corruption of human nature.* Writing of the evangelical preachers of the eighteenth century, he [Ryle] says, "They knew nothing of the modern notion that Christ is in every man and that all possess something good within, which they have only to stir up and use in order to be saved. They never flattered men and women in this fashion. They told them plainly they were dead and must be made alive again; that they were guilty, lost, helpless and hopeless and in imminent danger of eternal ruin. Strange and paradoxical as it may seem to some, their first step towards making men good was to show them that they were utterly bad; and their primary argument in persuading men to do something for their souls, was to convince them that they could do nothing all."

3. *Christ's Death on the Cross the only satisfaction for sin.* "We rest our souls on a 'finished work,' . . . we have a Saviour who has done all, paid all, accomplished all, performed all that is necessary for our salvation. When we look at our own works, we may well be ashamed of their imperfection. But when we look at the finished work of Christ, we may feel peace. We are 'complete in him,' if we believe."

4. *Justification by faith.* Bishop Ryle was rightly tremendously proud of Article XI. . . . He is never in better form than when he is explaining that we are accounted righteous before God, only for the merit of our Lord and Saviour, Jesus Christ, by faith. "Every one that believes on the Son of God is at once pardoned, forgiven, justified, counted righteous, reckoned innocent and freed from all liability to condemnation. His sins, however many, are at once cleansed away by Christ's precious blood. His soul, however guilty, is at once clothed with Christ's perfect righteousness. It matters not what he may have been in the past. His sins may have been of the worst kind. His former character may be of the blackest description. But does he believe on the Son of God? This is the one question. If he does believe, he is justified from all things in the sight of God."

5. *Universal necessity of heart conversion.* . . . "The change which our Lord Jesus Christ declares needful for salvation is evidently no light or superficial one. It is not merely reformation or amendment or moral change or outward alteration of life. It is a thorough change of heart, will and character. It is a resurrection. It is a passing from death unto life. It is the implanting in our dead hearts of a new principle from above. It is the calling into existence of a new creature,

with a new nature, new habits of life, new tastes, new desires, new appetites, new judgments, new opinions, new hopes, new fears. . . . nothing less than this, is implied, when our Lord declares that we all need a new birth."

6. *The connexion between true faith and personal holiness.* "We maintain that to tell a man he is born of God or regenerated while he is living in carelessness or sin, is a dangerous delusion. . . . Where there is the grace of the Spirit, there will always be more or less the fruit of the Spirit. Grace that cannot be seen is no grace at all, and nothing better than Antinomianism. In short, we believe that where there is nothing seen, there is nothing possessed."

7. *God's hatred against sin and God's love towards sinners.* "If men are not saved, it is not because God does not love them and is not willing to save them, but because they will not come to Christ. But we must not be wise above what is written. No morbid liberality, so called, must induce us to regret anything which God has revealed about the next world. Men sometimes talk exclusively about God's mercy and love and compassion as if he had no other attributes, and leave out of sight entirely his holiness and his purity, his justice and his unchangeableness and his hatred of sin. Let us beware of falling into this delusion. It is a growing evil in these latter days."[18]

In this extract both the core and the perspective of Ryle's evangelical theology are made utterly clear. As an Anglican clergyman, he was as he saw it committed to practice institutional evangelism through the parochial system, as part of the Church's pastoral care of Englishmen from the cradle to the grave, and of its never ending task of teaching true piety ("religion" was his word for it) to all, at every stage of their pilgrimage. As an Anglican evangelical, Ryle saw it as his job to inject into his ministry at every point the evangelical understanding of the knowledge of Christ and salvation, of communion with God the Father as a sinner saved by grace who is now an adopted child, and of the faith, hope, and love that are born of regeneration by the Holy Spirit; or, putting it differently and perhaps better, to teach everything he touched within the frame of steady emphasis on the seven points highlighted by Clark. So Ryle's exposition of evangelical beliefs was always angled as an account of the world of spiritual reality, within which we sinners are called to know the real God and live the real Christian life, according to the Bible, through faith in Jesus Christ. Ryle's skill in the pastoral angling of the evangelical belief system is one of the most valuable parts of his legacy.

Fourth comes Ryle's equally valuable demonstration of the evangelical way to meditate on the Bible.

Ryle wrote his comments ("Expository Thoughts") on the four Gospels in short sections that, as we noted, he hoped would be suitable for reading aloud at family prayers and in visitation ministry (each would take about ten minutes' reading time). He hoped, too, that they would make fruitful devotional reading for busy individuals, and in fact these pages contain many superb models of what in some circles is called discursive meditation. The Puritans in particular had described such meditation as doing for yourself, before the Lord, as a preface to prayer, what preachers should do for you from the pulpit each Sunday; namely, applying to yourself for guidance, comfort, correction, and motivation universal truths about God the Father, the Son, and the Spirit, and human relationship with the holy Three, as these truths emerge from the biblical text. Ryle's expository thoughts model this activity in classic fashion, as we saw in the comment on John 6 quoted earlier, and they remain as good a resource for priming the pump of meditation on the Bible as any I know. Too often in modern ministry we tell people to read and meditate on Scripture without showing them any method of meditation or offering them any examples of anyone actually doing it. This is a gap in today's Christian nurture that Ryle can still fill, I think to great advantage.

Fifth comes Ryle's vindication of evangelical Churchmanship.

This he achieved, as we have seen, by exegesis of the Thirty-nine Articles and Book of Common Prayer, plus his own glowing presentation of the evangelical tradition—Reformational, Puritan, and eighteenth-century evangelical. Historically, he made his case: there can be no question about that. But the spreading idea in his day was that the Church of England ought to broaden, and treat what was going on in the High and Broad camps as, in a general sense at least, coming from God and carrying his blessing. Ryle opposed this, as we have noted, but he was no more able to halt it then Canute could stop the tide coming in. Yet his argument that the ritualist and Broad Church traditions carried no spiritual power should not be forgotten, any more than should his demonstrations that doctrinal Anglicanism, as set forth in the Articles and Prayer Book, matches the didactic emphases and the delineation of spiritual life that the New Testament directly displays. In recent years, liturgical revision and charismatic novelties may seem to have carried the Anglican Church far away from Ryle's world, but his testimony stands as a reminder that as there was power in the past in the way marked out by the historic Anglican formularies, so there can be again, for neither God nor basic human nature and need change at all from one generation to another.

The strength, cogency, and clarity with which Ryle makes this point is another excellence of the legacy he has left us.

Sixth comes Ryle's vision of evangelical vitality, both individual and corporate.

I might illustrate this from his life, but I shall in fact take it from his books, where it appears with riveting force.

Ryle believed, and often said, that spiritual standards among his contemporaries in the faith were low, and a great deal of his writing about the Christian life was devoted to raising them. Here, for instance, is what he wrote about zeal:

> I want to strike a blow at the lazy, easy, sleepy Christianity of these latter days, which can see no beauty in zeal, and only uses the word "zealot" as a word of reproach. . . .
>
> Zeal in religion is a burning desire to please God, to do his will, and to advance his glory in the world in every possible way. It is a desire which no man feels by nature, which the Spirit puts in the heart of every believer when he is converted, but which some believers feel so much more strongly than others that they alone deserve to be called "zealous" men.
>
> This desire is so strong, when it really reigns in a man, that it impels him to make any sacrifice, to go through any trouble, to deny himself to any amount, to suffer, to work, to labour, to toil, to spend himself and be spent, and even to die, if only he can please God and honour Christ.
>
> A zealous man in religion is pre-eminently *a man of one thing*. It is not enough to say that he is earnest, hearty, uncompromising, thorough-going, wholehearted, fervent in spirit. He only sees one thing, he cares for one thing, he lives for one thing, he is swallowed up in one thing; and that one thing is to please God. Whether he lives or whether he dies, whether he has health or whether he has sickness, whether he is rich or whether he is poor, whether he pleases man or whether he gives offence, whether he is thought wise or whether he is thought foolish, whether he gets blame or whether he gets praise, whether he gets honour or whether he gets shame, for all this the zealous man cares nothing at all. He burns for one thing; and that one thing is to please God, and to advance God's glory. If he is consumed in the very burning, he cares not for it—he is content. He feels that, like a lamp, he is made to burn; and if consumed in burning, he has but done the work for which God appointed him. Such a one will always find a sphere for his zeal. If he cannot preach, and work, and give money, he will cry, and sigh, and pray. Yes: if he is only a pauper, on a perpetual bed of sickness, he will make the wheels of sin

around him drive heavily, by continually interceding against it. If he cannot fight in the valley with Joshua, he will do the work of Moses, Aaron and Hur, on the hill (Ex. 17:9-13). If he is cut off from working himself, he will give the Lord no rest till help is raised up from another quarter, and the work is done. This is what I mean when I speak of "zeal" in religion.[19]

We saw earlier how Ryle censured "Pearsall Smithism" as leading to self-deception and spiritual slackness and emptying key Bible terms of their true meaning. *Victory* was one of those terms. Here, now, is Ryle's own treatment of the victory theme, a further facet of his vision of Christian vitality. He is dealing with Christ's promises in Revelation 2 and 3 to those who overcome:

> If you would prove you are born again and going to heaven, you must be a victorious soldier of Christ. If you would make it clear that you have any title to Christ's precious promises, you must fight the good fight in Christ's cause, and in that fight you must conquer.
>
> Victory is the only satisfactory evidence that you have a saving religion. You like good sermons perhaps. You respect the Bible, and read it occasionally. You say your prayers night and morning. You have family prayers, and give to religious societies. I thank God for this. It is all very good. But how goes the battle? . . . Are you overcoming the love of the world and the fear of man? Are you overcoming the passions, tempers and lusts of your own heart? Are you resisting the devil and making him flee from you? How is it in this matter? You must either rule or serve sin and the devil and the world. There is no middle course. You must either conquer or be lost.
>
> I know well it is a hard battle that you have to fight, and I want you to know it, too. . . . You must make up your mind to a daily struggle if you would reach heaven. . . . Sin, the world and the devil must be actually mortified, resisted and overcome.
>
> This is the road that the saints of old have trodden. . . . Moses . . . overcame the love of pleasure. . . . Micaiah . . . overcame the love of ease. . . . Daniel . . . overcame the fear of death. . . . Matthew . . . overcame the love of money. . . . Peter and John . . . overcame the fear of man. . . . When Saul the Pharisee gave up all his prospects of preferment among the Jews, and preached that very Jesus whom he had once persecuted, this was overcoming: he overcame the love of man's praise.
>
> The same kind of thing which these men did you must also do if you would be saved. They were men of like passions with yourself, and yet they overcame. They had as many trials as you can possibly have, and yet they overcame. They fought. They wrestled. They struggled. You must do the same.

What was the secret of their victory? Their faith. They believed on Jesus and, believing, were made strong . . . and . . . were held up. In all their battles, they kept their eyes on Jesus, and he never left them nor forsook them. "They overcame by the blood of the Lamb, and by the word of their testimony" and so may you (Rev. 12:11).[20]

For Ryle's vision of Christian vitality we should surely thank God—and allow it to stir us to raise our sights.

As for corporate vitality, Ryle's understanding of how God brings the Church to life is embedded in *Christian Leaders of the Eighteenth Century*, where he shines his spotlight brilliantly on eleven—as far as he is concerned, the leading eleven—of the preachers who turned England and Wales upside down during the revival days.[21] The pattern of renewal that he detects begins with empowered preaching of the gospel and all that goes with it regarding the Christian life; this leads to transforming encounters with God; and these create a community with a passion to evangelize and spread the gospel everywhere, to root all evil out of society, and to establish standards of love, honesty, faithfulness, humility, steadiness, and service everywhere. In that book, which first appeared in 1869, Ryle expressed the view that community quickening must begin with the clergy, and he does not seem ever to have retreated from that very Puritan conviction during his time at Liverpool. Ryle's challenging vision of renewed vitality in Christians and churches is the last, and in one sense the climactic, excellence of his life and teaching to which I want to draw attention as I bring this celebration of him to a close.

There were giants in the earth in those days. That was how Ryle felt, contemplating the eighteenth-century evangelical leaders, and that is how we surely should feel as we contemplate Ryle himself. As he was a giant physically, so he was a giant spiritually: stable, alert, denying himself, driving himself; leaderlike, statesmanlike, enormously forceful, masterful in his style yet humble in his heart. Well did his successor, Bishop F. J. Chavasse, call him "that man of granite with the heart of a little child," and declare that he "lived so as to be missed."[22] But the supremely important things to say about him are that he held to the Bible and its gospel with absolute tenacity; that he never compromised on essentials,[23] such as biblical inspiration, or spiritual regeneration and conversion, or justification by faith in Christ, though he did not enjoy the controversial involvements into which his stance led him; and that his Puritan priorities were maintained intact throughout his episcopate, giving it a simple, down-to-earth, evangelical style that was and remains unique in modern times. I do not claim that he was flawless (he clearly was not), but I do claim that he was indeed great, as Canon Hobson affirmed. I invite my readers to consider whether they do not agree with me. And when today the questions that exercised Ryle, and that he answered in Puritan terms, arise in their modern form (How shall we understand and apply the Bible? What is the faith that we clergy should be systematically teaching, and all God's people systematically learning, day in and day out? What constitutes true spiritual life, true spiritual worship, true Christian holiness, and true Christian self-discipline? How can the word of Christ be effectively spoken and spread? How can preachers speak to consciences? How can sleepy churches be awakened, and dead churches revived, and weak churches become strong?)—when, as I said, these questions arise today, I invite my readers further to consider whether, at the level of principle and in a way that transcends cultural change, Ryle's answers to them, and Ryle's modeling of ministry in terms of those answers, do not still point the true way forward.

12

THE GREAT TRADITION

At this point I need, and wish, to come clean. It is, I think, high time I did.

It is now more than half a century since I began to discern in the developed Puritanism of history a definitive embodiment of New Testament Christianity. By the Puritanism of history I mean the Bible-based, Christ-centered, conversionist, devotional, Church-focused, community-oriented movement that began to take shape with the Elizabethans Greenham and Perkins and Richard Rogers, and that effectively ended with Baxter, Howe, and Henry, who saw the Stuarts out and toleration in, and that produced such as Sibbes, Owen, and Bunyan in old England and Thomas Hooker, Increase and Cotton Mather, and finally Jonathan Edwards in New England. By a definitive embodiment of New Testament Christianity I mean a body of beliefs and a style of life that combined on the grand scale the Trinitarian objectivism of the Fathers, the knowledge of self and sin set forth by Augustine, the knowledge of Christ, of the cross, and of justification by faith that the magisterial Reformers had and shared, and the universal Christian passion for the glory of God in the worshiping life of the Church, with the insight into regeneration, sanctification, and the inner life of the self that was the Puritans' distinctive contribution. I mean a body of beliefs and a style of life that was intensely practical, experiential, conscientious, determined, vigorous, hopeful, hardworking, and visionary in its struggle to achieve and maintain sanctity in all circumstances, walks of life, personal states, relationships, and life activities, and to establish that sanctity everywhere in England and Wales (Scotland and Ireland had their own parallel movements), and beyond Britain too, by every means available. My amazement at the rightness and richness of Puritan Christianity was great from the start, and has only increased as the years have gone by.

Seeing in this Puritan ideal, and in individual Puritan lives that I have studied, the most complete, profound, and magnificent realization of biblical religion that the world has yet known, and viewing German Lutheran pietism and the English-speaking evangelical movements of the eighteenth and nineteenth centuries as they viewed themselves—namely as partial though incomplete realizations of the Puritan vision of godliness—I have only been able to give two cheers for those many latter-day explorations of the evangelical heritage that treat evangelical religion as beginning in the eighteenth century. The truth is that evangelicalism, so-called, yesterday and today, should be seen as Puritanism continuing, but constantly narrowed—intellectually, culturally, humanistically, aesthetically, relationally—by secularizing pressures and perspectives in the Protestant world, so that increasingly it produces pygmies rather than giants. It is by Puritan standards that our stature should be measured, and our shortcomings detected, for those are the standards of the Bible. The pioneers of the Evangelical Revival in Britain and the Great Awakening in New England knew this well, and read, thought, prayed, spoke, and acted accordingly. The fact that today's evangelicals are so largely out of touch with their own history, and so cannot discern how small and dry and lightweight and superficial and childish they are compared with those from whom they take their name, is one of the more glaring of our current shortcomings, all the more so for going constantly unnoticed. As T. S. Eliot pictured his cultural generation as "the hollow men . . . filled with straw," so we must learn to see ourselves as the pygmy generation of miniaturized evangelicals, Christian Tiny Tims full of eager niceness but insipid to the palate of our alienated and desperate Western world. This is not a good state of affairs.

Latter-day giants there have been, however, in the Puritan mould, giants who knew, valued, and fed on the Puritan tradition as the benchmark of mainstream Christianity and the vitamin supply for their own souls. Among the Victorians Charles Haddon Spurgeon was one, and John Charles Ryle was another. Both fought to the last to keep the pure biblical gospel clear and central, in the face of doctrinal and devotional decline which they were almost lone voices in challenging; both were admired by their own constituencies but lacked successors of their own quality; and both leave readers of their work at the start of the twenty-first century wondering how, if they knew of us, they might sum us up. And we do well, I believe, to wonder, as I said above.

Dr. D. Martyn Lloyd-Jones, perhaps the only twentieth-century

British evangelical to match either of these Victorian flamethrowers in stature, used to insist that ours is an age of unparalleled confusion on spiritual matters, and that the basic question forced on us by the state of both the Church and the world is: What is a Christian? Surely he was right, and his words ring even truer today than they did a generation ago. Now Ryle, as we have seen, was a passionate exponent of the full biblical faith and a strategic thinker about the Church's mission into the bargain; but, like Lloyd-Jones, in his public ministry he was always high-lighting and enforcing the old, unchanging truth that real Christians are two things together; first, they are what we call Reformational in faith (that is, Bible-centered, God-centered, Christ-centered, cross-centered, and salvation-centered in the way that the New Testament models and requires, with neither addition nor subtraction); and, second, they are also what the Bible calls regenerate in heart and life (that is, manifesting motivations, values, goals, and behavior patterns that express the life-giving union with the risen Christ that changes character, and manifest-ing also the ability to do and endure, praising and praying, loving and serving, that the Holy Spirit brings about). If you think, as I do, that understanding, entering, and living this new life is everyone's prime vocation, and that helping people so to do is every church's prime task, then you will value Bishop Ryle the Puritan, as I do, as an icon and a beacon, recalling us from wrong roads and bypaths and showing us, three generations after his time, where to set our own feet. Here, as my last word on this, is Ryle's first, prefatory word on the "great truths . . . essential for salvation" that he sets forth in his volume *Old Paths*:

> The name which I have selected will prepare the reader to expect no new doctrines in this volume. It is simple, unadulterated, old-fashioned Evangelical theology. It contains nothing but the "Old Paths" in which the Apostolic Christians, the Reformers, the best English Churchmen for the last three hundred years, and the best Evangelical Christians of the present day, have persistently walked. From these "paths" I see no reason to depart. They are often sneered at and ridiculed. . . . "None of these things move me." I have yet to learn that there is any system of religious teaching, by whatever name it may be called, High, or Broad, or Romish, or Neologian, which produces one quarter of the effect on human nature that is produced by the old, despised system of doctrine which is commonly called Evangelical. . . . The longer I live the more I am convinced that the world needs no new Gospel, as some profess to think. I am thoroughly persuaded that the world needs nothing but a bold, full, unflinching teaching of the "old paths." The heart of man is

the same in every age. The spiritual medicine which it requires is always the same. The same Gospel which was preached by Latimer, and Hooper, and Bradford—by Halt, Davenant, Usher, Reynolds, and Hopkins—by Manton, Brooks, Charnock, Owen, Watson and Gurnall—by Romaine, Venn, Hervey, Grimshaw and Cecil—this is the gospel which alone wilt do real good in the present day. The leading doctrines of that gospel . . . are the doctrines, I firmly believe, of the Bible and the Thirty-nine Articles of the Church of England. They are doctrines which, I find, wear well, and in the faith of them I hope to live and die.[1]

Me, too; and you also, I trust. Here is the great tradition; here is the true path of wisdom and of life. Ryle has guided many along it; he has been a guide to me; may he now lead you. And to God be all the glory.

In saying this, I do not ask you to forget that Ryle was a child of his time, just as you and I are children of ours. His mind-set and rhetoric, his real brilliance and scholarship, and his self-understanding as an Englishman, a clergyman, and a bishop was early- and mid-Victorian, as we have already noted, and much water has flowed under the bridge since his day in academia, in Anglicanism, in Roman Catholicism, and in patterns of work, leisure, and family life, of technology and travel, of popular culture, reading habits, and attitudes to religion in general and Christianity in particular. However directly we find him speaking to our hearts, he is not in every respect our contemporary, and we would damage ourselves spiritually if we let ourselves imagine otherwise. Nor do I ask you to listen to Ryle as if he spoke the last words of human wisdom or achieved final formulations in Christian catechetics (not a Ryle word, be it said, but yet the right term for what he was doing most of the time). I simply ask you to tune in to Ryle as one who was himself attuned to the eternities and immensities, to use Carlyle's phrase, that belong to true faith: namely, knowledge of the truths of the gospel; knowledge of the grace of our Lord Jesus Christ; knowledge of the transforming reality of regeneration and the disciplines and delights of discipleship; knowledge of the God-sustained struggle against the world, the flesh, and the devil, and the enabling of the Holy Spirit in mission and ministry; and thus knowledge of God in the full biblical sense. Ryle spoke of himself, with sweet, grim wit, as "no more infallible than the Pope,"[2] and we may agree with that; but I do not think you can point to anyone, past or present, with better developed Christian instincts or greater skill in stating the first and fundamental words of divine wisdom for mankind according to Christ and the Scriptures. Take from Ryle, I urge, what Ryle has to give, that is, the basic Christianity that many fall short of and no one ever gets beyond, and thank God for such good food. You will not find a more nourishing diet this side of heaven.

> *Remember your leaders, those who spoke to you the word of God. Consider the outcome of their way of life, and imitate their faith. Jesus Christ is the same yesterday and today and forever* (Heb. 13:7-8, ESV).

FOR FURTHER READING

Ryle's books, which are constantly brought back into print, fall into five main categories:

1. Biblical Exposition:
Expository Thoughts on the Gospel of Matthew (1856)
Expository Thoughts on the Gospel of Mark (1858)
Expository Thoughts on the Gospel of Luke (2 vols., 1858)
Expository Thoughts on the Gospel of John (3 vols., 1865, 1869, 1873)

2. Devotional Studies:
Holiness (1877, 2nd enlarged edition 1879)
Practical Religion (1878)
The Upper Room (1888)
The Christian Race (1900)

3. Historical Studies:
Light from Old Times (1890; a new edition of *Bishops and Clergy of Other Days*, 1868, already republished as *Protestant Facts and Men*, 1882)
Christian Leaders of the Eighteenth Century (1869)

4. Doctrinal Studies:
Coming Events and Present Duties (1867, enlarged 1879)
Old Paths (1877)

5. Anglican Faith and Practice:
Knots Untied (1874)
Principles for Churchmen (1884)
Disestablishment Papers (1885)
Charges and Addresses (1903)

Also, there were several multi-volume printings of his tracts, under the title *Home Truths* (1851–); these Ryle cannibalized very freely in the books listed above.

The fullest life of Ryle is Eric Russell, *That Man of Granite with the Heart of a Child* (Fearn, UK: Christian Focus, 2001). The best life before this was Peter Toon and Michael Smout, *John Charles Ryle, Evangelical Bishop* (Cambridge: James Clarke; and Swengel, Pa.: Reiner, 1976). The most thorough study of Ryle's episcopate is Ian D. Farley, *J. C. Ryle, First Bishop of Liverpool* (Carlisle, England: Paternoster, 2000). A uniform centenary edition of Ryle's works has begun to appear from Charles Nolan Publishers, Moscow, Idaho: so far *Light from Old Times, Knots Untied,* and the large tract on the Bible, *How Readest Thou?* have become available.

HOLINESS

Its Nature, Hindrances, Difficulties, and Roots

⁌⦇⦈⁍

J. C. RYLE
(1877)

EPIGRAPH

*Extract from Ryle's Preface to the 1879
Enlarged Edition of* Holiness

The older I grow the more I am convinced that real practical *Holiness* does not receive the attention it deserves, and that there is a most painfully low standard of living among many high professors of religion in the land. But, at the same time, I am increasingly convinced that the zealous efforts of some well-meaning persons to promote a higher standard of spiritual life are often not "according to knowledge," and are really calculated to do more harm than good. Let me explain what I mean.

It is easy to get crowds together for what are called "Higher life" and "Consecration" meetings. Any one knows that, who has watched human nature, and read descriptions of American camp-meetings, and studied the curious phenomena of the "Religious affections." Sensational and exciting addresses by strange preachers or by women, loud singing, hot rooms, crowded tents, the constant sight of strong semi-religious feeling in the faces of all around you for several days, late hours, long protracted meetings, public profession of experience,—all this kind of thing is very interesting at the time, and seems to do good. But is the good real, deeply-rooted, solid, lasting? That is the point. And I should like to ask a few questions about it.

Do those who attend these meetings become more holy, meek, unselfish, kind, good tempered, self-denying, and Christ-like at home? Do they become more content with their position in life, and more free from restless craving after something different from that which God has given them? Do fathers, mothers, husbands, and other relatives and friends, find them more pleasant and easy to live with? Can they enjoy a *quiet* Sunday and *quiet* means of grace without noise, heat, and excitement? Above all, do they grow in charity, and especially in charity towards those who do not agree with them in every jot and tittle of their religion?

These are serious and searching questions, and deserve serious consideration. I hope I am as anxious to promote real practical *Holiness* in the land as any one. I admire and willingly acknowledge the zeal and earnestness of many with whom I cannot co-operate who are trying to promote it. But I cannot withhold a growing suspicion that the great "mass-meetings" of the present day, for the ostensible object of promoting spiritual life, do not tend to promote private home religion, private Bible-reading, private prayer, private usefulness, and private walking with God. If they are of any real value, they ought to make people better husbands, and wives, and fathers, and mothers, and sons, and daughters, and brothers, and sisters, and masters, and mistresses, and servants. But I should like to have clear proofs that they do. I only know it is far easier to be a Christian among singing, praying, sympathizing Christians in a public room, than to be a consistent Christian in a quiet, retired, out-of-the-way, uncongenial home. The first position is one in which there is a deal of *nature* to help us: the second is one which cannot be well filled without *grace*. But, alas, many talk now-a-days about *"Consecration,"* who seem to be ignorant of the "first principles of the oracles of God" about *"Conversion."*

I close this preface with the sorrowful feeling that probably some who read it will not agree with me. To the young especially I can see that the great gatherings of the so-called "spiritual-life" movement are sure to be attractive. They naturally like zeal and stir, and enthusiasm, and they say, "Where is the harm?" Be it so: we must agree to differ. When I was as young as they are, perhaps I should have thought as they do. When they are as old as I am, they will very likely agree with me.

To each and all of my readers, I say in conclusion, let us exercise charity in our judgments of one another. Towards those who think *Holiness* is to be promoted by the modern, so-called "spiritual life" movement, I feel nothing but charity. If they do good, I am thankful. Towards myself and those who agree with me, I ask them to feel charity in return. The last day will show who is right and who is wrong. In the meantime, I am quite certain that to exhibit bitterness and coldness towards those who cannot conscientiously work with us, is to prove ourselves very ignorant of real *Holiness*.

—*J. C. Ryle*

INTRODUCTION

The papers contained in this volume are a humble contribution to a cause which is exciting much interest in the present day—I mean the cause of *Scriptural holiness*. It is a cause which everyone who loves Christ, and desires to advance His kingdom in the world, should endeavour to help forward. Everyone can do something, and I wish to add my mite.

The reader will find little that is directly controversial in these papers. I have carefully abstained from naming modern teachers and modern books. I have been content to give the result of my own study of the Bible, my own private meditations, my own prayers for light, and my own reading of old divines. If in anything I am still in error, I hope I shall be shown it before I leave the world. We all see in part, and have a treasure in earthen vessels. I trust I am willing to learn.

I have had a deep conviction for many years that practical holiness and entire self-consecration to God are not sufficiently attended to by modern Christians in this country. Politics, or controversy, or party-spirit, or worldliness, have eaten out the heart of lively piety in too many of us. The subject of personal godliness has fallen sadly into the background. The standard of living has become painfully low in many quarters. The immense importance of "adorning the doctrine of God our Saviour" (Titus 2:10), and making it lovely and beautiful by our daily habits and tempers, has been far too much overlooked. Worldly people sometimes complain with reason that "religious" persons, so-called, are not so amiable and unselfish and good-natured as others who make no profession of religion. Yet sanctification, in its place and proportion, is quite as important as justification. Sound Protestant and Evangelical doctrine is useless if it is not accompanied by a holy life. It is worse than useless: it does positive harm. It is despised by keen-sighted and shrewd men of the world, as an unreal and hollow thing, and brings religion into contempt. It is my firm impression that we want a thorough revival about *Scriptural holiness*, and I am deeply thankful that attention is being directed to the point.

It is, however, of great importance that the whole subject should be placed on right foundations, and that the movement about it should not be damaged by crude, disproportioned, and one-sided statements. If such statements abound, we must not be surprised. Satan knows well the power of true holiness, and the immense injury which increased attention to it will do to his kingdom. It is his interest, therefore, to promote strife and controversy about this part of God's truth. Just as in time past he has succeeded in mystifying and confusing men's minds about justification, so he is labouring in the present day to make men "darken counsel by words without knowledge" about sanctification. May the Lord rebuke him! I cannot however give up the hope that good will be brought out of evil, that discussion will elicit truth, and that variety of opinion will lead us all to search the Scriptures more, to pray more, and to become more diligent in trying to find out what is "the mind of the Spirit."

I now feel it a duty, in sending forth this volume, to offer a few introductory hints to those whose attention is specially directed to the subject of sanctification in the present day. I know that I do so at the risk of seeming presumptuous, and possibly of giving offence. But something must be ventured in the interests of God's truth. I shall therefore put my hints into the form of questions, and I shall request my readers to take them as "Cautions for the Times on the subject of holiness."

(1) I ask, in the first place, whether it is wise to speak of *faith* as the one thing needful, and the only thing required, as many seem to do now-a-days in handling the doctrine of sanctification?—Is it wise to proclaim in so bald, naked, and unqualified a way as many do, that the holiness of converted people is *by faith only, and not at all by personal exertion?* Is it according to the proportion of God's Word? I doubt it.

That faith in Christ is the root of all holiness—that the first step towards a holy life is to believe on Christ—that until we believe we have not a jot of holiness—that union with Christ by faith is the secret of both beginning to be holy and continuing holy—that the life that we live in the flesh we must live by the faith of the Son of God—that faith purifies the heart—that faith is the victory which overcomes the world—that by faith the elders obtained a good report—all these are truths which no well-instructed Christian will ever think of denying. But surely the Scriptures teach us that in following holiness the true Christian needs personal exertion and work as well as faith. The very same Apostle who says in one place, "The life that I live in the flesh I live by the faith of the Son of God," says in another place, "I fight—I run—I keep under my body"; and in other places, "Let us cleanse ourselves—let us labour, let us lay aside every weight" (Gal. 2:20; 1 Cor. 9:26-27; 2 Cor. 7:1; Heb. 4:11; 12:1). Moreover, the Scriptures nowhere teach us that faith *sancti-fies* us in the same sense, and in the same manner, that faith *justifies* us! Justifying faith is a grace that "worketh not," but simply trusts, rests, and leans on Christ (Rom. 4:5). Sanctifying faith is a grace of which the very life is action: it "worketh by love," and, like a main-spring, moves the whole inward man (Gal. 5:6). After all, the precise phrase "sanctified by faith" is only found once in the New Testament. The Lord Jesus said to Saul, "I send thee, that they may receive forgiveness of sins and inheri-tance among them which are sanctified by faith that is in Me." Yet even there I agree with Alford, that *"by faith"* belongs to the whole sentence, and must not be tied to the word "sanctified." The true sense is, "that by faith in Me they may receive forgiveness of sins and inheritance among them that are sanctified" (compare Acts 26:18 with Acts 20:32).

As to the phrase "holiness by faith," I find it nowhere in the New Testament. Without controversy, in the matter of our justification before God, faith in Christ is the one thing needful. All that simply believe are justified. Righteousness is imputed "to him that worketh not but believeth" (Rom. 4:5). It is thoroughly Scriptural and right to say "faith alone justifies." But it is not equally Scriptural and right to say "faith alone sanctifies." The saying requires very large qualification. Let one fact suffice. We are frequently told that a man is "justified by faith with-out the deeds of the law," by St. Paul. But not once are we told that we are "sanctified by faith without the deeds of the law." On the contrary, we are expressly told by St. James that the faith whereby we are *visibly and demonstratively* justified before man, is a faith which "if it hath not works is dead, being alone"[1] (James 2:17). I may be told, in reply, that no one of course means to disparage "works" as an essential part of a holy life. It would be well, however, to make this more plain than many seem to make it in these days.

(2) I ask, in the second place, whether it is wise to make so little as some appear to do, comparatively, of the many *practical exhortations to holiness in daily life* which are to be found in the Sermon on the Mount, and in the latter part of most of St. Paul's epistles? Is it according to the proportion of God's Word? I doubt it.

That a life of daily self-consecration and daily communion with God should be aimed at by everyone who professes to be a believer—that we should strive to attain the habit of going to the Lord Jesus Christ with everything we find a burden, whether great or small, and casting it upon Him—all this, I repeat, no well-taught child of God will dream of disputing. But surely the New Testament teaches us that we want something more than *generalities* about holy living, which often prick no conscience and give no offence. The *details* and particular ingredients of which holiness is composed in daily life, ought to be fully set forth and pressed on believers by all who profess to handle the subject. True holiness does not consist merely of believing and feeling, but of doing and bearing, and a practical exhibition of active and passive grace. Our tongues, our tempers, our natural passions and inclinations—our conduct as parents and children, masters and servants, husbands and wives, rulers and subjects—our dress, our employment of time, our behaviour in business, our demeanour in sickness and health, in riches and in poverty—all, all these are matters which are fully treated by inspired writers. They are not content with a general statement of what we should believe and feel, and how we are to have the roots of holiness planted in our hearts. They dig down lower. They go into particulars. They specify minutely what a holy man ought to do and be in his own family, and by his own fireside, if he abides in Christ. I doubt whether this sort of teaching is sufficiently attended to in the movement of the present day. When people talk of having received "such a blessing," and of having found "the higher life," after hearing some earnest advocate of "holiness by faith and self-consecration," while their families and friends see no improvement and no increased sanctity in their daily tempers and behaviour, immense harm is done to the cause of Christ. True holiness, we surely ought to remember, does not consist merely of inward sensations and impressions. It is much more than tears, and sighs, and bodily excitement, and a quickened pulse, and a passionate feeling of attachment to our own favourite preachers and our own religious party, and a readiness to quarrel with everyone who does not agree with us. It is something of "the image of Christ," which can be seen and observed by others in our private life, and habits, and character, and doings (Rom. 8:29).

(3) I ask, in the third place, whether it is wise to use vague language about *perfection,* and to press on Christians a *standard of holiness,* as attainable in this world, for which there is no warrant to be shown either in Scripture or experience? I doubt it.

That believers are exhorted to "perfect holiness in the fear of God"—to "go on to perfection"—to "be perfect," no careful reader of his Bible will ever think of denying (2 Cor. 7:1; Heb. 6:1; 2 Cor. 13:11). But I have yet to learn that there is a single passage in Scripture which teaches that a literal perfection, a complete and entire freedom from sin, in thought, or word, or deed, is attainable, or ever has been attained, by any child of Adam in this world. A comparative perfection, a perfection in knowledge, an all-round consistency in every relation of life, a thorough soundness in every point of doctrine—this may be seen occasionally in some of God's believing people. But as to an *absolute literal perfection,* the most eminent saints of God in every age have always been the very last to lay claim to it! On the contrary, they have always had the deepest sense of their own utter unworthiness and imperfection. The more spiritual light they have enjoyed the more they have seen their own countless defects and shortcomings. The more grace they have had, the more they have been "clothed with humility" (1 Pet. 5:5).

What saint can be named in God's Word, of whose life many details are recorded, who was literally and absolutely perfect? Which of them all, when writing about himself, ever talks of feeling free from imperfection? On the contrary, men like David, and St. Paul, and St. John, declare in the strongest language that they feel in their own hearts weakness and sin. The holiest men of modern times have always been remarkable for deep humility. Have we ever seen holier men than the martyred John Bradford, or Hooker, or Usher, or Baxter, or Rutherford, or McCheyne? Yet no one can read the writings and letters of these men without seeing that they felt themselves "debtors to mercy and grace" every day, and the very last thing they ever laid claim to was perfection!

In the face of such facts as these I must protest against the language used in many quarters, in these last days, about *perfection.* I must think that those who use it either know very little of the nature of sin, or of the attributes of God, or of their own hearts, or of the Bible, or of the meaning of words. When a professing Christian coolly tells me that he has got beyond such hymns as "Just as I am," and that they are below his present experience, though they suited him when he first took up religion, I must think his soul is in a very unhealthy state! When a man can talk coolly of the possibility of "living without sin" while in the body, and can actually say that he has "never had an evil thought for three months," I can only say that in my opinion he is a very ignorant Christian! I protest against such teaching as this. It not only does no good, but does immense harm. It disgusts and alienates from religion far-seeing men of the world, who know it is incorrect and untrue. It depresses some of the best of God's children, who feel they never can attain to "perfection" of this kind. It puffs up many weak brethren, who fancy they are something when they are nothing. In short, it is a dangerous delusion.

(4) In the fourth place, is it wise to assert so positively and violently, as many do, that *the seventh chapter of the Epistle to the Romans* does

not describe the experience of the advanced saint, but the experience of the unregenerate man, or of the weak and unestablished believer? I doubt it.

I admit fully that the point has been a disputed one for eighteen centuries, in fact ever since the days of St. Paul. I admit fully that eminent Christians like John and Charles Wesley, and Fletcher, a hundred years ago, to say nothing of some able writers of our own time, maintain firmly that St. Paul was not describing his own present experience when he wrote this seventh chapter. I admit fully that many cannot see what I and many others do see: viz., that Paul says nothing in this chapter which does not precisely tally with the recorded experience of the most eminent saints in every age, and that he does say several things which no unregenerate man or weak believer would ever think of saying, and cannot say. So, at any rate, it appears to me. But I will not enter into any detailed discussion of the chapter.[2]

What I do lay stress upon is the broad fact that the best commentators in every era of the Church have almost invariably applied the seventh chapter of Romans to advanced believers. The commentators who do not take this view have been, with a few bright exceptions, the Romanists, the Socinians, and the Arminians. Against them is arrayed the judgment of almost all the Reformers, almost all the Puritans, and the best modern Evangelical divines. I shall be told, of course, that no man is infallible, that the Reformers, Puritans, and modern divines I refer to may have been entirely mistaken, and the Romanists, Socinians, and Arminians may have been quite right! Our Lord has taught us, no doubt, to "call no man master." But while I ask no man to call the Reformers and Puritans "masters," I do ask people to read what they say on this subject, and answer their arguments, if they can. This has not been done yet! To say, as some do, that they do not want human "dogmas" and "doctrines," is no reply at all. The whole point at issue is, "What is the meaning of a passage of Scripture? How is the seventh chapter of the Epistle to the Romans to be interpreted? What is the true sense of its words?" At any rate let us remember that there is a great fact which cannot be got over. On one side stand the opinions and interpretation of Reformers and Puritans, and on the other the opinions and interpretations of Romanists, Socinians, and Arminians. Let that be distinctly understood.

In the face of such a fact as this I must enter my protest against the sneering, taunting, contemptuous language which has been frequently used of late by some of the advocates of what I must call the Arminian view of the seventh of Romans, in speaking of the opinions of their opponents. To say the least, such language is unseemly, and only defeats its own end. A cause which is defended by such language is deservedly suspicious. Truth needs no such weapons. If we cannot agree with men, we need not speak of their views with discourtesy and contempt. An opinion which is backed and supported by such men as the best Reformers and Puritans may not carry conviction to all minds in the nineteenth century, but at any rate it would be well to speak of it with respect.

(5) In the fifth place, is it wise to use the language which is often used in the present day about the doctrine of *"Christ in us"*? I doubt it. Is not this doctrine often exalted to a position which it does not occupy in Scripture? I am afraid that it is.

That the true believer is one with Christ and Christ in him, no careful reader of the New Testament will think of denying for a moment. There is, no doubt, a mystical union between Christ and the believer. With Him we died, with Him we were buried, with Him we rose again, with Him we sit in heavenly places. We have five plain texts where we are distinctly taught that Christ is "in us" (Rom. 8:10; Gal. 2:20; 4:19; Eph. 3:17; Col. 3:11). But we must be careful that we understand what we mean by the expression. That "Christ dwells in our hearts by faith," and carries on His inward work by His Spirit, is clear and plain. But if we mean to say that beside, and over, and above this there is some mysterious indwelling of Christ in a believer, we must be careful what we are about. Unless we take care, we shall find ourselves ignoring the work of the Holy Ghost. We shall be forgetting that in the Divine economy of man's salvation election is the special work of God the Father—atonement, mediation, and intercession, the special work of God the Son—and sanctification, the special work of God the Holy Ghost. We shall be forgetting that our Lord said, when He went away, that He would send us another comforter, who should "abide with us" for ever, and, as it were, take His place (John 14:16). In short, under the idea that we are honouring Christ, we shall find that we are dishonouring His special and peculiar gift—the Holy Ghost. Christ, no doubt, as God, is everywhere—in our hearts, in heaven, in the place where two or three are met together in His name. But we really must remember that Christ, as our risen Head and High Priest, is *specially* at God's right hand interceding for us until He comes the second time; and that Christ carries on His work in the hearts of His people by the special work of His Spirit, whom He promised to send when He left the world (John 15:26). A comparison of the ninth and tenth verses of the eighth chapter of Romans seems to me to show this plainly. It convinces me that "Christ in us" means Christ in us "by His Spirit." Above all, the words of St. John are most distinct and express: "Hereby we know that He abideth in us by the Spirit which He hath given us" (1 John 3:24).

In saying all this, I hope no one will misunderstand me. I do not say that the expression, "Christ in us" is unscriptural. But I do say that I see great danger of giving an extravagant and unscriptural importance to the idea contained in the expression; and I do fear that many use it now-a-days without exactly knowing what they mean, and unwittingly, perhaps, dishonour the mighty work of the Holy Ghost. If any readers think that I am needlessly scrupulous about the point, I recommend to their notice a curious book by Samuel Rutherford (author of the well-known letters), called "The Spiritual Antichrist." They will there see that two centuries ago the wildest heresies arose out of an extravagant teaching of this very doctrine of the "indwelling of Christ" in believers. They will find that Saltmarsh, and Dell, and Towne, and other false teachers, against whom good Samuel Rutherford contended, began with strange notions of "Christ in us," and then proceeded to build on the doctrine antinomianism, and fanaticism of the worst description and vilest tendency. They maintained that the separate, personal life of the believer was so completely gone, that it was *Christ living in him* who repented, and believed, and acted! The root of this huge error was a forced and unscriptural interpretation of such texts as "I live: yet not I, but Christ liveth in me" (Gal. 2:20). And the natural result of it was that many of the unhappy followers of this school came to the comfortable conclusion that believers were not responsible, whatever they might do! Believers, forsooth, were dead and buried; and only Christ lived in them, and *undertook* everything for them! The ultimate consequence was, that some thought they might sit still in a carnal security, their personal accountableness being entirely gone, and might commit any kind of sin without fear! Let us never forget that truth, distorted and exaggerated, can become the mother of the most dangerous heresies. When we speak of "Christ being in us," let us take care to explain what we mean. I fear some neglect this in the present day.

(6) In the sixth place, is it wise to draw such a deep, wide, and distinct line of separation between conversion and *consecration, or the higher life,* so called, as many do draw in the present day? Is this according to the proportion of God's Word? I doubt it.

There is, unquestionably, nothing new in this teaching. It is well known that Romish writers often maintain that the Church is divided into three classes—sinners, penitents, and saints. The modern teachers of this day who tell us that professing Christians are of three sorts—the unconverted, the converted, and the partakers of the "higher life" of complete consecration—appear to me to occupy very much the same ground! But whether the idea be old or new, Romish or English, I am utterly unable to see that it has any warrant of Scripture. The Word of God always speaks of two great divisions of mankind, and two only. It speaks of the living and the dead in sin—the believer and the unbeliever— the converted and the unconverted—the travellers in the narrow way and the travellers in the broad—the wise and the foolish—the children of God and the children of the devil. *Within* each of these two great classes there are, doubtless, various measures of sin and of grace; but it is only the difference between the higher and lower end of an inclined plane. *Between* these two great classes there is an enormous gulf; they are as distinct as life and death, light and darkness, heaven and hell. But of a division into three classes the Word of God says nothing at all! I question the wisdom of making new-fangled divisions which the Bible has not made, and I thoroughly dislike the notion of a second conversion.

That there is a vast difference between one degree of grace and another—that spiritual life admits of growth, and that believers should be continually urged on every account to grow in grace—all this I fully concede. But the theory of a sudden, mysterious transition of a believer into a state of blessedness and *entire consecration,* at one mighty bound, I cannot receive. It appears to me to be a man-made invention; and I do not see a single plain text to prove it in Scripture. Gradual growth in grace, growth in knowledge, growth in faith, growth in love, growth in holiness, growth in humility, growth in spiritual-mindedness—all this I see clearly taught and urged in Scripture, and clearly exemplified in the lives of many of God's saints. But sudden, instantaneous leaps from conversion to *consecration* I fail to see in the Bible. I doubt, indeed, whether we have any warrant for saying that a man can possibly be *converted* without being consecrated to God! More consecrated he doubtless can be, and will be as his grace increases; but if he was not consecrated to God in the very day that he was converted and born again, I do not know what conversion means. Are not men in danger of undervaluing and underrating the immense blessedness of conversion? Are they not, when they urge on believers the "higher life" as a second conversion, underrating the length, and breadth, and depth, and height, of that great first change which Scripture calls the new birth, the new creation, the spiritual resurrection? I may be mistaken. But I have sometimes thought, while reading the strong language used by many about "consecration," in the last few years, that those who use it must have had previously a singularly low and inadequate view of "conversion," if indeed they knew anything about conversion at all. In short, I have almost suspected that when they were *consecrated,* they were in reality *converted* for the first time!

I frankly confess I prefer the old paths. I think it wiser and safer to press on all converted people the possibility of continual *growth* in grace, and the absolute necessity of going forward, increasing more and more, and every year dedicating and consecrating themselves more, in spirit, soul, and body, to Christ. By all means let us teach that there is more holiness to be attained, and more of heaven to be enjoyed upon earth than most believers now experience. But I decline to tell any converted man that he needs a *second conversion,* and that he may some day or other pass by one enormous step into a state of entire *consecration.* I decline to teach it, because I cannot see any warrant for such teaching in Scripture. I decline to teach it, because I think the tendency of the doctrine is thoroughly mischievous, depressing the humble-minded and meek, and puffing up the shallow, the ignorant, and the self-conceited, to a most dangerous extent.

(7) In the seventh and last place, is it wise to teach believers that they ought not to think so much of fighting and struggling against sin, but ought rather to *"yield themselves to God,"* and be passive in the hands of Christ? Is this according to the proportion of God's Word? I doubt it.

It is a simple fact that the expression "yield yourselves" is only to be found in one place in the New Testament, as a duty urged upon believers. That place is in the sixth chapter of Romans, and there within six verses the expression occurs five times (see Rom. 6:13-19). But even there the word will not bear the sense of "placing ourselves passively in the hands of another." Any Greek student can tell us that the sense is rather that of actively "presenting" ourselves for use, employment, and service (see Rom. 12:1). The expression therefore stands alone. But, on the other hand, it would not be difficult to point out at least twenty-five or thirty distinct passages in the Epistles where believers are plainly taught to use active personal exertion, and are addressed as responsible for doing energetically what Christ would have them do, and are not told to "yield themselves" up as passive agents and sit still, but to arise and work. A holy violence, a conflict, a warfare, a fight, a soldier's life, a wrestling, are spoken of as characteristic of the true Christian. The account of "the armour of God" in the sixth chapter of Ephesians, one might think, settles the question.[3]—Again, it would be easy to show that the doctrine of sanctification without personal exertion, by simply "yielding ourselves to God," is precisely the doctrine of the antinomian fanatics in the seventeenth century (to whom I have referred already, described in Rutherford's *Spiritual Antichrist*), and that the tendency of it is evil in the extreme.—Again, it would be easy to show that the doctrine is utterly subversive of the whole teaching of such tried and approved books as *Pilgrim's Progress,* and that if we receive it we cannot do better than put Bunyan's old book in the fire! If Christian in *Pilgrim's Progress* simply *yielded himself to God,* and never fought, or struggled, or wrestled, I have read the famous allegory in vain. But the plain truth is, that men will persist in confounding two things that differ—that is, justification and sanctification. In justification the word to be addressed to man is believe—only believe; in sanctification the word must be "watch, pray, and fight." What God has divided let us not mingle and confuse.

I leave the subject of my introduction here, and hasten to a conclusion. I confess that I lay down my pen with feelings of sorrow and anxiety. There is much in the attitude of professing Christians in this day which fills me with concern, and makes me full of fear for the future.

There is an amazing ignorance of Scripture among many, and a consequent want of established, solid religion. In no other way can I account for the ease with which people are, like children, "tossed to and fro, and carried about by every wind of doctrine" (Eph. 4:14). There is an Athenian love of novelty abroad, and a morbid distaste for anything old and regular, and in the beaten path of our forefathers. Thousands will crowd to hear a new voice and a new doctrine, without considering for a moment whether what they hear is true.—There is an incessant craving after any teaching which is sensational, and exciting, and rousing to the feelings.—There is an unhealthy appetite for a sort of spasmodic and hysterical Christianity. The religious life of many is little better than spiritual dram-drinking, and the "meek and quiet spirit" which St. Peter commends is clean forgotten (1 Pet. 3:4). Crowds, and crying, and hot rooms, and high-flown singing, and an incessant rousing of the emotions, are the only things which many care for.—Inability to distinguish differences in doctrine is spreading far and wide, and so long as the preacher is "clever" and "earnest," hundreds seem to think it must be all right, and call you dreadfully "narrow and uncharitable" if you hint that he is unsound! Moody and Haweis, Dean Stanley and Canon Liddon, Mackonochie and Pearsall Smith, all seem to be alike in the eyes of such people. All this is sad, very sad. But if, in addition to this, the true-hearted advocates of increased holiness are going to fall out by the way and misunderstand one another, it will be sadder still. We shall indeed be in evil plight.

For myself, I am aware that I am no longer a young minister. My mind perhaps stiffens, and I cannot easily receive any new doctrine. "The old is better." I suppose I belong to the old school of Evangelical theology, and I am therefore content with such teaching about sanctification as I find in the *Life of Faith* of Sibbes and of Manton, and in *The Life, Walk, and Triumph of Faith* of William Romaine. But I must express a hope that my younger brethren who have taken up new views of holiness will beware of multiplying causeless divisions. Do they think that a higher standard of Christian living is needed in the present day? So do I.—Do they think that clearer, stronger, fuller teaching about holiness is needed? So do I.—Do they think that Christ ought to be more exalted as the root and author of sanctification as well as justification? So do I.—Do they think that believers should be urged more and more to live by faith? So do I.—Do they think that a very close walk with God should be more pressed on believers as the secret of happiness and usefulness? So do I.—In all these things we agree. But if they want to go further, then I ask them to take care where they tread, and to explain very clearly and distinctly what they mean.

Finally, I must deprecate, and I do it in love, the use of uncouth and new-fangled terms and phrases in teaching sanctification. I plead that a movement in favour of holiness cannot be advanced by new-coined phraseology, or by disproportioned and one-sided statements—or by overstraining and isolating particular texts—or by exalting one truth at the expense of another—or by allegorizing and accommodating texts, and squeezing out of them meanings which the Holy Ghost never put in them—or by speaking contemptuously and bitterly of those who do not entirely see things with our eyes, and do not work exactly in our ways. These things do not make for peace: they rather repel many and keep them at a distance. The cause of true sanctification is not helped, but hindered, by such weapons as these. A movement in aid of holiness which produces strife and dispute among God's children is somewhat suspicious. For Christ's sake, and in the name of truth and charity, let us endeavour to follow after peace as well as holiness. "What God has joined together let not man put asunder."

It is my heart's desire, and prayer to God daily, that personal holiness may increase greatly among professing Christians in England. But I trust that all who endeavour to promote it will adhere closely to the proportion of Scripture, will carefully distinguish things that differ, and will separate "the precious from the vile" (Jer. 15:19).

1

SIN

"Sin is the transgression of the law."

— I JOHN 3:4

He that wishes to attain right views about Christian holiness, must begin by examining the vast and solemn subject of *sin*. He must dig down very low if he would build high. A mistake here is most mischievous. Wrong views about holiness are generally traceable to wrong views about human corruption. I make no apology for beginning this volume of papers about holiness by making some plain statements about *sin*.

The plain truth is that a right knowledge of sin lies at the root of all saving Christianity. Without it such doctrines as justification, conversion, sanctification, are "words and names" which convey no meaning to the mind. The first thing, therefore, that God does when He makes anyone a new creature in Christ, is to send light into his heart, and show him that he is a guilty sinner. The material creation in Genesis began with "light," and so also does the spiritual creation. God "shines into our hearts" by the work of the Holy Ghost, and then spiritual life begins (2 Cor. 4:6).—Dim or indistinct views of sin are the origin of most of the errors, heresies, and false doctrines of the present day. If a man does not realize the dangerous nature of his soul's disease, you cannot wonder if he is content with false or imperfect remedies. I believe that one of the chief wants of the Church in the nineteenth century has been, and is, clearer, fuller teaching about sin.

(1) I shall begin the subject by supplying some definition of sin. We are all of course familiar with the terms "sin" and "sinners." We talk frequently of "sin" being in the world, and of men committing "sins." But what do we mean by these terms and phrases? Do we really know?

I fear there is much mental confusion and haziness on this point. Let me try, as briefly as possible, to supply an answer.

I say, then, that "sin," speaking generally, is, as the Ninth Article of our Church declares, "the fault and corruption of the nature of every man that is naturally engendered of the offspring of Adam; whereby man is very far gone (*quam longissime* is the Latin) from original righteousness, and is of his own nature inclined to evil, so that the flesh lusteth alway against the spirit; and, therefore, in every person born into the world, it deserveth God's wrath and damnation." Sin, in short, is that vast moral disease which affects the whole human race, of every rank, and class, and name, and nation, and people, and tongue; a disease from which there never was but one born of woman that was free. Need I say that One was Christ Jesus the Lord?

I say, furthermore, that "a sin," to speak more particularly, consists in doing, saying, thinking, or imagining, anything that is not in perfect conformity with the mind and law of God. "Sin," in short, as the Scripture saith, is "the transgression of the law" (1 John 3:4). The slightest outward or inward departure from absolute mathematical parallelism with God's revealed will and character constitutes a sin, and at once makes us guilty in God's sight.

Of course I need not tell anyone who reads his Bible with attention, that a man may break God's law in heart and thought, when there is no overt and visible act of wickedness. Our Lord has settled that point beyond dispute in the Sermon on the Mount (Matt. 5:21-28). Even a poet of our own has truly said, "A man may smile and smile, and be a villain."

Again, I need not tell a careful student of the New Testament, that there are sins of omission as well as commission, and that we sin, as our Prayer-book justly reminds us, by "leaving undone the things we ought to do," as really as by "doing the things we ought not to do." The solemn words of our Master in the Gospel of St. Matthew place this point also beyond dispute. It is there written, "Depart, ye cursed, into everlasting fire:—for I was an hungered, and ye gave Me no meat; I was thirsty, and ye gave Me no drink" (Matt. 25:41, 42). It was a deep and thoughtful saying of holy Archbishop Usher, just before he died—"Lord, forgive me all my sins, and specially my sins of omission."

But I do think it necessary in these times to remind my readers that a man may commit sin and yet be ignorant of it, and fancy himself innocent when he is guilty. I fail to see any Scriptural warrant for the modern assertion that "Sin is not sin to us until we discern it and are conscious of it." On the contrary, in the 4th and 5th chapters of that unduly neglected book, Leviticus, and in the 15th of Numbers, I find Israel distinctly taught that there were sins of *ignorance* which rendered people unclean, and needed atonement (Lev. 4:1-35; 5:14-19; Num. 15:25-29). And I find our Lord expressly teaching that "the servant who knew not his master's will and did it not," was not excused on account of his ignorance, but was "beaten" or punished (Luke 12:48). We shall do well to remember, that when we make our own miserably imperfect knowledge and consciousness the measure of our sinfulness, we are on very dangerous ground. A deeper study of Leviticus might do us much good.

(2) Concerning the origin and source of this vast moral disease called "sin" I must say something. I fear the views of many professing Christians on this point are sadly defective and unsound. I dare not pass it by. Let us, then, have it fixed down in our minds that the sinfulness of man does not begin from without, but from within. It is not the result of bad training in early years. It is not picked up from bad companions and bad examples, as some weak Christians are too fond of saying. No! It is a family disease, which we all inherit from our first parents, Adam and Eve, and with which we are born. Created "in the image of God," innocent and righteous at first, our parents fell from original righteousness and became sinful and corrupt. And from that day to this all men and women are born in the image of fallen Adam and Eve, and inherit a heart and nature inclined to evil. "By one man sin entered into the world."—"That which is born of the flesh is flesh."—"We are by nature children of wrath."—"The carnal mind is enmity against God."—"Out of the heart (naturally, as out of a fountain) proceed evil thoughts, adulteries," and the like (Rom. 5:12; John 3:6; Eph. 2:3; Rom. 8:7; Mark 7:21). The fairest babe that has entered life this year, and become the sunbeam of a family, is not, as its mother perhaps fondly calls it, a little "angel," or a little "innocent," but a little "sinner." Alas! As it lies smiling and crowing in its cradle, that little creature carries in its heart the seeds of every kind of wickedness! Only watch it carefully, as it grows in stature and its mind develops, and you will soon detect in it an incessant tendency to that which is bad, and a backwardness to that which is good. You will see in it the buds and germs of deceit, evil temper, selfishness, self-will, obstinacy, greediness, envy, jealousy, passion—which, if indulged and let alone, will shoot up with painful rapidity. Who taught the child these things? Where did he learn them? The Bible alone can answer these questions!—Of all the foolish things that parents say about their children there is none worse than the common saying, "My son *has a good heart at the bottom.* He is not what he ought to be; but he has fallen into bad hands. Public schools are bad places. The tutors neglect

the boys. Yet he has a good heart at the bottom."—The truth, unhappily, is diametrically the other way. The first cause of all sin lies in the natural corruption of the boy's own heart, and not in the school.

(3) Concerning the extent of this vast moral disease of man called sin, let us beware that we make no mistake. The only safe ground is that which is laid for us in Scripture. "Every imagination of the thoughts of his heart" is by nature "evil, and that continually."—"The heart is deceitful above all things, and desperately wicked" (Gen. 6:5; Jer. 17:9). Sin is a disease which pervades and runs through every part of our moral constitution and every faculty of our minds. The understanding, the affections, the reasoning powers, the will, are all more or less infected. Even the conscience is so blinded that it cannot be depended on as a sure guide, and is as likely to lead men wrong as right, unless it is enlightened by the Holy Ghost. In short, "from the sole of the foot even unto the head there is no soundness" about us (Isa. 1:6). The disease may be veiled under a thin covering of courtesy, politeness, good manners, and outward decorum; but it lies deep down in the constitution.

I admit fully that man has many grand and noble faculties left about him, and that in arts and sciences and literature he shows immense capacity. But the fact still remains that in spiritual things he is utterly "dead," and has no natural knowledge, or love, or fear of God. His best things are so interwoven and intermingled with corruption, that the contrast only brings out into sharper relief the truth and extent of *the fall.* That one and the same creature should be in some things so high and in others so low—so great and yet so little—so noble and yet so mean—so grand in his conception and execution of material things, and yet so grovelling and debased in his affections—that he should be able to plan and erect buildings like those to Carnac and Luxor in Egypt, and the Parthenon at Athens, and yet worship vile gods and goddesses, and birds, and beasts, and creeping things—that he should be able to produce tragedies like those of Aeschylus and Sophocles, and histories like that of Thucydides, and yet be a slave to abominable vices like those described in the first chapter of the Epistle to the Romans—all this is a sore puzzle to those who sneer at "God's Word written," and scoff at us as Bibliolaters. But it is a knot that we can untie with the Bible in our hands. We can acknowledge that man has all the marks of a majestic temple about him—a temple in which God once dwelt, but a temple which is now in utter ruins—a temple in which a shattered window here, and a doorway there, and a column there, still give some faint idea of the magnificence of the original design, but a temple which from end to end has lost its glory and fallen from its high estate. And we say that nothing solves the complicated problem of man's condition but the doctrine of original or birth-sin and the crushing effects of the fall.

Let us remember, besides this, that every part of the world bears testimony to the fact that sin is the *universal disease of all mankind*. Search the globe from east to west and from pole to pole—search every nation of every clime in the four quarters of the earth—search every rank and class in our own country from the highest to the lowest—and under every circumstance and condition, the report will be always the same. The remotest islands in the Pacific Ocean, completely separate from Europe, Asia, Africa, and America, beyond the reach alike of Oriental luxury and Western arts and literature—islands inhabited by people ignorant of books, money, steam, and gunpowder—uncontaminated by the vices of modern civilization—these very islands have always been found, when first discovered, the abode of the vilest forms of lust, cruelty, deceit, and superstition. If the inhabitants have known nothing else, they have always known how to sin! Everywhere the human heart is naturally "deceitful above all things, and desperately wicked" (Jer. 17:9). For my part, I know no stronger proof of the inspiration of Genesis and the Mosaic account of the origin of man, than the power, extent, and universality of sin. Grant that mankind have all sprung from one pair, and that this pair fell (as Gen. 3 tells us), and the state of human nature everywhere is easily accounted for. Deny it, as many do, and you are at once involved in inexplicable difficulties. In a word, the uniformity and universality of human corruption supply one of the most unanswerable instances of the enormous "difficulties of infidelity."

After all, I am convinced that the greatest proof of the extent and power of sin is the pertinacity with which it cleaves to man even after he is converted and has become the subject of the Holy Ghost's operations. To use the language of the Ninth Article, "this infection of nature doth remain—yea, even in them that are regenerate." So deeply planted are the roots of human corruption, that even after we are born again, renewed, "washed, sanctified, justified," and made living members of Christ, these roots remain alive in the bottom of our hearts, and, like the leprosy in the walls of the house, we never get rid of them until the earthly house of this tabernacle is dissolved. Sin, no doubt, in the believer's heart, has no longer *dominion*. It is checked, controlled, mortified, and crucified by the expulsive power of the new principle of grace. The life of a believer is a life of victory, and not of failure. But the very struggles which go on within his bosom, the fight that he finds it needful to fight daily, the watchful jealousy which he is obliged to exercise over his inner man, the contest between the flesh and the spirit, the inward "groanings" which no one knows but he who has experienced them—all, all testify to the same great truth, all show the enormous power and vitality of sin. Mighty indeed must that foe be who even when crucified is still alive! Happy is that believer who understands it, and while he rejoices in Christ Jesus has no confidence in the flesh; and while he says, "Thanks be unto God who giveth us the victory," never forgets to watch and pray lest he fall into temptation!

(4) Concerning the guilt, vileness, and offensiveness of sin in the sight of God, my words shall be few. I say "few" advisedly. I do not think, in the nature of things, that mortal man can at all realize the exceeding sinfulness of sin in the sight of that holy and perfect One with whom we have to do. On the one hand, God is that eternal Being who "chargeth His angels with folly," and in whose sight the very "heavens are not clean." He is One who reads thoughts and motives as well as actions, and requires "truth in the inward parts" (Job 4:18; 15:15; Ps. 51:6). We, on the other hand—poor blind creatures, here to-day and gone to-morrow, born in sin, surrounded by sinners, living in a constant atmosphere of weakness, infirmity, and imperfection—can form none but the most inadequate conceptions of the hideousness of evil. We have no line to fathom it, and no measure by which to gauge it. The blind man can see no difference between a masterpiece of Titian or Raphael, and the Queen's Head on a village signboard. The deaf man cannot distinguish between a penny whistle and a cathedral organ. The very animals whose smell is most offensive to us have no idea that they are offensive, and are not offensive to one another. And man, fallen man, I believe, can have no just idea what a vile thing sin is in the sight of that God whose handiwork is absolutely perfect—perfect whether we look through telescope or microscope—perfect in the formation of a mighty planet like Jupiter, with his satellites, keeping time to a second as he rolls round the sun—perfect in the formation of the smallest insect that crawls over a foot of ground. But let us nevertheless settle it firmly in our minds that sin is "the abominable thing that God hateth"—that God "is of purer eyes than to behold iniquity, and cannot look upon that which is evil"—that the least transgression of God's law makes us "guilty of all"—that "the soul that sinneth shall die"—that "the wages of sin is death"—that God shall "judge the secrets of men"—that there is a worm that never dies, and a fire that is not quenched—that "the wicked shall be turned into hell"—and "shall go away into everlasting punishment"—and that "nothing that defiles shall in any wise enter heaven" (Jer. 44:4; Hab. 1:13; James 2:10; Ezek.

18:4; Rom. 6:23; Rom. 2:16; Mark 9:44; Ps. 9:17; Matt. 25:46; Rev. 21:27). These are indeed tremendous words, when we consider that they are written in the Book of a most merciful God!

No proof of the fulness of sin, after all, is so overwhelming and unanswerable as the cross and passion of our Lord Jesus Christ, and the whole doctrine of His substitution and atonement. Terribly black must that guilt be for which nothing but the blood of the Son of God could make satisfaction. Heavy must that weight of human sin be which made Jesus groan and sweat drops of blood in agony at Gethsemane, and cry at Golgotha, "My God, My God, why hast Thou forsaken Me?" (Matt. 27:46). Nothing, I am convinced, will astonish us so much, when we awake in the resurrection day, as the view we shall have of sin, and the retrospect we shall take of our own countless shortcomings and defects. Never till the hour when Christ comes the second time shall we fully realize the "sinfulness of sin." Well might George Whitfield say, "The anthem in heaven will be, What hath God wrought!"

(5) One point only remains to be considered on the subject of sin, which I dare not pass over. That point is its deceitfulness. It is a point of most serious importance, and I venture to think it does not receive the attention which it deserves. You may see this deceitfulness in the wonderful proneness of men to regard sin as less sinful and dangerous than it is in the sight of God; and in their readiness to extenuate it, make excuses for it, and minimize its guilt.—"It is but a little one! God is merciful! God is not extreme to mark what is done amiss! We mean well! One cannot be so particular! Where is the mighty harm? We only do as others!" Who is not familiar with this kind of language?—You may see it in the long string of smooth words and phrases which men have coined in order to designate things which God calls downright wicked and ruinous to the soul. What do such expressions as "fast," "gay," "wild," "unsteady," "thoughtless," "loose" mean? They show that men try to cheat themselves into the belief that sin is not quite so sinful as God says it is, and that they are not so bad as they really are.—You may see it in the tendency even of believers to indulge their children in questionable practices, and to blind their own eyes to the inevitable result of the love of money, of tampering with temptation, and sanctioning a low standard of family religion.—I fear we do not sufficiently realize the extreme subtlety of our soul's disease. We are too apt to forget that temptation to sin will rarely present itself to us in its true colours, saying, "I am your deadly enemy, and I want to ruin you for ever in hell." Oh, no! Sin comes to us, like Judas, with a kiss; and like Joab, with an outstretched hand and flattering words. The forbidden

fruit seemed good and desirable to Eve; yet it cast her out of Eden. The walking idly on his palace roof seemed harmless enough to David; yet it ended in adultery and murder. Sin rarely seems sin at first beginnings. Let us then watch and pray, lest we fall into temptation. We may give wickedness smooth names, but we cannot alter its nature and character in the sight of God. Let us remember St. Paul's words: "Exhort one another daily, lest any be hardened through the deceitfulness of sin" (Heb. 3:13). It is a wise prayer in our Litany: "From the *deceits* of the world, the flesh, and the devil, good Lord, deliver us."

And now, before I go further, let me briefly mention two thoughts which appear to me to rise with irresistible force out of the subject.

On the one hand, I ask my readers to observe what deep reasons we all have *for humiliation and self-abasement*. Let us sit down before the picture of sin displayed to us in the Bible, and consider what guilty, vile, corrupt creatures we all are in the sight of God. What need we all have of that entire change of heart called regeneration, new birth, or conversion! What a mass of infirmity and imperfection cleaves to the very best of us at our very best! What a solemn thought it is, that "without holiness no man shall see the Lord!" (Heb. 12:14). What cause we have to cry with the publican, every night in our lives, when we think of our sins of omission as well as commission, "God be merciful to me a sinner!" (Luke 18:13). How admirably suited are the general and Communion Confessions of the Prayer-book to the actual condition of all professed Christians! How well that language suits God's children which the Prayer-book puts in the mouth of every Churchman before he goes up to the Communion Table—"The remembrance of our misdoings is grievous unto us; the burden is intolerable. Have mercy upon us, have mercy upon us, most merciful Father; for Thy Son our Lord Jesus Christ's sake, forgive us all that is past." How true it is that the holiest saint is in himself a "miserable sinner," and a debtor to mercy and grace to the last moment of his existence!

With my whole heart I subscribe to that passage in Hooker's sermon on Justification, which begins, "Let the holiest and best things we do be considered. We are never better affected unto God than when we pray; yet when we pray, how are our affections many times distracted! How little reverence do we show unto the grand majesty of God unto whom we speak! How little remorse of our own miseries! How little taste of the sweet influence of His tender mercies do we feel! Are we not as unwilling many times to begin, and as glad to make an end, as if in saying, 'Call upon Me,' He had set us a very burdensome task? It may seem somewhat extreme, which I will speak; therefore, let every one judge of it, even as his own heart shall tell him, and not otherwise; I will but only make a demand! If God should yield unto us, not as unto Abraham—If fifty, forty, thirty, twenty—yea, or if ten good persons could be found in a city, for their sakes this city should not be destroyed; but, and if He should make us an offer thus large, search all the generations of men since the fall of our father Adam, find one man that hath done one action which hath passed from him pure, without any stain or blemish at all; and for that one man's only action neither man nor angel should feel the torments which are prepared for both. Do you think that this ransom to deliver men and angels could be found to be among the sons of men? The best things which we do have somewhat in them to be pardoned."[1]

That witness is true. For my part I am persuaded the more light we have, the more we see our own sinfulness; the nearer we get to heaven, the more we are clothed with humility. In every age of the Church you will find it true, if you will study biographies, that the most eminent saints—men like Bradford, Rutherford, and McCheyne—have always been the humblest men.

On the other hand, I ask my readers to observe *how deeply thankful we ought to be for the glorious Gospel of the grace of God.* There is a remedy revealed for man's need, as wide and broad and deep as man's disease. We need not be afraid to look at sin, and study its nature, origin, power, extent, and vileness, if we only look at the same time at the Almighty medicine provided for us in the salvation that is in Jesus Christ. Though sin has abounded, grace has much more abounded. Yes: in the everlasting covenant of redemption, to which Father, Son, and Holy Ghost are parties—in the Mediator of that covenant, Jesus Christ the righteous, perfect God and perfect Man in one Person—in the work that He did by dying for our sins and rising again for our justification—in the offices that He fills as our Priest, Substitute, Physician, Shepherd, and Advocate—in the precious blood He shed which can cleanse from all sin—in the everlasting righteousness that he brought in—in the perpetual intercession that He carries on as our Representative at God's right hand—in His power to save to the uttermost the chief of sinners, His willingness to receive and pardon the vilest, His readiness to bear with the weakest—in the grace of the Holy Spirit which He plants in the hearts of all His people, renewing, sanctifying and causing old things to pass away and all things to become new—in all this—and oh, what a brief sketch it is!—in all this, I say, there is a full, perfect, and complete medicine for the hideous disease of sin. Awful and tremendous as the right view of sin undoubtedly is, no one need faint and despair if he will take a right view of Jesus Christ at the same time. No wonder that old Flavel ends many a chapter of his admirable "Fountain of Life" with the touching words, "Blessed be God for Jesus Christ."

In bringing this mighty subject to a close, I feel that I have only touched the surface of it. It is one which cannot be thoroughly handled in a paper like this. He that would see it treated fully and exhaustively must turn to such masters of experimental theology as Owen, and Burgess, and Manton, and Charnock, and the other giants of the Puritan school. On subjects like this there are no writers to be compared to the Puritans. It only remains for me to point out some practical uses to which the whole doctrine of sin may be profitably turned in the present day.

(a) I say, then, in the first place, that a Scriptural view of sin is one of the *best antidotes to that vague, dim, misty, hazy kind of theology* which is so painfully current in the present age. It is vain to shut our eyes to the fact that there is a vast quantity of so-called Christianity now-a-days which you cannot declare positively unsound, but which, nevertheless, is not full measure, good weight, and sixteen ounces to the pound. It is a Christianity in which there is undeniably "something about Christ, and something about grace, and something about faith, and something about repentance, and something about holiness"; but it is not the real "thing as it is" in the Bible. Things are out of place, and out of proportion. As old Latimer would have said, it is a kind of "mingle-mangle," and does no good. It neither exercises influence on daily conduct, nor comforts in life, nor gives peace in death; and those who hold it often awake too late to find that they have got nothing solid under their feet. Now I believe the likeliest way to cure and mend this defective kind of religion is to bring forward more prominently the old Scriptural truth about the sinfulness of sin. People will never set their faces decidedly towards heaven, and live like pilgrims, until they really feel that they are in danger of hell. Let us all try to revive the old teaching about sin, in nurseries, in schools, in training colleges, in Universities. Let us not forget that "the law is good if we use it lawfully," and that "by the law is the knowledge of sin" (1 Tim. 1:8; Rom. 3:20; 7:7). Let us bring the law to the front and press it on men's attention. Let us expound and beat out the Ten Commandments, and show the length, and breadth, and depth, and height of their requirements. This is the way of our Lord in the Sermon on the Mount. We cannot do better than follow His plan. We may depend upon it, men will never come to Jesus, and stay with Jesus, and live for Jesus, unless they really know why they are to come, and what is their need. Those whom the Spirit draws to Jesus are those whom the Spirit has convinced of sin. Without thorough conviction of sin, men may seem to come to Jesus and follow Him for a season, but they will soon fall away and return to the world.

(b) In the next place, a Scriptural view of sin is one of the *best antidotes to the extravagantly broad and liberal theology* which is so much in vogue at the present time. The tendency of modern thought is to reject dogmas, creeds, and every kind of bounds in religion. It is thought grand and wise to condemn no opinion whatsoever, and to pronounce all earnest and clever teachers to be trustworthy, however heterogeneous and mutually destructive their opinions may be.—Everything forsooth is true, and nothing is false! Everybody is right, and nobody is wrong! Everybody is likely to be saved, and nobody is to be lost!—The Atonement and Substitution of Christ, the personality of the devil, the miraculous element in Scripture, the reality and eternity of future punishment, all these mighty foundation-stones are coolly tossed overboard, like lumber, in order to lighten the ship of Christianity, and enable it to keep pace with modern science.—Stand up for these great verities, and you are called narrow, illiberal, old-fashioned, and a theological fossil! Quote a text, and you are told that all truth is not confined to the pages of an ancient Jewish Book, and that free inquiry has found out many things since the Book was completed!—Now, I know nothing so likely to counteract this modern plague as constant clear statements about the nature, reality, vileness, power, and guilt of sin. We must charge home into the consciences of these men of broad views, and demand a plain answer to some plain questions. We must ask them to lay their hands on their hearts, and tell us whether their favourite opinions comfort them in the day of sickness, in the hour of death, by the bedside of dying parents, by the grave of a beloved wife or child. We must ask them whether a vague *earnestness,* without definite doctrine, gives them peace at seasons like these. We must challenge them to tell us whether they do not sometimes feel a gnawing "something" within, which all the free inquiry and philosophy and science in the world cannot satisfy. And then we must tell them that this gnawing "something" is the sense of sin, guilt, and corruption, which they are leaving out in their calculations. And, above all, we must tell them that nothing will ever make them feel rest, but submission to the old doctrines of man's ruin and Christ's redemption, and simple childlike faith in Jesus.

(c) In the next place, a right view of sin is the *best antidote to that sensuous, ceremonial, formal kind of Christianity,* which has swept over England like a flood in the last twenty-five years, and carried away so many before it. I can well believe that there is much that is attractive in this system of religion, to a certain order of minds, so long as the conscience is not fully enlightened. But when that wonderful part of our constitution called conscience is really awake and alive, I find it hard to believe that sensuous ceremonial Christianity will thoroughly satisfy us. A little child is easily quieted and amused with gaudy toys, and dolls, and rattles, so long as it is not hungry; but once let it feel the cravings of nature within, and we know that nothing will satisfy it but *food*. Just so it is with man in the matter of his soul. Music, and flowers, and candles, and incense, and banners, and processions, and beautiful vestments, and confessionals, and man-made ceremonies of a semi-Romish character, may do well enough for him under certain conditions. But once let him "awake and arise from the dead," and he will not rest content with these things. They will seem to him mere solemn triflings, and a waste of time. Once let him see his sin, and he must see his *Saviour*. He feels stricken with a deadly disease, and nothing will satisfy him but the great Physician. He hungers and thirsts, and he must have nothing less than the bread of life. I may seem bold in what I am about to say; but I fearlessly venture the assertion, that four-fifths of the semi-Romanism of the last quarter of a century would never have existed if English people had been taught more fully and clearly the nature, vileness, and sinfulness of sin.

(d) In the next place, a right view of sin is one of the *best antidotes to the overstrained theories of Perfection,* of which we hear so much in these times. I shall say but little about this, and in saying it I trust I shall not give offence. If those who press on us perfection mean nothing more than an all-round consistency, and a careful attention to all the graces which make up the Christian character, reason would that we should not only bear with them, but agree with them entirely. By all means let us aim high.—But if men really mean to tell us that here in this world a believer can attain to entire freedom from sin, live for years in unbroken and uninterrupted communion with God, and feel for months together not so much as one evil thought, I must honestly say that such an opinion appears to me very *unscriptural*.—I go even further. I say that the opinion is very dangerous to him that holds it, and very likely to depress, discourage, and keep back inquirers after salvation. I cannot find the slightest warrant in God's Word for expecting such perfection as this while we are in the body. I believe the words of our Fifteenth Article are strictly true—that "Christ alone is without sin; and that all we, the rest, though baptized and born again in Christ, offend in many things; and if we say that we have no sin, we deceive ourselves, and the truth is not in us."—To use the language of our first Homily, "There be imperfections in our best works: we do not love God so much as we are bound to do, with all our hearts, mind, and power; we do not fear God so much as we ought to do; we do not pray to God but with many and great imperfections. We give, forgive, believe, live, and hope imperfectly; we speak, think, and do imperfectly; we fight against the devil, the world, and the flesh imperfectly. Let us, therefore, not be ashamed to confess plainly our state of imperfections."—Once more I repeat what I have said, the best preservative against this temporary delusion about perfection which clouds some minds—for such I hope I may call it—is a clear, full, distinct understanding of the nature, sinfulness, and deceitfulness of sin.

(e) In the last place, a Scriptural view of sin will prove an admirable *antidote to the low views of personal holiness* which are so painfully prevalent in these last days of the Church. This is a very painful and delicate subject, I know; but I dare not turn away from it. It has long been my sorrowful conviction that the standard of daily life among professing Christians in this country has been gradually falling. I am afraid that Christ-like charity, kindness, good-temper, unselfishness, meekness, gentleness, good-nature, self-denial, zeal to do good, and separation from the world, are far less appreciated than they ought to be, and than they used to be in the days of our fathers.

Into the causes of this state of things I cannot pretend to enter fully, and can only suggest conjectures for consideration. It may be that a certain profession of religion has become so fashionable and comparatively easy in the present age, that the streams which were once narrow and deep have become wide and shallow, and what we have gained in outward show we have lost in quality. It may be that the vast increase of wealth in the last twenty-five years has insensibly introduced a plague of worldliness, and self-indulgence, and love of ease into social life. What were once called luxuries are now comforts and necessaries, and self-denial and "enduring hardness" are consequently little known. It may be that the enormous amount of controversy which marks this age has insensibly dried up our spiritual life. We have too often been content with zeal for orthodoxy, and have neglected the sober realities of daily practical godliness. Be the causes what they may, I must declare my own belief that the result remains. There has been of late years a lower standard of personal holiness among believers than there used to be in the days of our fathers. The whole result is that the Spirit is grieved! And the matter calls for much humiliation and searching of heart.

As to the best remedy for the state of things I have mentioned, I shall venture to give an opinion. Other schools of thought in the Churches must judge for themselves. The cure for Evangelical Churchmen, I am convinced, is to be found in a clearer apprehension of the nature and sinfulness of sin. We need not go back to Egypt, and borrow semi-Romish practices in order to revive our spiritual life. We need not restore the confessional, or return to monasticism or asceticism. Nothing of the kind! We must simply repent and do our first works. We must return to first principles. We must go back to "the old paths." We must sit down humbly in the presence of God, look the whole subject in the face, examine clearly what the Lord Jesus calls sin, and what the Lord Jesus calls "doing His will." We must then try to realize that it is *terribly possible* to live a careless, easy-going, half-worldly life, and yet at the same time to maintain Evangelical principles and call ourselves Evangelical people! Once let us see that sin is far viler, and far nearer to us, and sticks more closely to us than we supposed, and we shall be led, I trust and believe, to get nearer to Christ. Once drawn nearer to Christ, we shall drink more deeply out of His fulness, and learn more thoroughly to "live the life of faith" in Him, as St. Paul did. Once taught to live the life of faith in Jesus, and abiding in Him, we shall bear more fruit, shall find ourselves more strong for duty, more patient in trial, more watchful over our poor weak hearts, and more like our Master in all our little daily ways. Just in proportion as we realize how much Christ has done for us, shall we labour to do much for Christ. Much forgiven, we shall love much. In short, as the Apostle says, "with open face beholding as in a glass the glory of the Lord, we are changed into the same image even as by the Spirit of the Lord" (2 Cor. 3:18).

Whatever some may please to think or say, there can be no doubt that an increased feeling about holiness is one of the signs of the times. Conferences for the promotion of "spiritual life" are becoming common in the present day. The subject of "spiritual life" finds a place on Congress platforms almost every year. It has awakened an amount of interest and general attention throughout the land, for which we ought to be thankful. Any movement, based on sound principles, which helps to deepen our spiritual life and increase our personal holiness, will be a real blessing to the Church of England. It will do much to draw us together and heal our unhappy divisions. It may bring down some fresh out-pouring of the grace of the Spirit, and be "life from the dead" in these later times. But sure I am, as I said in the beginning of this paper, we must begin low, if we would build high. I am convinced that the first step towards attaining a higher standard of holiness is to realize more fully the amazing sinfulness of sin.

2

SANCTIFICATION

"Sanctify them through Thy truth."

—JOHN 17:17

"This is the will of God, even your sanctification."

—1 THESSALONIANS 4:3

The subject of sanctification is one which many, I fear, dislike exceedingly. Some even turn from it with scorn and disdain. The very last thing they would like is to be a "saint," or a "sanctified" man. Yet the subject does not deserve to be treated in this way. It is not an enemy, but a friend.

It is a subject of the utmost importance to our souls. If the Bible be true, it is certain that unless we are "sanctified," we shall not be saved. There are three things which, according to the Bible, are absolutely necessary to the salvation of every man and woman in Christendom. These three are, justification, regeneration, and sanctification. All three meet in every child of God: he is both born again, and justified, and sanctified. He that lacks any one of these three things is not a true Christian in the sight of God, and dying in that condition will not be found in heaven and glorified in the last day.

It is a subject which is peculiarly seasonable in the present day. Strange doctrines have risen up of late upon the whole subject of sanctification. Some appear to confound it with justification. Others fritter it away to nothing, under the pretence of zeal for free grace, and practically neglect it altogether. Others are so much afraid of "works" being made a part of justification, that they can hardly find any place at all for "works" in their religion. Others set up a wrong standard of sanctification before their eyes, and failing to attain it, waste their lives in repeated secessions from Church to Church, chapel to chapel, and sect to sect, in the vain hope that they will find what they want. In a day like this, a calm examination of the subject, as a great leading doctrine of the Gospel, may be of great use to our souls.

I. Let us consider, firstly, *the true nature of sanctification.*
II. Let us consider, secondly, *the visible marks of sanctification.*
III. Let us consider, lastly, *wherein justification and sanctification agree and are like one another, and wherein they differ and are unlike.*

If, unhappily, the reader of these pages is one of those who care for nothing but this world, and make no profession of religion, I cannot expect him to take much interest in what I am writing. You will probably think it an affair of "words, and names," and nice questions, about which it matters nothing what you hold and believe. But if you are a thoughtful, reasonable, sensible Christian, I venture to say that you will find it worth while to have some clear ideas about sanctification.

I. In the first place, we have to consider *the nature of sanctification.* What does the Bible mean when it speaks of a "sanctified" man?

Sanctification is that inward spiritual work which the Lord Jesus Christ works in a man by the Holy Ghost, when He calls him to be a true believer. He not only washes him from his sins in His own blood, but He also *separates* him from his natural love of sin and the world, puts a new principle in his heart, and makes him practically godly in life. The instrument by which the Spirit effects this work is generally the Word of God, though He sometimes uses afflictions and providential visitations "without the Word" (1 Pet. 3:1). The subject of this work of Christ by His Spirit is called in Scripture a "sanctified" man.[1]

He who supposes that Jesus Christ only lived and died and rose again in order to provide justification and forgiveness of sins for His people, has yet much to learn. Whether he knows it or not, he is dishonouring our blessed Lord, and making Him only a half Saviour. The Lord Jesus has undertaken everything that His people's souls require; not only to deliver them from the *guilt* of their sins by His atoning death, but from the *dominion* of their sins, by placing in their hearts the Holy Spirit; not only to justify them, but also to sanctify them. He is, thus, not only their "righteousness," but their "sanctification" (1 Cor. 1:30). Let us hear what the Bible says: "For their sakes I sanctify myself, that they also might be sanctified."—"Christ loved the Church, and gave Himself for it; that He might sanctify and cleanse it."—"Christ gave Himself for us, that He might redeem us from all iniquity, and purify unto Himself a peculiar people, zealous of good works."—"Christ bore our sins in His own body on the tree, that we, being dead to sins, should live unto righteousness."—"Christ hath reconciled (you) in the body of His flesh through death, to present you holy and unblameable and unreproveable in His sight" (John 17:19; Eph. 5:25-26; Titus 2:14; 1 Pet. 2:24; Col. 1:22). Let the meaning of these five texts be carefully considered. If words mean anything, they teach that Christ undertakes the sanctification, no less than the justification of His believing people. *Both* are alike provided for in that "everlasting covenant ordered in all things and sure," of which the Mediator is Christ. In fact, Christ in one place is called "He that sanctifieth," and His People, "they who are sanctified" (Heb. 2:11).

The subject before us is of such deep and vast importance, that it requires fencing, guarding, clearing up, and marking out on every side. A doctrine which is needful to salvation can never be too sharply developed, or brought too fully into light. To clear away the confusion between doctrines and doctrines, which is so unhappily common among Christians, and to map out the precise relation between truths and truths in religion, is one way to attain accuracy in our theology. I shall therefore not hesitate to lay before my readers a series of connected propositions or statements, drawn from Scripture, which I think will be found useful in defining the exact nature of sanctification.

(1) Sanctification, then, is the invariable *result of that vital union with Christ* which true faith gives to a Christian.—"He that abideth in Me, and I in him, the same bringeth forth much fruit" (John 15:5). The branch which bears no fruit is no living branch of the vine. The union with Christ which produces no effect on heart and life is a mere formal union, which is worthless before God. The faith which has not a sanctifying influence on the character is no better than the faith of devils. It is a "dead faith, because it is alone." It is not the gift of God. It is not the faith of God's elect. In short, where there is no sanctification of life, there is no real faith in Christ. True faith worketh by love. It constrains a man to live unto the Lord from a deep sense of gratitude for redemption. It makes him feel that he can never do too much for Him that died for him. Being much forgiven, he loves much. He whom the blood cleanses, walks in the light. He who has real lively hope in Christ, purifieth himself even as He is pure (James 2:17-20; Titus 1:1; Gal. 5:6; 1 John 1:7; 3:3).

(2) Sanctification, again, is the *outcome and inseparable consequence*

of regeneration. He that is born again and made a new creature, receives a new nature and a new principle, and always lives a new life. A regeneration which man can have, and yet live carelessly in sin or worldliness, is a regeneration invented by uninspired theologians, but never mentioned in Scripture. On the contrary, St. John expressly says, that "He that is born of God doth not commit sin—doeth righteousness—loveth the brethren—keepeth himself—and overcometh the world" (1 John 2:29; 3:9-14; 5:4-18). In a word, where there is no sanctification there is no regeneration, and where there is no holy life there is no new birth. This is, no doubt, a hard saying to many minds; but, hard or not, it is simple Bible truth. It is written plainly, that when one is born of God, God's "seed remaineth in him, and he cannot sin, because he is born of God" (1 John 3:9).

(3) Sanctification, again, is the only *certain evidence of that indwelling of the Holy Spirit* which is essential to salvation. "If any man have not the Spirit of Christ, he is none of His" (Rom. 8:9). The Spirit never lies dormant and idle within the soul: He always makes His presence known by the fruit He causes to be borne in heart, character, and life. "The fruit of the Spirit," says St. Paul, "is love, joy, peace, long-suffering, gentleness, goodness, faith, meekness, temperance," and such like (Gal. 5:22-23). Where these things are to be found, there is the Spirit: where these things are wanting, men are dead before God. The Spirit is compared to the wind, and, like the wind, He cannot be seen by our bodily eyes. But just as we know there is a wind by the effect it produces on waves, and trees, and smoke, so we may know the Spirit is in a man by the effects He produces in the man's conduct. It is nonsense to suppose that we have the Spirit, if we do not also "walk in the Spirit" (Gal. 5:25). We may depend on it as a positive certainty, that where there is no holy living, there is no Holy Ghost. The seal that the Spirit stamps on Christ's people is sanctification. As many as are actually "led by the Spirit of God, they," and they only, "are the sons of God" (Rom. 8:14).

(4) Sanctification, again, is the *only sure mark of God's election.* The names and number of the elect are a secret thing, no doubt, which God has wisely kept in His own power, and not revealed to man. It is not given to us in this world to study the pages of the book of life, and see if our names are there. But if there is one thing clearly and plainly laid down about election, it is this—that elect men and women may be known and distinguished by holy lives. It is expressly written that they are "elect through sanctification—chosen unto salvation through sanctification—predestinated to be conformed to the image of God's Son—and chosen in Christ before the foundation of the world that they should be holy."—

Hence, when St. Paul saw the working "faith" and labouring "love" and patient "hope" of the Thessalonian believers, he says, "I know your election of God" (1 Pet. 1:2; 2 Thess. 2:13; Rom. 8:29; Eph. 1:4; 1 Thess. 1:3, 4). He that boasts of being one of God's elect, while he is willfully and habitually living in sin, is only deceiving himself, and talking wicked blasphemy. Of course it is hard to know what people *really* are, and many who make a fair show outwardly in religion, may turn out at last to be rotten-hearted hypocrites. But where there is not, at least, some appearance of sanctification, we may be quite certain there is no election. The Church Catechism correctly and wisely teaches that the Holy Ghost *"sanctifieth* all the elect people of God."

(5) Sanctification, again, is *a thing that will always be seen*. Like the Great Head of the Church, from whom it springs, it "cannot be hid." "Every tree is known by his own fruit" (Luke 6:44). A truly sanctified person may be so clothed with humility, that he can see in himself nothing but infirmity and defects. Like Moses, when he came down from the Mount, he may not be conscious that his face shines. Like the righteous, in the mighty parable of the sheep and the goats, he may not see that he has done anything worthy of his Master's notice and commendation: "When saw we Thee an hungered, and fed Thee?" (Matt. 25:37). But whether he sees it himself or not, others will always see in him a tone, and taste, and character, and habit of life unlike that of other men. The very idea of a man being "sanctified," while no holiness can be seen in his life, is flat nonsense and a misuse of words. Light may be very dim; but if there is only a spark in a dark room it will be seen. Life may be very feeble; but if the pulse only beats a little, it will be felt. It is just the same with a sanctified man: his sanctification will be something felt and seen, though he himself may not understand it. A "saint" in whom nothing can be seen but worldliness or sin, is a kind of monster not recognised in the Bible!

(6) Sanctification, again, is *a thing for which every believer is responsible*. In saying this I would not be mistaken. I hold as strongly as anyone that every man on earth is accountable to God, and that all the lost will be speechless and without excuse at the last day. Every man has power to "lose his own soul" (Matt. 16:26). But while I hold this, I maintain that believers are eminently and peculiarly responsible, and under a special obligation to live holy lives. They are not as others, dead and blind and unrenewed: they are alive unto God, and have light and knowledge, and a new principle within them. Whose fault is it if they are not holy, but their own? On whom can they throw the blame if they are not sanctified, but themselves? God, who has given them grace and a new heart, and a new

nature, has deprived them of all excuse if they do not live for His praise. This is a point which is far too much forgotten. A man who professes to be a true Christian, while he sits still, content with a very low degree of sanctification (if indeed he has any at all), and coolly tells you he "can do nothing," is a very pitiable sight, and a very ignorant man. Against this delusion let us watch and be on our guard. The Word of God always addresses its precepts to believers as accountable and responsible beings. If the Saviour of sinners gives us renewing grace, and calls us by His Spirit, we may be sure that he expects us to use our grace, and not to go to sleep. It is forgetfulness of this which causes many believers to "grieve the Holy Spirit," and makes them very useless and uncomfortable Christians.

(7) Sanctification, again, is *a thing which admits of growth and degrees*. A man may climb from one step to another in holiness, and be far more sanctified at one period of his life than another. More pardoned and more justified than he is when he first believes, he cannot be, though he may feel it more. More sanctified he certainly may be, because every grace in his new character may be strengthened, enlarged, and deepened. This is the evident meaning of our Lord's last prayer for His disciples, when He used the words, "Sanctify them"; and of St. Paul's prayer for the Thessalonians, "The very God of peace sanctify you" (John 17:17; 1 Thess. 5:23). In both cases the expression plainly implies the possibility of increased sanctification, while such an expression as "justify them" is never once in Scripture applied to a believer, because he cannot be more justified than he is. I can find no warrant in Scripture for the doctrine of "imputed sanctification." It is a doctrine which seems to me to confuse things that differ, and to lead to very evil consequences. Not least, it is a doctrine which is flatly contradicted by the experience of all the most eminent Christians. If there is any point on which God's holiest saints agree it is this: that they see more, and know more, and feel more, and do more, and repent more, and believe more, as they get on in spiritual life, and in proportion to the closeness of their walk with God. In short, they "grow in grace," as St. Peter exhorts believers to do; and "abound more and more," according to the words of St. Paul (2 Pet. 3:18; 1 Thess. 4:1).

(8) Sanctification, again, is *a thing which depends greatly on a diligent use of Scriptural means*. When I speak of "means," I have in view Bible-reading, private prayer, regular attendance on public worship, regular hearing of God's Word, and regular reception of the Lord's Supper. I lay it down as a simple matter of fact, that no one who is careless about such things must ever expect to make much progress in sanctification. I can find no record of any eminent saint who ever neglected them. They

are appointed channels through which the Holy Spirit conveys fresh supplies of grace to the soul, and strengthens the work which He has begun in the inward man. Let men call this legal doctrine if they please, but I will never shrink from declaring my belief that there are no "spiritual gains without pains." I should as soon expect a farmer to prosper in business who contented himself with sowing his fields and never looking at them till harvest, as expect a believer to attain much holiness who was not diligent about his Bible-reading, his prayers, and the use of his Sundays. Our God is a God who works by means, and He will never bless the soul of that man who pretends to be so high and spiritual that he can get on without them.

(9) Sanctification, again, is *a thing which does not prevent a man having a great deal of inward spiritual conflict.* By conflict I mean a struggle within the heart between the old nature and the new, the flesh and spirit, which are to be found together in every believer (Gal. 5:17). A deep sense of that struggle, and a vast amount of mental discomfort from it, are no proof that a man is not sanctified. Nay, rather, I believe they are healthy symptoms of our condition, and prove that we are not dead, but alive. A true Christian is one who has not only peace of conscience, but war within. He may be known by his warfare as well as by his peace. In saying this, I do not forget that I am contradicting the views of some well-meaning Christians, who hold the doctrine called "sinless perfection." I cannot help that. I believe that what I say is confirmed by the language of St. Paul in the seventh chapter of Romans. That chapter I commend to the careful study of all my readers. I am quite satisfied that it does not describe the experience of an unconverted man, or of a young and unestablished Christian; but of an old experienced saint in close communion with God. None but such a man could say, "I delight in the law of God after the inward man" (Rom. 7:22). I believe, furthermore, that what I say is proved by the experience of all the most eminent servants of Christ that have ever lived. The full proof is to be seen in their journals, their autobiographies, and their lives.—Believing all this, I shall never hesitate to tell people that inward conflict is no proof that a man is not holy, and that they must not think they are not sanctified because they do not feel entirely free from inward struggle. Such freedom we shall doubtless have in heaven; but we shall never enjoy it in this world. The heart of the best Christian, even at his best, is a field occupied by two rival camps, and the "company of two armies" (Song 6:13). Let the words of the Thirteenth and Fifteenth Articles be well considered by all Churchmen: "The infection of nature doth remain in them that are

regenerated." "Although baptized and born again in Christ, we offend in many things; and if we say that we have no sin, we deceive ourselves, and the truth is not in us."[2]

(10) Sanctification, again, is *a thing which cannot justify a man, and yet it pleases God.* This may seem wonderful, and yet it is true. The holiest actions of the holiest saint that ever lived are all more or less full of defects and imperfections. They are either wrong in their motive or defective in their performance, and in themselves are nothing better than "splendid sins," deserving God's wrath and condemnation. To suppose that such actions can stand the severity of God's judgment, atone for sin, and merit heaven, is simply absurd. "By the deeds of the law shall no flesh be justified."—"We conclude that a man is justified by faith without the deeds of the law" (Rom. 3:20-28). The only righteousness in which we can appear before God is the righteousness of another—even the perfect righteousness of our Substitute and Representative, Jesus Christ the Lord. His work, and not our work, is our only title to heaven. This is a truth which we should be ready to die to maintain.—For all this, however, the Bible distinctly teaches that the holy actions of a sanctified man, although imperfect, are pleasing in the sight of God. "With such sacrifices God is well pleased" (Heb. 13:16). "Obey your parents, for this is well pleasing to the Lord" (Col. 3:20). "We do those things that are pleasing in His sight" (1 John 3:22). Let this never be forgotten, for it is a very comfortable doctrine. Just as a parent is pleased with the efforts of his little child to please him, though it be only by picking a daisy or walking across a room, so is our Father in heaven pleased with the poor performances of His believing children. He looks at the motive, principle, and intention of their actions, and not merely at their quantity and quality. He regards them as members of His own dear Son, and for His sake, wherever there is a single eye, He is well-pleased. Those Churchmen who dispute this would do well to study the Twelfth Article of the Church of England.

(11) Sanctification, again, is *a thing which will be found absolutely necessary as a witness to our character in the great day of judgment.* It will be utterly useless to plead that we believed in Christ, unless our faith has had some sanctifying effect, and been seen in our lives. Evidence, evidence, evidence, will be the one thing wanted when the great white throne is set, when the books are opened, when the graves give up their tenants, when the dead are arraigned before the bar of God. Without some evidence that our faith in Christ was real and genuine, we shall only rise again to be condemned. I can find no evidence that will be admitted in that day, except sanctification. The question will not be how

we talked and what we professed, but how we lived and what we did. Let no man deceive himself on this point. If anything is certain about the future, it is certain that there will be a judgment; and if anything is certain about judgment, it is certain that men's "works" and "doings" will be considered and examined in it (John 5:29; 2 Cor. 5:10; Rev. 20:13). He that supposes works are of no importance, because they cannot justify us, is a very ignorant Christian. Unless he opens his eyes, he will find to his cost that if he comes to the bar of God without some evidence of grace, he had better never have been born.

(12) Sanctification, in the last place, is *absolutely necessary, in order to train and prepare us for heaven.* Most men hope to go to heaven when they die; but few, it may be feared, take the trouble to consider whether they would enjoy heaven if they got there. Heaven is essentially a holy place; its inhabitants are all holy; its occupations are all holy. To be really happy in heaven, it is clear and plain that we must be somewhat trained and made ready for heaven while we are on earth. The notion of a purgatory after death, which shall turn sinners into saints, is a lying invention of man, and is nowhere taught in the Bible. We must be saints before we die, if we are to be saints afterwards in glory. The favourite idea of many, that dying men need nothing except absolution and forgiveness of sins to fit them for their great change, is a profound delusion. We need the work of the Holy Spirit as well as the work of Christ; we need renewal of the heart as well as the atoning blood; we need to be sanctified as well as to be justified. It is common to hear people saying on their death-beds, "I only want the Lord to forgive me my sins, and take me to rest." But those who say such things forget that the rest of heaven would be utterly useless if we had no heart to enjoy it! What could an unsanctified man do in heaven, if by any chance he got there? Let that question be fairly looked in the face, and fairly answered. No man can possibly be happy in a place where he is not in his element, and where all around him is not congenial to his tastes, habits, and character. When an eagle is happy in an iron cage, when a sheep is happy in the water, when an owl is happy in the blaze of noonday sun, when a fish is happy on the dry land—then, and not till then, will I admit that the unsanctified man could be happy in heaven.[3]

I lay down these twelve propositions about sanctification with a firm persuasion that they are true, and I ask all who read these pages to ponder them well. Each of them would admit of being expanded and handled more fully, and all of them deserve private thought and consideration. Some of them may be disputed and contradicted; but I doubt whether any of them can be overthrown or proved untrue. I only ask for them a fair and impartial hearing. I believe in my conscience that they are likely to assist men in attaining clear views of sanctification.

II. I now proceed to take up the second point which I proposed to consider. That point is the *visible evidence of sanctification*. In a word, what are the visible marks of a sanctified man? What may we expect to see in him?

This is a very wide and difficult department of our subject. It is wide, because it necessitates the mention of many details which cannot be handled fully in the limits of a paper like this. It is difficult, because it cannot possibly be treated without giving offence. But at any risk truth ought to be spoken; and there is some kind of truth which especially requires to be spoken in the present day.

(1) True sanctification then does not consist in *talk about religion*. This is a point which ought never to be forgotten. The vast increase of education and preaching in these latter days makes it absolutely necessary to raise a warning voice. People hear so much of Gospel truth that they contract an unholy familiarity with its words and phrases, and sometimes talk so fluently about its doctrines that you might think them true Christians. In fact it is sickening and disgusting to hear the cool and flippant language which may pour out about "conversion—the Saviour—the Gospel—finding peace—free grace," and the like, while they are notoriously serving sin or living for the world. Can we doubt that such talk is abominable in God's sight, and is little better than cursing, swearing, and taking God's name in vain? The tongue is not the only member that Christ bids us give to His service. God does not want His people to be mere empty tubs, sounding brass and tinkling cymbals. We must be sanctified, not only "in word and in tongue, but in deed and truth" (1 John 3:18).

(2) True sanctification does not consist in temporary *religious feelings*. This again is a point about which a warning is greatly needed. Mission services and revival meetings are attracting great attention in every part of the land, and producing a great sensation. The Church of England seems to have taken a new lease of life, and exhibits a new activity; and we ought to thank God for it. But these things have their attendant dangers as well as their advantages. Wherever wheat is sown the devil is sure to sow tares. Many, it may be feared, appear moved and touched and roused under the preaching of the Gospel, while in reality their hearts are not changed at all. A kind of animal excitement from the contagion of seeing others weeping, rejoicing, or affected, is the true account of their case. Their wounds are only skin deep, and the peace they profess to feel is skin deep also. Like

the stony-ground hearers, they "receive the Word with joy" (Matt. 13:20); but after a little they fall away, go back to the world, and are harder and worse than before. Like Jonah's gourd, they come up suddenly in a night and perish in a night. Let these things not be forgotten. Let us beware in this day of healing wounds slightly, and crying, "Peace, peace," when there is no peace. Let us urge on every one who exhibits new interest in religion to be content with nothing short of the deep, solid, sanctifying work of the Holy Ghost. Reaction, after false religious excitement, is a most deadly disease of soul. When the devil is only temporarily cast out of a man in the heat of a revival, and by and by returns to his house, the last state becomes worse than the first. Better a thousand times begin more slowly, and then "continue in the word" steadfastly, than begin in a hurry, without counting the cost, and by and by look back, with Lot's wife, and return to the world. I declare I know no state of soul more dangerous than to imagine we are born again and sanctified by the Holy Ghost, because we have picked up a few religious feelings.

(3) True sanctification does not consist in *outward formalism* and external devoutness. This is an enormous delusion, but unhappily a very common one. Thousands appear to imagine that true holiness is to be seen in an excessive quantity of bodily religion—in constant attendance on Church services, reception of the Lord's Supper, and observance of fasts and saints' days—in multiplied bowings and turnings and gestures and postures during public worship—in self-imposed austerities and petty self-denials—in wearing peculiar dresses, and the use of pictures and crosses. I freely admit that some people take up these things from conscientious motives, and actually believe that they help their souls. But I am afraid that in many cases this external *religiousness* is made a substitute for inward holiness; and I am quite certain that it falls utterly short of sanctification of heart. Above all, when I see that many followers of this outward, sensuous, and formal style of Christianity are absorbed in worldliness, and plunge headlong into its pomps and vanities, without shame, I feel that there is need of very plain speaking on the subject. There may be an immense amount of "bodily service," while there is not a jot of real sanctification.

(4) Sanctification does not consist *in retirement from our place in life,* and the renunciation of our social duties. In every age it has been a snare with many to take up this line in the pursuit of holiness. Hundreds of hermits have buried themselves in some wilderness, and thousands of men and women have shut themselves up within the walls of monasteries and convents, under the vain idea that by so doing they would escape sin

and become eminently holy. They have forgotten that no bolts and bars can keep out the devil, and that, wherever we go, we carry that root of all evil, our own hearts. To become a monk, or a nun, or to join a House of Mercy, is not the high road to sanctification. True holiness does not make a Christian evade difficulties, but face and overcome them. Christ would have His people show that His grace is not a mere hot-house plant, which can only thrive under shelter, but a strong, hardy thing which can flourish in every relation of life. It is doing our duty in that state to which God has called us—like salt in the midst of corruption, and light in the midst of darkness—which is a primary element in sanctification. It is not the man who hides himself in a cave, but the man who glorifies God as master or servant, parent or child, in the family and in the street, in business and in trade, who is the Scriptural type of a sanctified man. Our Master Himself said in His last prayer, "I pray not that Thou shouldest take them out of the world, but that Thou shouldest keep them from the evil" (John 17:15).

(5) Sanctification does not consist in the *occasional performance of right actions*. It is the habitual working of a new heavenly principle within, which runs through all a man's daily conduct, both in great things and in small. Its seat is in the heart, and like the heart in the body, it has a regular influence on every part of the character. It is not like a pump, which only sends forth water when worked up from without, but like a perpetual fountain, from which a stream is ever flowing spontaneously and naturally. Even Herod, when he heard John the Baptist, "did many things," while his heart was utterly wrong in the sight of God (Mark 6:20). Just so there are scores of people in the present day who seem to have spasmodical fits of "goodness," as it is called, and do many right things under the influence of sickness, affliction, death in the family, public calamities, or a sudden qualm of conscience. Yet all the time any intelligent observer can see plainly that they are not converted, and that they know nothing of "sanctification." A true saint, like Hezekiah, will be whole-hearted. He will count God's commandments concerning all things to be right, and "hate every false way" (2 Chron. 31:21; Ps. 119:104).

(6) Genuine sanctification will show itself in *habitual respect to God's law,* and habitual effort to live in obedience to it as the rule of life. There is no greater mistake than to suppose that a Christian has nothing to do with the law and the Ten Commandments, because he cannot be justified by keeping them. The same Holy Ghost who convinces the believer of sin by the law, and leads him to Christ for justification, will always lead him to a spiritual use of the law, as a friendly guide, in the pursuit of sanctification. Our Lord Jesus Christ never made light of the Ten Commandments; on

the contrary, in His first public discourse, the Sermon on the Mount, He expounded them, and showed the searching nature of their requirements. St. Paul never made light of the law: on the contrary, he says, "The law is good, if a man use it lawfully."—"I delight in the law of God after the inward man" (1 Tim. 1:8; Rom. 7:22). He that pretends to be a saint, while he sneers at the Ten Commandments, and thinks nothing of lying, hypocrisy, swindling, ill-temper, slander, drunkenness, and breach of the seventh commandment, is under a fearful delusion. He will find it hard to prove that he is a "saint" in the last day!

(7) Genuine sanctification will show itself in an *habitual endeavour* to do Christ's will, and to live by His practical precepts. These precepts are to be found scattered everywhere throughout the four Gospels, and especially in the Sermon on the Mount. He that supposes they were spoken without the intention of promoting holiness, and that a Christian need not attend to them in his daily life, is really little better than a lunatic, and at any rate is a grossly ignorant person. To hear some men talk, and read some men's writings, one might imagine that our blessed Lord, when He was on earth, never taught anything but *doctrine,* and left practical duties to be taught by others! The slightest knowledge of the four Gospels ought to tell us that this is a complete mistake. What His disciples ought to be and to do is continually brought forward in our Lord's teaching. A truly sanctified man will never forget this. He serves a Master who said, "Ye are My friends if ye do whatsoever I command you" (John 15:14).

(8) Genuine sanctification will show itself in an habitual desire to live up to *the standard which St. Paul sets before the Churches* in his writings. That standard is to be found in the closing chapters of nearly all his Epistles. The common idea of many persons that St. Paul's writings are full of nothing but doctrinal statements and controversial subjects—justification, election, predestination, prophecy, and the like—is an entire delusion, and a melancholy proof of the ignorance of Scripture which prevails in these latter days. I defy anyone to read St. Paul's writings carefully without finding in them a large quantity of plain, practical directions about the Christian's duty in every relation of life, and about our daily habits, temper, and behaviour to one another. These directions were written down by inspiration of God for the perpetual guidance of professing Christians. He who does not attend to them may possibly pass muster as a member of a Church or a chapel, but he certainly is not what the Bible calls a "sanctified" man.

(9) Genuine sanctification will show itself in habitual *attention to the active graces* which our Lord so beautifully exemplified, and especially to

the grace of charity. "A new commandment I give unto you, that ye love one another; as I have loved you, that ye also love one another. By this shall all men know that ye are My disciples, if ye have love one to another" (John 13:34-35). A sanctified man will try to do good in the world, and to lessen the sorrow and increase the happiness of all around him. He will aim to be like his Master, full of kindness and love to every one; and this not in word only, by calling people "dear," but by deeds and actions and self-denying work, according as he has opportunity. The selfish Christian professor, who wraps himself up in his own conceit of superior knowledge, and seems to care nothing whether others sink or swim, go to heaven or hell, so long as he walks to Church or chapel in his Sunday best, and is called a "sound member"—such a man knows nothing of sanctification. He may think himself a saint on earth, but he will not be a saint in heaven. Christ will never be found the Saviour of those who know nothing of following His example. Saving faith and real converting grace will always produce some conformity to the image of Jesus[4] (Col. 3:10).

(10) Genuine sanctification, in the last place, will show itself in *habitual attention to the passive graces* of Christianity. When I speak of passive graces, I mean those graces which are especially shown in submission to the will of God, and in bearing and forbearing towards one another. Few people, perhaps, unless they have examined the point, have an idea how much is said about these graces in the New Testament, and how important a place they seem to fill. This is the special point which St. Peter dwells upon in commending our Lord Jesus Christ's example to our notice: "Christ also suffered for us, leaving us an example, that we should follow His steps: Who did no sin, neither was guile found in His mouth: Who, when He was reviled, reviled not again; when He suffered, He threatened not; but committed Himself to Him that judgeth righteously" (1 Pet. 2:21-23).—This is the one piece of profession which the Lord's prayer requires us to make: "Forgive us our trespasses, as we forgive them that trespass against us"; and the one point that is commented upon at the end of the prayer.—This is the point which occupies one-third of the list of the fruits of the Spirit, supplied by St. Paul. Nine are named, and three of these, "long-suffering, gentleness, and meekness," are unquestionably passive graces (Gal. 5:22-23). I must plainly say that I do not think this subject is sufficiently considered by Christians. The passive graces are no doubt harder to attain than the active ones, but they are precisely the graces which have the greatest influence on the world. Of one thing I feel very sure—it is nonsense to pretend to sanctification unless we follow after the meekness, gentleness, long-suffering, and forgiveness of which

the Bible makes so much. People who are habitually giving way to peevish and cross tempers in daily life, and are constantly sharp with their tongues, and disagreeable to all around them—spiteful people, vindictive people, revengeful people, malicious people—of whom, alas, the world is only too full!—all such know little, as they should know, about sanctification.

Such are the visible marks of a sanctified man. I do not say that they are all to be seen equally in all God's people. I freely admit that in the best they are not fully and perfectly exhibited. But I do say confidently, that the things of which I have been speaking are the Scriptural marks of sanctification, and that they who know nothing of them may well doubt whether they have any grace at all. Whatever others may please to say, I will never shrink from saying that genuine sanctification is a thing that can be seen, and that the marks I have endeavoured to sketch out are more or less the marks of a sanctified man.

III. I now propose to consider, in the last place, the *distinction between justification and sanctification*. Wherein do they agree, and wherein do they differ?

This branch of our subject is one of great importance, though I fear it will not seem so to all my readers. I shall handle it briefly, but I dare not pass it over altogether. Too many are apt to look at nothing but the surface of things in religion, and regard nice distinctions in theology as questions of "words and names," which are of little real value. But I warn all who are in earnest about their souls, that the discomfort which arises from not "distinguishing things that differ" in Christian doctrine is very great indeed; and I especially advise them, if they love peace, to seek clear views about the matter before us. Justification and sanctification are two distinct things we must always remember. Yet there are points in which they *agree* and points in which they *differ*. Let us try to find out what they are.

In what, then, are justification and sanctification alike?

(a) Both proceed originally from the free grace of God. It is of His gift alone that believers are justified or sanctified at all.

(b) Both are part of that great work of salvation which Christ, in the eternal covenant, has undertaken on behalf of His people. Christ is the fountain of life, from which pardon and holiness both flow. The root of each is Christ.

(c) Both are to be found in the same persons. Those who are justified are always sanctified, and those who are sanctified are always justified. God has joined them together, and they cannot be put asunder.

(d) Both begin at the same time. The moment a person begins to be a justified person, he also begins to be a sanctified person. He may not feel it, but it is a fact.

(e) Both are alike necessary to salvation. No one ever reached heaven without a renewed heart as well as forgiveness, without the Spirit's grace as well as the blood of Christ, without a meetness for eternal glory as well as a title. The one is just as necessary as the other.

Such are the points on which justification and sanctification agree. Let us now reverse the picture, and see wherein they differ.

(a) Justification is the *reckoning* and counting a man to be righteous for the sake of another, even Jesus Christ the Lord. Sanctification is the actual *making* a man inwardly righteous, though it may be in a very feeble degree.

(b) The righteousness we have by our justification is *not our own,* but the everlasting perfect righteousness of our great Mediator Christ, imputed to us, and made our own by faith. The righteousness we have by sanctification is *our own* righteousness, imparted, inherent, and wrought in us by the Holy Spirit, but mingled with much infirmity and imperfection.

(c) In justification our own works have no place at all, and simple faith in Christ is the one thing needful. In sanctification our own works are of vast importance and God bids us fight, and watch, and pray, and strive, and take pains, and labour.

(d) Justification is a finished and complete work, and a man is perfectly justified the moment he believes. Sanctification is an imperfect work, comparatively, and will never be perfected until we reach heaven.

(e) Justification admits of no growth or increase: a man is as much justified the hour he first comes to Christ by faith as he will be to all eternity. Sanctification is eminently a progressive work, and admits of continual growth and enlargement so long as a man lives.

(f) Justification has special reference to our *persons,* our standing in God's sight, and our deliverance from guilt. Sanctification has special reference to our *natures,* and the moral renewal of our hearts.

(g) Justification gives us our title to heaven, and boldness to enter in. Sanctification gives us our meetness for heaven, and prepares us to enjoy it when we dwell there.

(h) Justification is the act of God *about* us, and is not easily discerned by others. Sanctification is the work of God *within* us, and cannot be hid in its outward manifestation from the eyes of men.

I commend these distinctions to the attention of all my readers, and I ask them to ponder them well. I am persuaded that one great cause of the darkness and uncomfortable feelings of many well-meaning people in the matter of religion, is their habit of confounding, and not distinguishing, justification and sanctification. It can never be too strongly impressed on our minds that they are two separate things. No doubt they cannot be divided, and everyone that is a partaker of either is a partaker of both. But never, never ought they to be confounded, and never ought the distinction between them to be forgotten.

It only remains for me now to bring this subject to a conclusion by a few plain words of application. The nature and visible marks of sanctification have been brought before us. What practical reflections ought the whole matter to raise in our minds?

(1) For one thing, let us all awake to a sense of *the perilous state of many professing Christians.* "Without holiness no man shall see the Lord"; without sanctification there is no salvation (Heb. 12:14). Then what an enormous amount of so-called religion there is which is perfectly useless! What an immense proportion of Church-goers and chapel-goers are in the broad road that leadeth to destruction! The thought is awful, crushing, and overwhelming. Oh, that preachers and teachers would open their eyes and realize the condition of souls around them! Oh, that men could be persuaded to "flee from the wrath to come"! If unsanctified souls can be saved and go to heaven, the Bible is not true. Yet the Bible is true and cannot lie! What must the end be!

(2) For another thing, let us *make sure work of our own condition,* and never rest till we feel and know that we are "sanctified" ourselves. What are our tastes, and choices, and likings, and inclinations? This is the great testing question. It matters little what we wish, and what we hope, and what we desire to be before we die. What are we now? What are we doing? Are we sanctified or not? If not, the fault is all our own.

(3) For another thing, if we would be sanctified, our course is clear and plain—*we must begin with Christ.* We must go to Him as sinners, with no plea but that of utter need, and cast our souls on Him by faith, for peace and reconciliation with God. We must place ourselves in His hands, as in the hands of a good physician, and cry to Him for mercy and grace. We must wait for nothing to bring with us as a recommendation. The very first step towards sanctification, no less than justification, is to come with faith to Christ. We must first live and then work.

(4) For another thing, if we would grow in holiness and become more sanctified, we must *continually go on as we began,* and be ever making fresh applications to Christ. He is the Head from which every member must be supplied (Eph. 4:16). To live the life of daily faith in the Son of

God, and to be daily drawing out of His fulness the promised grace and strength which He has laid up for His people—this is the grand secret of progressive sanctification. Believers who seem at a standstill are generally neglecting close communion with Jesus, and so grieving the Spirit. He that prayed, "Sanctify them," the last night before His crucifixion, is infinitely willing to help everyone who by faith applies to Him for help, and desires to be made more holy.

(5) For another thing, *let us not expect too much* from our own hearts here below. At our best we shall find in ourselves daily cause for humiliation, and discover that we are needy debtors to mercy and grace every hour. The more light we have, the more we shall see our own imperfection. Sinners we were when we began, sinners we shall find ourselves as we go on; renewed, pardoned, justified—yet sinners to the very last. Our absolute perfection is yet to come, and the expectation of it is one reason why we should long for heaven.

(6) Finally, let us never be ashamed of *making much of sanctification,* and contending for a high standard of holiness. While some are satisfied with a miserably low degree of attainment, and others are not ashamed to live on without any holiness at all—content with a mere round of Church-going and chapel-going, but never getting on, like a horse in a mill—let us stand fast in the old paths, follow after eminent holiness ourselves, and recommend it boldly to others. This is the only way to be really happy.

Let us feel convinced, whatever others may say, that holiness is happiness, and that the man who gets through life most comfortably is the *sanctified* man. No doubt there are some true Christians who from ill-health, or family trials, or other secret causes, enjoy little sensible comfort, and go mourning all their days on the way to heaven. But these are exceptional cases. As a general rule, in the long run of life, it will be found true that "sanctified" people are the happiest people on earth. They have solid comforts which the world can neither give nor take away. "The ways of wisdom are ways of pleasantness."—"Great peace have they that love Thy law."—It was said by One who cannot lie, "My yoke is easy, and My burden is light."—But it is also written, "There is no peace unto the wicked" (Prov. 3:17; Ps. 119:165; Matt. 11:30; Isa. 48:22).

P. S.

The subject of sanctification is of such deep importance, and the mistakes made about it so many and great, that I make no apology for strongly recommending "Owen on the Holy Spirit" to all who want to study more thoroughly the whole doctrine of sanctification. No single paper like this can embrace it all.

I am quite aware that Owen's writings are not fashionable in the present day, and that many think fit to neglect and sneer at him as a Puritan! Yet the great divine who in Commonwealth times was Dean of Christ Church, Oxford, does not deserve to be treated in this way. He had more learning and sound knowledge of Scripture in his little finger than many who depreciate him have in their whole bodies. I assert unhesitatingly that the man who wants to study experimental theology will find no books equal to those of Owen and some of his contemporaries, for complete, Scriptural, and exhaustive treatment of the subjects they handle.

3

HOLINESS

"Holiness, without which no man shall see the Lord . . ."
—HEBREWS 12:14

The text which heads this page opens up a subject of deep importance. That subject is practical holiness. It suggests a question which demands the attention of all professing Christians—Are we holy? Shall we see the Lord?

That question can never be out of season. The wise man tells us, "There is a time to weep, and a time to laugh—a time to keep silence, and a time to speak" (Eccles. 3:4, 7); but there is no time, no, not a day, in which a man ought not to be holy. Are we?

That question concerns all ranks and conditions of men. Some are rich and some are poor—some learned and some unlearned—some masters, and some servants; but there is no rank or condition in life in which a man ought not to be holy. Are we?

I ask to be heard to-day about this question. How stands the account between our souls and God? In this hurrying, bustling world, let us stand still for a few minutes and consider the matter of holiness. I believe I might have chosen a subject more popular and pleasant. I am sure I might have found one more easy to handle. But I feel deeply I could not have chosen one more seasonable and more profitable to our souls. It is a solemn thing to hear the Word of God saying, "Without holiness no man shall see the Lord" (Heb. 12:14).

I shall endeavour, by God's help, to examine what true holiness is, and the reason why it is so needful. In conclusion, I shall try to point out the only way in which holiness can be attained. I have already, in the second paper in this volume, approached this subject from a doctrinal side. Let me now try to present it to my readers in a more plain and practical point of view.

I. First, then, let me try to show *what true practical holiness is—what sort of persons are those whom God calls holy.*

A man may go great lengths, and yet never reach true holiness. It is not knowledge—Balaam had that; nor great profession—Judas Iscariot had that; nor doing many things—Herod had that; nor zeal for certain matters in religion—Jehu had that; nor morality and outward respectability of conduct—the young ruler had that; nor taking pleasure in hearing preachers—the Jews in Ezekiel's time had that; nor keeping company with godly people—Joab and Gehazi and Demas had that. Yet none of these was holy! These things are not holiness. A man may have any one of them, and yet never see the Lord.

What then is true practical holiness? It is a hard question to answer. I do not mean that there is any want of Scriptural matter on the subject. But I fear lest I should give a defective view of holiness, and not say all that ought to be said; or lest I should say things about it that ought not to be said, and so do harm. Let me, however, try to draw a picture of holiness, that we may see it clearly before the eyes of our minds. Only let it never be forgotten, when I have said all, that my account is but a poor imperfect outline at the best.

(a) Holiness is *the habit of being of one mind with God,* according as we find His mind described in Scripture. It is the habit of agreeing in God's judgment—hating what He hates—loving what He loves—and measuring everything in this world by the standard of His Word. He who most entirely agrees with God, he is the most holy man.

(b) A holy man will *endeavour to shun every known sin, and to keep every known commandment.* He will have a decided bent of mind toward God, a hearty desire to do His will—a greater fear of displeasing Him than of displeasing the world, and a love to all His ways. He will feel what Paul felt when he said, "I delight in the law of God after the inward man" (Rom. 7:22), and what David felt when he said, "I esteem *all* Thy precepts concerning all things to be right, and I hate *every* false way" (Ps. 119:128).

(c) A holy man will *strive to be like our Lord Jesus Christ.* He will not only live the life of faith in Him, and draw from Him all his daily peace and strength, but he will also labour to have the mind that was in Him, and to be "conformed to His image" (Rom. 8:29). It will be his aim to bear with and forgive others, even as Christ forgave us—to be unselfish, even as Christ pleased not Himself—to walk in love, even as Christ loved us—to be lowly-minded and humble, even as Christ made Himself of no reputation and humbled Himself. He will remember that Christ was a faithful witness for the truth—that He came not to do His own will—that it was His meat and drink to do His Father's will—that He would continually deny Himself in order to minister to others—that He was meek and patient under undeserved insults—that He thought more of godly poor men than of kings—that He was full of love and compassion to sinners—that He was bold and uncompromising in denouncing sin—that He sought not the praise of men, when He might have had it—that He went about doing good—that He was separate from worldly people—that He continued instant in prayer—that He would not let even His nearest relations stand in His way when God's work was to be done. These things a holy man will try to remember. By them he will endeavour to shape his course in life. He will lay to heart the saying of John, "He that saith he abideth in Christ ought himself also so to walk, even as He walked" (1 John 2:6); and the saying of Peter, that "Christ suffered for us, leaving us an example that ye should follow His steps" (1 Pet. 2:21). Happy is he who has learned to make Christ his "all," both for salvation and example! Much time would be saved, and much sin prevented, if men would oftener ask themselves the question, "What would Christ have said and done, if He were in my place?"

(d) A holy man will follow after *meekness,* longsuffering, gentleness, patience, kind tempers, government of his tongue. He will bear much, forbear much, overlook much and be slow to talk of standing on his rights. We see a bright example of this in the behaviour of David when Shimei cursed him—and of Moses when Aaron and Miriam spake against him (2 Sam. 16:10; Num. 12:3).

(e) A holy man will follow after *temperance and self-denial.* He will labour to mortify the desires to his body—to crucify his flesh with his affections and lusts—to curb his passions—to restrain his carnal inclinations, lest at any time they break loose. Oh, what a word is that of the Lord Jesus to the Apostles: "Take heed to yourselves, lest at any time your hearts be overcharged with surfeiting and drunkenness, and cares of this life" (Luke 21:34); and that of the Apostle Paul: "I keep under my body, and bring it into subjection, lest that by any means when I have preached to others, I myself should be a castaway" (1 Cor. 9:27).

(f) A holy man will follow after *charity and brotherly kindness.* He will endeavour to observe the golden rule of doing as he would have men do to him, and speaking as he would have men speak to him. He will be full of affection towards his brethren—towards their bodies, their property, their characters, their feelings, their souls. "He that loveth another," says Paul, "hath fulfilled the law" (Rom. 13:8). He will abhor all lying, slandering, backbiting, cheating, dishonesty, and unfair dealing, even in the least things. The shekel and cubit of the sanctuary were larger than those in common use. He will strive to adorn his religion by all his outward demeanour, and to make it lovely and beautiful in the eyes of all around him. Alas, what condemning words are the 13th chapter of 1 Corinthians, and the Sermon on the Mount, when laid alongside the conduct of many professing Christians!

(g) A holy man will follow after a spirit of *mercy and benevolence towards others*. He will not stand all the day idle. He will not be content with doing no harm—he will try to do good. He will strive to be useful in his day and generation, and to lessen the spiritual wants and misery around him, as far as he can. Such was Dorcas, "full of good works and almsdeeds, which she did,"—not merely purposed and talked about, *but did*. Such an one was Paul: "I will very gladly spend and be spent for you," he says, "though the more abundantly I love you the less I be loved" (Acts 9:36; 2 Cor. 12:15).

(h) A holy man will follow after *purity of heart*. He will dread all filthiness and uncleanness of spirit, and seek to avoid all things that might draw him into it. He knows his own heart is like tinder, and will diligently keep clear of the sparks of temptation. Who shall dare to talk of strength when David can fall? There is many a hint to be gleaned from the ceremonial law. Under it the man who only *touched* a bone, or a deadly body, or a grave, or a diseased person, became at once unclean in the sight of God. And these things were emblems and figures. Few Christians are ever too watchful and too particular about this point.

(i) A holy man will follow after *the fear of God*. I do not mean the fear of a slave, who only works because he is afraid of punishment, and would be idle if he did not dread discovery. I mean rather the fear of a child, who wishes to live and move as if he was always before his father's face, because he loves him. What a noble example Nehemiah gives us of this! When he became Governor at Jerusalem he might have been chargeable to the Jews and required of them money for his support. The former Governors had done so. There was none to blame him if he did. But he says, "So did not I, because of the fear of God" (Neh. 5:15).

(j) A holy man will follow after *humility*. He will desire, in lowliness of mind, to esteem all others better than himself. He will see more evil in his own heart than in any others in the world. He will understand something of Abraham's feeling, when he says, "I am dust and ashes";—and

Jacob's, when he says, "I am less than the least of all Thy mercies";—and Job's, when he says, "I am vile";—and Paul's, when he says, "I am chief of sinners." Holy Bradford, that faithful martyr of Christ, would sometimes finish his letters with these words: "A most miserable sinner, John Bradford." Good old Mr. Grimshaw's last words, when he lay on his death-bed, were these: "Here goes an unprofitable servant."

(k) A holy man will follow after *faithfulness in all the duties and relations in life.* He will try, not merely to fill his place as well as others who take no thought for their souls, but even better, because he has higher motives, and more help than they. Those words of Paul should never be forgotten: "Whatever ye do, do it heartily, as unto the Lord,"—"Not slothful in business, fervent in spirit, serving the Lord" (Col. 3:23; Rom. 12:11). Holy persons should aim at doing everything well, and should be ashamed of allowing themselves to do anything ill if they can help it. Like Daniel, they should seek to give no "occasion" against themselves, except "concerning the law of their God" (Dan. 6:5). They should strive to be good husbands and good wives, good parents and good children, good masters and good servants, good neighbours, good friends, good subjects, good in private and good in public, good in the place of business and good by their firesides. Holiness is worth little indeed, if it does not bear this kind of fruit. The Lord Jesus puts a searching question to His people, when He says, "What do ye more than others?" (Matt. 5:47).

(l) Last, but not least, a holy man will follow after *spiritual mindedness.* He will endeavour to set his affections entirely on things above, and to hold things on earth with a very loose hand. He will not neglect the business of the life that now is; but the first place in his mind and thoughts will be given to the life to come. He will aim to live like one whose treasure is in heaven, and to pass through this world like a stranger and pilgrim travelling to his home. To commune with God in prayer, in the Bible, and in the assembly of His people—these things will be the holy man's chiefest enjoyments. He will value every thing and place and company, just in proportion as it draws him nearer to God. He will enter into something of David's feeling, when he says, "My soul followeth hard after Thee." "Thou art my portion" (Ps. 63:8; 119:57).

Such is the outline of holiness which I venture to sketch out. Such is the character which those who are called "holy" *follow after.* Such are the main features of a holy man.

But here let me say, I trust no man will misunderstand me. I am not without fear that my meaning will be mistaken, and the description I have given of holiness will discourage some tender conscience. I would not willingly make one righteous heart sad, or throw a stumbling-block in any believer's way.

I do not say for a moment that holiness shuts out the presence of *indwelling* sin. No: far from it. It is the greatest misery of a holy man that he carries about with him a "body of death";—that often when he would do good "evil is present with him"; that the old man is clogging all his movements, and, as it were, trying to draw him back at every step he takes (Rom. 7:21). But it is the excellence of a holy man that he is not at peace with indwelling sin, as others are. He hates it, mourns over it, and longs to be free from its company. The work of sanctification within him is like the wall of Jerusalem—the building goes forward "even in troublous times" (Dan. 9:25).

Neither do I say that holiness comes to ripeness and perfection all at once, or that these graces I have touched on must be found in full bloom and vigour before you can call a man holy. No: far from it. Sanctification is always a *progressive work*. Some men's graces are in the blade, some in the ear, and some are like full corn in the ear. All must have a beginning. We must never despise "the day of small things." And sanctification in the very best is an *imperfect work*. The history of the brightest saints that ever lived will contain many a "but," and "howbeit," and "notwithstanding," before you reach the end. The gold will never be without some dross—the light will never shine without some clouds, until we reach the heavenly Jerusalem. The sun himself has spots upon his face. The holiest men have many a blemish and defect when weighed in the balance of the sanctuary. Their life is a continual warfare with sin, the world, and the devil; and sometimes you will see them not overcoming, but overcome. The flesh is ever lusting against the spirit, and the spirit against the flesh, and "in many things they offend all" (Gal. 5:17; James 3:2).

But still, for all this, I am sure that to have such a character as I have faintly drawn, is the heart's desire and prayer of all true Christians. They press towards it, if they do not reach it. They may not attain to it, but they always aim at it. It is what they strive and labour to be, if it is not what they are.

And this I do boldly and confidently say, that true holiness is a great *reality*. It is something in a man that can be seen, and known, and marked, and felt by all around him. It is light: if it exists, it will show itself. It is salt: if it exists, its savour will be perceived. It is a precious ointment: if it exists, its presence cannot be hid.

I am sure we should all be ready to make allowance for much backsliding, for much occasional deadness in professing Christians. I know a road may lead from one point to another, and yet have many a winding and turn; and a man may be truly holy, and yet be drawn aside by many an infirmity. Gold is not the less gold because mingled with alloy, nor light the less light because faint and dim, nor grace the less grace because young and weak. But after every allowance, I cannot see how any man deserves to be called "holy," who wilfully allows himself in sins, and is not humbled and ashamed because of them. I dare not call anyone "holy" who makes a habit of wilfully neglecting known duties, and wilfully doing what he knows God has commanded him not to do. Well says Owen, "I do not understand how a man can be a true believer unto whom sin is not the greatest burden, sorrow, and trouble."

Such are the leading characteristics of practical holiness. Let us examine ourselves and see whether we are acquainted with it. Let us prove our own selves.

II. Let me try, in the next place, *to show some reasons why practical holiness is so important.*

Can holiness save us? Can holiness put away sin—cover iniquities—make satisfaction for transgressions—pay our debt to God? No: not a whit. God forbid that I should ever say so. Holiness can do none of these things. The brightest saints are all "unprofitable servants." Our purest works are no better than filthy rags, when tried by the light of God's holy law. The white robe which Jesus offers, and faith puts on, must be our only righteousness—the name of Christ our only confidence—the Lamb's book of life our only title to heaven. With all our holiness we are no better than *sinners.* Our best things are stained and tainted with imperfection. They are all more or less incomplete, wrong in the motive or defective in the performance. By the deeds of the law shall no child of Adam ever be justified. "By grace are ye saved through faith, and that not of yourselves, it is the gift of God: not of works, lest any man should boast" (Eph. 2:8-9).

Why then is holiness so important? Why does the Apostle say, "Without it no man shall see the Lord"? Let me set out in order a few reasons.

(a) For one thing, we must be holy, because *the voice of God in Scripture plainly commands it.* The Lord Jesus says to His people, "Except your righteousness shall exceed the righteousness of the scribes and Pharisees, ye shall in no case enter into the kingdom of heaven" (Matt. 5:20). "Be ye perfect, even as your Father which is in heaven is perfect" (Matt. 5:48). Paul tells the Thessalonians, "This is the will of God, even your sanctification" (1 Thess. 4:3). And Peter says, "As He which hath called you is holy, so be ye holy in all manner of conversation; because it is written, Be ye holy, for I am holy" (1 Pet. 1:15-16). "In this," says Leighton, "law and Gospel agree."

(b) We must be holy, because this is one grand *end and purpose for which Christ came into the world.* Paul writes to the Corinthians, "He died for all, that they which live should not henceforth live unto themselves, but unto Him which died for them and rose again" (2 Cor. 5:15). And to the Ephesians, "Christ loved the Church, and gave Himself for it, that He might sanctify and cleanse it" (Eph. 5:25-26). And to Titus, "He gave Himself for us, that He might redeem us from all iniquity, and purify unto Himself a peculiar people, zealous of good works" (Titus 2:14). In short, to talk of men being saved from the guilt of sin, without being at the same time saved from its dominion in their hearts, is to contradict the witness of all Scripture. Are believers said to be elect?—it is "through sanctification of the Spirit." Are they predestinated?—it is "to be conformed to the image of God's Son." Are they chosen?—it is "that they may be holy." Are they called?—it is "with a holy calling." Are they afflicted?—it is that they may be "partakers of holiness." Jesus is a complete Saviour. He does not merely take away the guilt of a believer's sin, He does more—He breaks its power (1 Pet. 1:2; Rom. 8:29; Eph. 1:4; Heb. 12:10).

(c) We must be holy, because this is the *only sound evidence that we have saving faith in our Lord Jesus Christ.* The Twelfth Article of our Church says truly, that "Although good works cannot put away our sins, and endure the severity of God's judgment, yet are they pleasing and acceptable to God in Christ, and do spring out necessarily of a true and lively faith; insomuch that by them a lively faith may be as evidently known as a tree discerned by its fruits." James warns us there is such a thing as a dead faith—a faith which goes no further than the profession of the lips, and has no influence on a man's character (James 2:17). True saving faith is a very different kind of thing. True faith will always show itself by its fruits—it will sanctify, it will work by love, it will overcome the world, it will purify the heart. I know that people are fond of talking about death-bed evidences. They will rest on words spoken in the hours of fear, and pain, and weakness, as if they might take comfort in them about the friends they lose. But I am afraid in ninety-nine cases out of a hundred such evidences are not to be depended on. I suspect that, with rare exceptions, men die just as they have lived. The only safe evidence that we are one with Christ, and Christ in us, is holy life. They that live unto the Lord are generally the only people who die in the Lord. If we would die the death of the righteous, let us not rest in slothful desires only; let us seek to live His life. It is a true saying of Traill's, "That man's state is naught, and his faith unsound, that find not his hopes of glory purifying to his heart and life."

(d) We must be holy, because this is the *only proof that we love the Lord Jesus Christ in sincerity*. This is a point on which He has spoken most plainly, in the fourteenth and fifteenth chapters of John. "If ye love Me, keep My commandments."—"He that hath My commandments and keepeth them, he it is that loveth Me."—"If a man love Me he will keep My words."—"Ye are My friends if ye do whatsoever I command you" (John 14:15, 21, 23; 15:14).—Plainer words than these it would be difficult to find, and woe to those who neglect them! Surely that man must be in an unhealthy state of soul who can think of all that Jesus suffered, and yet cling to those sins for which that suffering was undergone. It was sin that wove the crown of thorns—it was sin that pierced our Lord's hands, and feet, and side—it was sin that brought Him to Gethsemane and Calvary, to the cross and to the grave. Cold must our hearts be if we do not hate sin and labour to get rid of it, though we may have to cut off the right hand and pluck out the right eye in doing it.

(e) We must be holy, because this is the *only sound evidence that we are true children of God*. Children in this world are generally like their parents. Some, doubtless, are more so, and some less—but it is seldom indeed that you cannot trace a kind of family likeness. And it is much the same with the children of God. The Lord Jesus says, "If ye were Abraham's children ye would do the works of Abraham."—"If God were your Father ye would love Me" (John 8:39, 42). If men have no likeness to the Father in heaven, it is vain to talk of their being His "sons." If we know nothing of holiness we may flatter ourselves as we please, but we have not got the Holy Spirit dwelling in us: we are dead, and must be brought to life again—we are lost, and must be found. "As many as are led by the Spirit of God, they," and they only, "are the sons of God" (Rom. 8:14). We must show by our lives the family we belong to.—We must let men see by our good conversation that we are indeed the children of the Holy One, or our son-ship is but an empty name. "Say not," says Gurnall, "that thou hast royal blood in thy veins, and are born of God, except thou canst prove thy pedigree by daring to be holy."

(f) We must be holy, because this is the *most likely way to do good to others*. We cannot live to ourselves only in this world. Our lives will always be doing either good or harm to those who see them. They are a silent sermon which all can read. It is sad indeed when they are a sermon for the devil's cause, and not for God's. I believe that far more is done for

Christ's kingdom by the holy living of believers than we are at all aware of. There is a reality about such living which makes men feel, and obliges them to think. It carries a weight and influence with it which nothing else can give. It makes religion beautiful, and draws men to consider it, like a lighthouse seen afar off. The day of judgment will prove that many besides husbands have been won *"without the word"* by a holy life (1 Pet. 3:1). You may talk to persons about the doctrines of the Gospels, and few will listen, and still fewer understand. But your life is an argument that none can escape. There is a meaning about holiness which not even the most unlearned can help taking in. They may not understand justification, but they can understand charity.

I believe there is far more harm done by unholy and inconsistent Christians than we are aware of. Such men are among Satan's best allies. They pull down by their lives what ministers build with their lips. They cause the chariot wheels of the Gospel to drive heavily. They supply the children of this world with a never ending excuse for remaining as they are.—"I cannot see the use of so much religion," said an irreligious tradesman not long ago; "I observe that some of my customers are always talking about the Gospel, and faith, and election, and the blessed promises, and so forth; and yet these very people think nothing of cheating me of pence and half-pence, when they have an opportunity. Now, if religious persons can do such things, I do not see what good there is in religion."—I grieve to be obliged to write such things, but I fear that Christ's name is too often blasphemed because of the lives of Christians. Let us take heed lest the blood of souls should be required at our hands. From murder of souls by inconsistency and loose walking, good Lord, deliver us! Oh, for the sake of others, if for no other reason, let us strive to be holy!

(g) We must be holy, *because our present comfort depends much upon it.* We cannot be too often reminded of this. We are sadly apt to forget that there is a close connection between sin and sorrow, holiness and happiness, sanctification and consolation. God has so wisely ordered it, that our well-being and our well-doing are linked together. He has mercifully provided that even in this world it shall be man's *interest* to be holy. Our justification is not by works—our calling and election are not according to our works—but it is vain for anyone to suppose that he will have a lively *sense* of his justification, or an *assurance* of his calling, so long as he neglects good works, or does not strive to live a holy life. "Hereby we do know that we know Him, if we keep His commandments."—"Hereby we know that we are of the truth, and shall assure our hearts" (1 John 2:3; 3:19). A believer may as soon expect to feel the sun's rays upon a dark and cloudy day, as to feel strong consolation in Christ while he does not follow Him fully. When the disciples forsook the Lord and fled, they escaped danger, but they were miserable and sad. When, shortly after, they confessed Him boldly before men, they were cast into prison and beaten; but we are told "they rejoiced that they were counted worthy to suffer shame for His name" (Acts 5:41). Oh, for our own sakes, if there were no other reason, let us strive to be holy! He that follows Jesus most fully will always follow Him most comfortably.

(h) Lastly, we must be holy, *because without holiness on earth we shall never be prepared to enjoy heaven.* Heaven is a holy place. The Lord of heaven is a holy Being. The angels are holy creatures. Holiness is written on everything in heaven. The book of Revelation says expressly, "There shall in no wise enter into it anything that defileth, neither whatsoever worketh abomination, or maketh a lie" (Rev. 21:27).

I appeal solemnly to everyone who reads these pages, How shall we ever be at home and happy in heaven, if we die unholy? Death works no change. The grave makes no alteration. Each will rise again with the same character in which he breathed his last. Where will our place be if we are strangers to holiness now?

Suppose for a moment that you were allowed to enter heaven without holiness. What would you do? What possible enjoyment could you feel there? To which of all the saints would you join yourself, and by whose side would you sit down? Their pleasures are not your pleasures, their tastes not your tastes, their character not your character. How could you possibly be happy, if you had not been holy on earth?

Now perhaps you love the company of the light and careless, the worldly-minded and the covetous, the reveller and the pleasure-seeker, the ungodly and the profane. There will be none such in heaven.

Now perhaps you think the saints of God too strict and particular, and serious. You rather avoid them. You have no delight in their society. There will be no other company in heaven.

Now perhaps you think praying, and Scripture-reading, and hymn singing, dull and melancholy, and stupid work—a thing to be tolerated now and then, but not enjoyed. You reckon the Sabbath a burden and weariness; you could not possibly spend more than a small part of it in worshipping God. But remember, heaven is a never-ending Sabbath. The inhabitants thereof rest not day or night, saying, "Holy, holy, holy, Lord God Almighty," and singing the praise of the Lamb. How could an unholy man find pleasure in occupation such as this?

Think you that such an one would delight to meet David, and Paul, and John, after a life spent in doing the very things they spoke against? Would he take sweet counsel with them, and find that he and they had much in common?—Think you, above all, that he would rejoice to meet Jesus, the Crucified One, face to face, after cleaving to the sins for which He died, after loving His enemies and despising His friends? Would he stand before Him with confidence, and join in the cry, "This is our God; we have waited for Him, we will be glad and rejoice in His salvation"? (Isa. 25:9). Think you not rather that the tongue of an unholy man would cleave to the roof of his mouth with shame, and his only desire would be to be cast out! He would feel a stranger in a land he knew not, a black sheep amidst Christ's holy flock. The voice of Cherubim and Seraphim, the song of Angels and Archangels and all the company of heaven, would be a language he could not understand. The very air would seem an air he could not breathe.

I know not what others may think, but to me it does seem clear that heaven would be a miserable place to an unholy man. It cannot be otherwise. People may say, in a vague way, "they hope to go to heaven"; but they do not consider what they say. There must be a certain "meetness for the inheritance of the saints in light." Our hearts must be somewhat in tune. To reach the holiday of glory, we must pass through the training school of grace. We must be heavenly-minded, and have heavenly tastes, in the life that now is, or else we shall never find ourselves in heaven, in the life to come.

And now, before I go any further, let me say a few words by way of application.

(1) For one thing, let me ask everyone who may read these pages, *Are you holy?* Listen, I pray you, to the question I put to you this day. Do you know anything of the holiness of which I have been speaking?

I do not ask whether you attend your Church regularly—whether you have been baptized, and received the Lord's Supper—whether you have the name of Christian—I ask something more than all this: *Are you holy, or are you not?*

I do not ask whether you approve of holiness in others—whether you like to read the lives of holy people, and to talk of holy things, and to have on your table holy books—whether you mean to be holy, and hope you will be holy some day—I ask something further: *Are you yourself holy this very day, or are you not?*

And why do I ask so straitly, and press the question so strongly? I do it because the Scripture says, "Without holiness no man shall see the Lord." It is written, it is not my fancy—it is the Bible, not my private opinion—it is the word of God, not of man—"*Without holiness no man shall see the Lord*" (Heb. 12:14).

Alas, what searching, sifting words are these! What thoughts come across my mind, as I write them down! I look at the world, and see the greater part of it lying in wickedness. I look at professing Christians, and see the vast majority having nothing of Christianity but the name. I turn to the Bible, and I hear the Spirit saying, "Without holiness no man shall see the Lord."

Surely it is a text that ought to make us consider our ways, and search our hearts. Surely it should raise within us solemn thoughts, and send us to prayer.

You may try to put me off by saying you feel much, and think much about these things: far more than many suppose. I answer, "This is not the point. The poor lost souls in hell do as much as this. The great question is not what you *think,* and what you *feel,* but what you DO."

You may say, it was never meant that all Christians should be holy, and that holiness, such as I have described, is only for great saints, and people of uncommon gifts. I answer, "I cannot see that in Scripture. I read that *every man* who hath hope in Christ purifieth himself" (1 John 3:3).—"Without holiness *no man* shall see the Lord."

You may say, it is impossible to be so holy and to do our duty in this life at the same time: the thing cannot be done. I answer, "You are mistaken. It *can* be done. With Christ on your side nothing is impossible. It *has* been done by many. David, and Obadiah, and Daniel, and the servants of Nero's household, are all examples that go to prove it."

You may say, "If I were so holy I would be unlike other people." I answer, "I know it well. It is just what you ought to be. Christ's true servants always were unlike the world around them—a separate nation, a peculiar people;—and you must be so too, if you would be saved!"

You may say, "At this rate very few will be saved." I answer, "I know it. It is precisely what we are told in the Sermon on the Mount." The Lord Jesus said so 1,900 years ago. "Strait is the gate, and narrow is the way, that leadeth unto life, and few there be that find it" (Matt. 7:14). Few will be saved, because few will take the trouble to seek salvation. Men will not deny themselves the pleasures of sin and their own way for a little season. They turn their backs on an "inheritance incorruptible, undefiled, and that fadeth not away." "Ye will not come unto Me," says Jesus, "that ye might have life" (John 5:40).

You may say, "These are hard sayings: the way is very narrow." I answer, "I know it. So says the Sermon on the Mount." The Lord Jesus said so 1,900 years ago. He always said that men must take up the cross daily, and that they must be ready to cut off hand or foot, if they would be His disciples. It is in religion as it is in other things, "there are no gains without pains." That which costs nothing is worth nothing.

Whatever we may think fit to say, we must be holy, if we would see the Lord. Where is our Christianity if we are not? We must not merely have a Christian name, and Christian knowledge, we must have a Christian *character* also. We must be saints on earth, if ever we mean to be saints in heaven. God has said it, and He will not go back: "Without holiness no man shall see the Lord." "The Pope's calendar," says Jenkyn, "only makes saints of the dead, but Scripture requires sanctity in the *living*." "Let not men deceive themselves," says Owen; "sanctification is a qualification indispensably necessary unto those who will be under the conduct of the Lord Christ unto salvation. He leads none to heaven but whom He sanctifies on the earth. This living Head will not admit of dead members."

Surely we need not wonder that Scripture says, "Ye must be born again" (John 3:7). Surely it is clear as noon-day that many professing Christians need a complete change—new hearts, new natures—if ever they are to be saved. Old things must pass away—they must become new creatures. "Without holiness no man," be he who he may, "shall see the Lord."

(2) Let me, for another thing, speak a little to believers. I ask you this question: *"Do you think you feel the importance of holiness as much as you should?"*

I own I fear the temper of the times about this subject. I doubt exceedingly whether it holds that place which it deserves in the thoughts and attention of some of the Lord's people. I would humbly suggest that we are apt to overlook the doctrine of growth in grace, and that we do not sufficiently consider how very far a person may go in a profession of religion, and yet have no grace, and be dead in God's sight after all. I believe that Judas Iscariot seemed very like the other Apostles. When the Lord warned them that one would betray Him, no one said, "Is it Judas?" We had better think more about the Churches of Sardis and Laodicea than we do.

I have no desire to make an idol of holiness. I do not wish to dethrone Christ, and put holiness in His place. But I must candidly say, I wish sanctification was more thought of in this day than it seems to be, and I therefore take occasion to press the subject on all believers into whose hands these pages may fall. I fear it is sometimes forgotten that God has married together justification and sanctification. They are distinct and different things, beyond question, but one is never found without the other. All justified people are sanctified, and all sanctified are justified. What God has joined together let no man dare to put asunder. Tell me not of your justification, unless you have also some marks of sanctification. Boast not of Christ's work *for you*, unless you can show us the Spirit's work *in you*. Think not that Christ and the Spirit can ever be divided. I doubt not that many believers know these things, but I think it good for us to be put in remembrance of them. Let us prove that we know them by our lives. Let us try to keep in view this text more continually: "Follow holiness, without which no man shall see the Lord."

I must frankly say I wish there was not such an excessive *sensitiveness* on the subject of holiness as I sometimes perceive in the minds of believers. A man might really think it was a dangerous subject to handle, so cautiously is it touched! Yet surely when we have exalted Christ as "the way, the truth, and the life," we cannot err in speaking strongly about what should be the character of His people. Well says Rutherford, "The way that crieth down duties and sanctification, is not the way of grace. Believing and doing are blood-friends."

I would say it with all reverence, but say it I must—I sometimes fear if Christ were on earth now, there are not a few who would think His preaching *legal*; and if Paul were writing his Epistles, there are those who would think he had better not write the latter part of most of them as he did. But let us remember that the Lord Jesus *did* speak the Sermon on the Mount, and that the Epistle to the Ephesians contains six chapters and not four. I grieve to feel obliged to speak in this way, but I am sure there is a cause.

That great divine, John Owen, the Dean of Christ Church, used to say, more than two hundred years ago, that there were people whose whole religion seemed to consist in going about complaining of their own corruptions, and telling everyone that they could do nothing of themselves. I am afraid that after two centuries the same thing might be said with truth of some of Christ's professing people in this day. I know there are texts in Scripture which warrant such complaints. I do not object to them when they come from men who walk in the steps of the Apostle Paul, and fight a good fight, as he did, against sin, the devil, and the world. But I never like such complaints when I see ground for suspecting, as I often do, that they are only a cloak to cover spiritual laziness, and an excuse for spiritual sloth. If we say with Paul, "O wretched man that I am," let us also be able to say with him, "I would press toward the mark." Let us not quote his example in one thing, while we do not follow him in another (Rom. 7:24; Phil. 3:14).

I do not set up myself to be better than other people, and if anyone asks, "What are you, that you write in this way?" I answer, "I am a very poor creature indeed." But I say that I cannot read the Bible without desiring to see many believers more spiritual, more holy, more single-eyed, more heavenly-minded, more whole-hearted than they are in the nineteenth century. I want to see among believers more of a pilgrim spirit, a more decided separation from the world, a conversation more evidently in heaven, a closer walk with God—and therefore I have written as I have.

Is it not true that we need a higher standard of personal holiness in this day? Where is our patience? Where is our zeal? Where is our love? Where are our works? Where is the power of religion to be seen, as it was in times gone by? Where is that unmistakable tone which used to distinguish the saints of old, and shake the world? Verily our silver has become dross, our wine mixed with water, and our salt has very little savour. We are all more than half asleep. The night is far spent, and the day is at hand. Let us awake, and sleep no more. Let us open our eyes more widely than we have done hitherto. "Let us lay aside every weight, and the sin that doth so easily beset us."—"Let us cleanse ourselves from all filthiness of flesh and spirit, and perfect holiness in the fear of God"—(Heb. 12:1; 2 Cor. 7:1). "Did Christ die," says Owen, "and shall sin live? Was He crucified in the world, and shall our affections to the world be quick and lively? Oh, where is the spirit of him, who by the cross of Christ was crucified to the world, and the world to him!"

III. Let me, in the last place, offer a *word of advice to all who desire to be holy.*

Would you be holy? Would you become a new creature? Then you must *begin with Christ.* You will do just nothing at all, and make no progress till you feel your sin and weakness, and flee to Him. He is the root and beginning of all holiness, and the way to be holy is to come to Him by faith and be joined to Him. Christ is not wisdom and righteousness only to His people, but sanctification also. Men sometimes try to make themselves holy first of all, and sad work they make of it. They toil and labour, and turn over new leaves, and make many changes; and yet, like the woman with the issue of blood, before she came to Christ, they feel "nothing bettered, but rather worse" (Mark 5:26). They run in vain, and labour in vain; and little wonder, for they are beginning at the wrong end. They are building up a wall of sand; their work runs down as fast as they throw it up. They are baling water out of a leaky vessel; the leak gains on them, not they on the leak. Other foundation of "holiness" can no man lay than that which Paul laid, even Christ Jesus. "Without Christ we can do nothing" (John 15:5). It is a strong but true saying of Traill's, "Wisdom out of Christ is damning folly—righteousness out of Christ is guilt and condemnation—sanctification out of Christ is filth and sin— redemption out of Christ is bondage and slavery."

Do you want to attain holiness? Do you feel this day a real hearty desire to be holy? Would you be a partaker of the Divine nature? Then *go to Christ*. Wait for nothing. Wait for nobody. Linger not. Think not to make yourself ready. Go and say to Him, in the words of that beautiful hymn—

"Nothing in my hand I bring,
Simply to Thy cross I cling;
Naked, flee to Thee for dress;
Helpless, look to Thee for grace."

There is not a brick nor a stone laid in the work of our sanctification till we go to Christ. Holiness is His special gift to His believing people. Holiness is the work He carries on in their hearts, by the Spirit whom He puts within them. He is appointed a "Prince and a Saviour, to give repentance" as well as remission of sins.—"To as many as receive Him, He gives power to become sons of God" (Acts 5:31; John 1:12). Holiness comes not of blood—parents cannot give it to their children: nor yet of the will of the flesh—man cannot produce it in himself: nor yet of the will of man—ministers cannot give it you by baptism. Holiness comes from Christ. It is the result of vital union with Him. It is the fruit of being a living branch of the True Vine. Go then to Christ and say, "Lord, not only save me from the guilt of sin, but send the Spirit, whom Thou didst promise, and save me from its power. Make me holy. Teach me to do Thy will."

Would you continue holy? Then *abide in Christ*. He says Himself, "Abide in Me and I in you,—he that abideth in Me and I in him, the same beareth much fruit" (John 15:4, 5). It pleased the Father that in Him should all fulness dwell—a full supply for all a believer's wants. He is the Physician to whom you must daily go, if you would keep well. He is the Manna which you must daily eat, and the Rock of which you must daily drink. His arm is the arm on which you must daily lean, as you come up out of the wilderness of this world. You must not only be rooted, you must also be *built up* in Him. Paul was a man of God indeed—a holy man—a growing, thriving Christian—and what was the secret of it all? He was one to whom Christ was "all in all." He was ever "looking unto Jesus." "I can do all things," he says, "through Christ which strengtheneth me." "I live, yet not I, but Christ liveth in me. The life that I now live, I live by the faith of the Son of God." Let us go and do likewise (Heb. 12:2; Phil. 4:13; Gal. 2:20).

May all who read these pages know these things by experience, and not by hearsay only. May we all feel the importance of holiness, far more than we have ever done yet! May our years be *holy years* with our souls, and then they will be happy ones! Whether we live, may we live unto the Lord; or whether we die, may we die unto the Lord; or if He comes for us, may we be found in peace, without spot, and blameless!

4

THE FIGHT

"Fight the good fight of faith."

— 1 TIMOTHY 6:12

It is a curious fact that there is no subject about which most people feel such deep interest as "fighting." Young men and maidens, old men and little children, high and low, rich and poor, learned and unlearned, all feel a deep interest in wars, battles, and fighting.

This is a simple fact, whatever way we may try to explain it. We should call that Englishman a dull fellow who cared nothing about the story of Waterloo, or Inkermann, or Balaclava or Lucknow. We should think that heart cold and stupid which was not moved and thrilled by the struggles at Sedan and Strasburg, and Metz, and Paris, during the war between France and Germany.

But there is another warfare of far greater importance than any war that was ever waged by man. It is a warfare which concerns not two or three nations only, but every Christian man and woman born into the world. The warfare I speak of is the *spiritual* warfare. It is the fight which everyone who would be saved must fight about his soul.

This warfare, I am aware, is a thing of which many know nothing. Talk to them about it, and they are ready to set you down as a madman, an enthusiast, or a fool. And yet it is as real and true as any war the world has ever seen. It has its hand-to-hand conflicts and its wounds. It has its watchings and fatigues. It has its sieges and assaults. It has its victories and its defeats. Above all, it has *consequences* which are awful, tremendous, and most peculiar. In earthly warfare the consequences to nations are often temporary and remediable. In the spiritual warfare it is very different. Of that warfare, the consequences, when the fight is over, are unchangeable and eternal.

It is of this warfare that St. Paul spoke to Timothy, when he wrote those burning words, "Fight the good fight of faith; lay hold on eternal life." It is of this warfare that I propose to speak in this paper. I hold the subject to be closely connected with that of sanctification and holiness. He that would understand the nature of true holiness must know that the Christian is "a man of war." If we would be holy we must fight.

I. The first thing I have to say is this: *True Christianity is a fight.*

True Christianity! Let us mind that word "true." There is a vast quantity of religion current in the world which is not true, genuine Christianity. It passes muster; it satisfies sleepy consciences; but it is not good money. It is not the real thing which was called Christianity eighteen hundred years ago. There are thousands of men and women who go to Churches and chapels every Sunday, and call themselves Christians. Their names are in the baptismal register. They are reckoned Christians while they live. They are married with a Christian marriage service. They mean to be buried as Christians when they die. But you never see any "fight" about their religion! Of spiritual strife, and exertion, and conflict, and self-denial, and watching, and warring, they know literally nothing at all. Such Christianity may satisfy man, and those who say anything against it may be thought very hard and uncharitable; but it certainly is not the Christianity of the Bible. It is not the religion which the Lord Jesus founded, and His Apostles preached. It is not the religion which produces real holiness. True Christianity is "a fight."

The true Christian is called to be a soldier, and must behave as such from the day of his conversion to the day of his death. He is not meant to live a life of religious ease, indolence, and security. He must never imagine for a moment that he can sleep and doze along the way to heaven, like one travelling in an easy carriage. If he takes his standard of Christianity from the children of this world, he may be content with such notions; but he will find no countenance for them in the Word of God. If the Bible is the rule of his faith and practice, he will find his course laid down very plainly in this matter. He must "fight."

With whom is the Christian soldier meant to fight? Not with other Christians. Wretched indeed is that man's idea of religion who fancies that it consists in perpetual controversy! He who is never satisfied unless he is engaged in some strife between Church and Church, chapel and chapel, sect and sect, faction and faction, party and party, knows nothing yet as he ought to know. No doubt it may be absolutely needful sometimes to appeal to law courts, in order to ascertain the right interpretation of a Church's Articles, and rubrics, and formularies. But, as a general rule, the cause of sin is never so much helped as when Christians waste their strength in quarrelling with one another, and spend their time in petty squabbles.

No, indeed! The principal fight of the Christian is with the world, the flesh, and the devil. These are his never-dying foes. These are the three chief enemies against whom he must wage war. Unless he gets the victory over these three, all other victories are useless and vain. If he had a nature like an angel, and were not a fallen creature, the warfare would not be so essential. But with a corrupt heart, a busy devil, and an ensnaring world, he must either "fight" or be lost.

He must fight *the flesh*. Even after conversion he carries within him a nature prone to evil, and a heart weak and unstable as water. That heart will never be free from imperfection in this world, and it is a miserable delusion to expect it. To keep that heart from going astray, the Lord Jesus bids us "watch and pray." The spirit may be ready, but the flesh is weak. There is need of a daily struggle and a daily wrestling in prayer. "I keep under my body," cries St. Paul, "and bring it into subjection."—"I see a law in my members warring against the law of my mind, and bringing me into captivity."—"O wretched man that I am, who shall deliver me from the body of this death?"—"They that are Christ's have crucified the flesh with the affections and lusts."—"Mortify your members which are upon the earth" (Mark 14:38; 1 Cor. 9:27; Rom. 7:23, 24; Gal. 5:24; Col. 3:5).

He must fight *the world*. The subtle influence of that mighty enemy must be daily resisted, and without a daily battle can never be overcome. The love of the world's good things—the fear of the world's laughter or blame—the secret desire to keep in with the world—the secret wish to do as others in the world do, and not to run into extremes—all these are spiritual foes which beset the Christian continually on his way to heaven, and must be conquered. "The friendship of the world is enmity with God: whosoever therefore will be a friend of the world is the enemy of God."—"If any man love the world, the love of the Father is not in him."—"The world is crucified to me, and I unto the world."—"Whatsoever is born of God overcometh the world."—"Be not conformed to this world" (James 4:4; 1 John 2:15; Gal. 6:14; 1 John 5:4; Rom. 12:2).

He must fight *the devil*. That old enemy of mankind is not dead. Ever since the fall of Adam and Eve he has been "going to and fro in the earth, and walking up and down in it," and striving to compass one great end—the ruin of man's soul. Never slumbering and never sleeping, he is always "going about as a lion seeking whom he may devour." An unseen enemy, he is always near us, about our path and about our bed, and spying out all our ways. A "murderer and a liar" from the beginning, he labours night and day to cast us down to hell. Sometimes by leading into superstition, sometimes by suggesting infidelity, sometimes by one kind of tactics and sometimes by another, he is always carrying on a campaign against our souls. "Satan hath desired to have you, that he may sift you as wheat." This mighty adversary must be daily resisted if we wish to be saved. But "this kind goeth not out" but by watching and praying, and fighting, and putting on the whole armour of God. The strong man armed will never be kept out of our hearts without a daily battle (Job 1:7; 1 Pet. 5:8; John 8:44; Luke 22:31; Eph. 6:11).

Some men may think these statements too strong. You fancy that I am going too far, and laying on the colours too thickly. You are secretly saying to yourself, that men and women in England may surely get to heaven without all this trouble and warfare and fighting. Listen to me for a few minutes and I will show you that I have something to say on God's behalf. Remember the maxim of the wisest General that ever lived in England—"In time of war it is the worst mistake to underrate your enemy, and try to make a little war." This Christian warfare is no light matter. Give me your attention and consider what I say. What saith the Scripture?—"Fight the good fight of faith. Lay hold on eternal life."—"Endure hardness as a good soldier of Jesus Christ."—"Put on the whole armour of God, that ye may be able to stand against the wiles of the devil. For we wrestle not against flesh and blood, but against principalities, against powers, against the rulers of the darkness of this world, against spiritual wickedness in high places. Wherefore take unto you the whole armour of God, that you may be able to withstand in the evil day, and having done all to stand."—"Strive to enter in at the straight gate."—"Labour for the meat that endureth unto everlasting life."—"Think not that I came to send peace on the earth: I came not to send peace but a sword."—"He that hath no sword let him sell his garment and buy one."—"Watch ye, stand fast in the faith: quit you like men, be strong."—"War a good warfare, holding faith and a good conscience" (1 Tim. 6:12; 2 Tim. 2:3; Eph. 6:11-13; Luke 13:24; John 6:27; Matt. 10:34; Luke 22:36; 1 Cor. 16:13; 1 Tim. 1:18-19). Words such as these appear to me clear, plain, and unmistakable. They all teach one and the same great lesson, if we are willing to receive it. That lesson is, that true Christianity is a struggle, a fight, and a warfare. He that pretends to condemn "fighting" and teaches that we ought to sit still and "yield ourselves to God," appears to me to misunderstand his Bible, and to make a great mistake.

What says the Baptismal Service of the Church of England? No doubt that Service is uninspired, and, like every uninspired composition, it has its defects; but to the millions of people all over the globe, who profess and call themselves English Churchmen, its voice ought to speak with some weight. And what does it say? It tells us that over every new member who is admitted into the Church of England the following words are used—"I baptize thee in the name of the Father, the Son, and the Holy Ghost."—"I sign this child with the sign of the cross, in token that hereafter he shall not be ashamed to confess the faith of Christ crucified, and manfully to *fight* under His banner against sin, the world, and the devil, and to continue Christ's faithful soldier and servant unto his life's end."—Of course we all know that in myriads of cases baptism is a mere form, and that parents bring their children to the font without faith or prayer or thought, and consequently receive no blessing. The man who supposes that baptism in such cases acts *mechanically,* like a medicine, and that godly and ungodly, praying and prayerless parents, all alike get the same benefit for their children, must be in a strange state of mind. But one thing, at any rate, is very certain. Every baptized Churchman is by his profession a "soldier of Jesus Christ," and is pledged "to fight under His banner against sin, the world, and the devil." He that doubts it had better take up his Prayer-book, and read, mark, and learn its contents. The worst thing about many very zealous Churchmen is their total ignorance of what their own Prayer-book contains.

Whether we are Churchmen or not, one thing is certain—this Christian warfare is a great reality, and a subject of vast importance. It is not a matter like Church government and ceremonial, about which men may differ, and yet reach heaven at last. Necessity is laid upon us. We must fight. There are no promises in the Lord Jesus Christ's Epistles to the Seven Churches, except to those who "overcome." Where there is grace there will be conflict. The believer is a soldier. There is no holiness without a warfare. Saved souls will always be found to have fought a fight.

It is a fight of *absolute necessity.* Let us not think that in this war we can remain neutral and sit still. Such a line of action may be possible in the strife of nations, but it is utterly impossible in that conflict which concerns the soul. The boasted policy of non-interference—the "masterly inactivity" which pleases so many statesmen—the plan of keeping quiet and letting things alone—all this will never do in the Christian warfare. Here at any rate no one can escape serving under the plea that he is "a man of peace." To be at peace with the world, the flesh, and the devil, is to be at enmity with God, and in the broad way that leadeth to destruction. We have no choice or option. We must either fight or be lost.

It is a fight of *universal necessity*. No rank, or class, or age, can plead exemption, or escape the battle. Ministers and people, preachers and hearers, old and young, high and low, rich and poor, gentle and simple, kings and subjects, landlords and tenants, learned and unlearned—all alike must carry arms and go to war. All have by nature a *heart* full of pride, unbelief, sloth, worldliness, and sin. All are living in a *world* beset with snares, traps, and pitfalls for the soul. All have near them a busy, restless, malicious *devil*. All, from the queen in her palace down to the pauper in the workhouse, all must fight, if they would be saved.

It is a fight of *perpetual necessity*. It admits of no breathing time, no armistice, no truce. On week-days as well as on Sundays—in private as well as in public—at home by the family fireside as well as abroad—in little things like management of tongue and temper, as well as in great ones like the government of kingdoms—the Christian's warfare must unceasingly go on. The foe we have to do with keeps no holidays, never slumbers, and never sleeps. So long as we have breath in our bodies we must keep on our armour, and remember we are on an enemy's ground. "Even on the brink of Jordan," said a dying saint, "I find Satan nibbling at my heels." We must fight till we die.

Let us consider well these propositions. Let us take care that our own personal religion is real, genuine, and true. The saddest symptom about many so-called Christians is the utter absence of anything like conflict and fight in their Christianity. They eat, they drink, they dress, they work, they amuse themselves, they get money, they spend money, they go through a scanty round of formal religious services once or twice every week. But the great spiritual warfare—its watchings and strugglings, its agonies and anxieties, its battles and contests—of all this they appear to know nothing at all. Let us take care that this case is not our own. The worst state of soul is when the strong man armed keepeth the house, and his goods are at peace—when he leads men and women "captive at his will," and they make no resistance. The worst chains are those which are neither felt nor seen by the prisoner (Luke 11:21; 2 Tim. 2:26).

We may take comfort about our souls if we know anything of an inward fight and conflict. It is the invariable companion of genuine Christian holiness. It is not everything, I am well aware, but it is something. Do we find in our heart of hearts a spiritual struggle? Do we feel anything of the flesh lusting against the spirit and the spirit against the flesh, so that we cannot do the things we would? (Gal. 5:17). Are we conscious of two principles within us, contending for the mastery? Do we feel anything of war in our inward man? Well, let us thank God for it! It is a good sign. It is strongly probable evidence of the great work of sanctification. All true saints are soldiers. Anything is better than apathy, stagnation, deadness, and indifference. We are in a better state than many. The most part of so-called Christians have no feeling at all. We are evidently no friends of Satan. Like the kings of this world, he wars not against his own subjects. The very fact that he assaults us should fill our minds with hope. I say again, let us take comfort. The child of God has two great marks about him, and of these two we have one. HE MAY BE KNOWN BY HIS INWARD WARFARE, AS WELL AS BY HIS INWARD PEACE.

II. I pass on to the second thing which I have to say in handling my subject: *True Christianity is the fight of faith.*

In this respect the Christian warfare is utterly unlike the conflicts of this world. It does not depend on the strong arm, the quick eye, or the swift foot. It is not waged with carnal weapons, but with spiritual. Faith is the hinge on which victory turns. Success depends entirely on believing.

A *general faith in the truth of God's written Word* is the primary foundation of the Christian soldier's character. He is what he is, does what he does, thinks as he thinks, acts as he acts, hopes as he hopes, behaves as he behaves, for one simple reason—he believes certain propositions revealed and laid down in Holy Scripture. "He that cometh to God must believe that He is, and that He is a Rewarder of them that diligently seek Him" (Heb. 11:5-6).

A religion without doctrine or dogma is a thing which many are fond of talking of in the present day. It sounds very fine at first. It looks very pretty at a distance. But the moment we sit down to examine and consider it, we shall find it a simple impossibility. We might as well talk of a body without bones and sinews. No man will ever be anything or do anything in religion, unless he believes *something*. Even those who profess to hold the miserable and uncomfortable views of the Deists are obliged to confess that they believe something. With all their bitter sneers against dogmatic theology and Christian credulity, as they call it, they themselves have a kind of faith.

As for true Christians, faith is the very backbone of their spiritual existence. No one ever fights earnestly against the world, the flesh, and the devil, unless he has engraven on his heart certain great principles which he believes. What they are he may hardly know, and may certainly not be able to define or write down. But there they are, and, consciously or unconsciously, they form the roots of his religion. Wherever you see a man, whether rich or poor, learned or unlearned, wrestling manfully with sin, and trying to overcome it, you may be sure there are certain great principles which that man believes. The poet who wrote the famous lines,

> "For modes of faith let graceless zealots fight,
> He can't be wrong whose life is in the right,"

was a clever man, but a poor divine. There is no such thing as right living without faith and believing.

A special faith in our Lord Jesus Christ's person, work, and office, is the life, heart, and mainspring of the Christian soldier's character.

He sees by faith an unseen Saviour, who loved him, gave Himself for him, paid his debts for him, bore his sins, carried his transgressions, rose again for him, and appears in heaven for him as his Advocate at the right hand of God. He sees Jesus, and clings to Him. Seeing this Saviour and trusting in Him, he feels peace and hope, and willingly does battle against the foes of his soul.

He sees his own many sins—his weak heart, a tempting world, a busy devil; and if he looked only at them he might well despair. But he sees also a mighty Saviour, an interceding Saviour, a sympathizing Saviour—His blood, His righteousness, His everlasting priesthood—and he believes that all this is his own. He sees Jesus, and casts his whole weight on Him. Seeing Him he cheerfully fights on, with a full confidence that he will prove "more than conqueror through Him that loved him" (Rom. 8:37).

Habitual lively faith in Christ's presence and readiness to help is the secret of the Christian soldier fighting successfully.

It must never be forgotten that faith admits of degrees. All men do not believe alike, and even the same person has his ebbs and flows of faith, and believes more heartily at one time than another. According to the degree of his faith the Christian fights well or ill, wins victories, or suffers occasional repulses, comes off triumphant, or loses a battle. He that has most faith will always be the happiest and most comfortable soldier. Nothing makes the anxieties of warfare sit so lightly on a man as the assurance of Christ's love and continual protection. Nothing enables him to bear the fatigue of watching, struggling, and wrestling against sin, like the indwelling confidence that Christ is on his side and success is sure. It is the "shield of faith" which quenches all the fiery darts of the wicked one.—It is the man who can say, "I know whom I have believed"—who can say in time of suffering, "I am not ashamed."—He who wrote those glowing words, "We faint not,"—"Our light affliction which endureth but for a moment worketh in us a far more exceeding and eternal weight of glory"—was the man who wrote with the same pen, "We look not at the things which are seen, but at the things which are not seen; for the things which are seen are temporal, but the things which are not seen are eternal."—It is the man who said, "I live by the faith of the Son of God," who said, in the same Epistle, "the world is crucified unto me, and I unto the world."—It is the man who said, "To me to live is Christ," who said, in the same Epistle, "I have learned in whatsoever state I am therewith to be content."—"I can do all things through Christ."—The more faith the more victory! The more faith the more inward peace! (Eph. 6:16; 2 Tim. 1:12; 2 Cor. 4:17, 18; Gal. 2:20; 6:14; Phil. 1:21; 4:11, 13).

I think it impossible to overrate the value and importance of faith. Well may the Apostle Peter call it "precious" (2 Pet. 1:1). Time would fail me if I tried to recount a hundredth part of the victories which by faith Christian soldiers have obtained.

Let us take down our Bibles and read with attention the eleventh chapter of the Epistle to the Hebrews. Let us mark the long list of worthies whose names are thus recorded, from Abel down to Moses, even before Christ was born of the Virgin Mary, and brought life and immortality into full light by the Gospel. Let us note well what battles they won against the world, the flesh, and the devil. And then let us remember that *believing* did it all. These men looked forward to the promised Messiah. They saw Him that is invisible. "By faith the elders obtained a good report" (Heb. 11:2).

Let us turn to the pages of early Church history. Let us see how the primitive Christians held fast their religion even unto death, and were not shaken by the fiercest persecutions of heathen Emperors. For centuries there were never wanting men like Polycarp and Ignatius, who were ready to die rather than deny Christ. Fines, and prisons, and torture, and fire, and sword, were unable to crush the spirit of the noble army of martyrs. The whole power of imperial Rome, the mistress of the world, proved unable to stamp out the religion which began with a few fishermen and publicans in Palestine! And then let us remember that *believing* in an unseen Jesus was the Church's strength. They won their victory by faith.

Let us examine the story of the Protestant Reformation. Let us study the lives of its leading champions—Wycliffe, and Huss, and Luther, and Ridley, and Latimer, and Hooper. Let us mark how these gallant soldiers of Christ stood firm against a host of adversaries, and were ready to die for their principles. What battles they fought! What controversies they maintained! What contradiction they endured! What tenacity of purpose they exhibited against a world in arms! And then let us remember that *believing* in an unseen Jesus was the secret of their strength. They overcame by faith.

Let us consider the men who have made the greatest marks in Church history in the last hundred years. Let us observe how men like Wesley, and Whitfield, and Venn, and Romaine, stood alone in their day and generation, and revived English religion in the face of opposition from men high in office, and in the face of slander, ridicule, and persecution from nine-tenths of professing Christians in our land. Let us observe how men like William Wilberforce, and Havelock, and Hedley Vicars, have witnessed for Christ in the most difficult positions, and displayed a banner for Christ even at the regimental mess-table, or on the floor of the House of Commons. Let us mark how these noble witnesses never flinched to the end, and won the respect even of their worst adversaries. And then let us remember that *believing* in an unseen Christ is the key to all their characters. By faith they lived, and walked, and stood, and overcame.

Would anyone live the life of a Christian soldier? Let him pray for faith. It is the gift of God, and a gift which those who ask shall never ask for in vain. You must believe before you do. If men do nothing in religion, it is because they do not believe. Faith is the first step toward heaven.

Would anyone fight the fight of a Christian soldier successfully and prosperously? Let him pray for a continual increase of faith. Let him abide in Christ, get closer to Christ, tighten his hold on Christ every day that he lives. Let his daily prayer be that of the disciples—"Lord, increase my faith" (Luke 17:5). Watch jealously over your faith, if you have any. It is the citadel of the Christian character, on which the safety of the whole fortress depends. It is the point which Satan loves to assail. All lies at his mercy if faith is overthrown. Here, if we love life, we must especially stand on our guard.

III. The last thing I have to say is this: *True Christianity is a good fight.*

"Good" is a curious word to apply to any warfare. All worldly war is more or less evil. No doubt it is an absolute necessity in many cases—to procure the liberty of nations, to prevent the weak from being trampled down by the strong—but still it is an evil. It entails an awful amount of bloodshed and suffering. It hurries into eternity myriads who are completely unprepared for their change. It calls forth the worst passions of man. It causes enormous waste and destruction of property. It fills peaceful homes with mourning widows and orphans. It spreads far and wide poverty, taxation, and national distress. It disarranges all the order of society. It interrupts the work of the Gospel and the growth of Christian missions. In short, war is an immense and incalculable evil, and every praying man should cry night and day, "Give peace in our time." And yet there is one warfare which is emphatically "good," and one fight in which there is no evil. That warfare is the Christian warfare. That fight is the fight of the soul.

Now what are the reasons why the Christian's fight is a "good fight"? What are the points in which his warfare is superior to the warfare of this world? Let me examine this matter, and open it out in order. I dare not pass the subject and leave it unnoticed. I want no one to begin the life of a Christian soldier without counting the cost. I would not keep back from anyone that if he would be holy and see the Lord he must fight, and that the Christian fight though spiritual is real and severe. It needs courage, boldness, and perseverance. But I want my readers to know that there is abundant encouragement, if they will only begin the battle. The Scripture does not call the Christian fight "a good fight" without reason and cause. Let me try to show what I mean.

(a) The Christian's fight is good, *because fought under the best of generals.* The Leader and Commander of all believers is our Divine Saviour, the Lord Jesus Christ—a Saviour of perfect wisdom, infinite love, and almighty power. The Captain of our salvation never fails to lead His soldiers to victory. He never makes any useless movements, never errs in judgment, never commits any mistake. His eye is on all His followers, from the greatest of them even to the least. The humblest servant in His army is not forgotten. The weakest and most sickly is cared for, remembered, and kept unto salvation. The souls whom He has purchased and redeemed with His own blood are far too precious to be wasted and thrown away. Surely this is good!

(b) The Christian's fight is good, *because fought with the best of helps.* Weak as each believer is in himself, the Holy Spirit dwells in him, and his body is a temple of the Holy Ghost. Chosen by God the Father, washed in the blood of the Son, renewed by the Spirit, he does not go to warfare at his own charges, and is never alone. God the Holy Ghost daily teaches, leads, guides, and directs him. God the Father guards him by His almighty power. God the Son intercedes for him every moment, like Moses on the mount, while he is fighting in the valley below. A threefold cord like this can never be broken! His daily provisions and supplies never fail. His commissariat is never defective. His bread and his water are sure. Weak as he seems in himself, like a worm, he is strong in the Lord to do great exploits. Surely this is good!

(c) The Christian fight is a good fight, *because fought with the best of promises.* To every believer belong exceeding great and precious promises—all Yea and Amen in Christ—promises sure to be fulfilled, because made by One who cannot lie, and has power as well as will to keep His word. "Sin shall not have dominion over you."—"The God of peace shall bruise Satan under your feet shortly."—"He that has begun a good work will perform it until the day of Jesus Christ."—"When thou passeth through the waters I will be with thee, and through the floods, they shall not overflow thee."—"My sheep shall never perish, neither shall anyone pluck them out of My hand."—"Him that cometh unto Me I will in no wise cast out."—"I will never leave thee, nor forsake thee."—"I am persuaded that neither death, nor life, nor things present, nor things to come, shall be able to separate us from the love of God, which is in Christ Jesus" (Rom. 6:14; Rom. 16:20; Phil. 1:6; Isa. 43:2; John 10:28; John 6:37; Heb. 13:5; Rom. 8:38-39). Words like these are worth their weight in gold! Who does not know that promises of coming aid have cheered the defenders of besieged cities, like Lucknow, and raised them above their natural strength? Have we never heard that the promise of "help before night" had much to say to the mighty victory of Waterloo? Yet all such promises are as nothing compared to the rich treasure of believers, the eternal promises of God. Surely this is good!

(d) The Christian's fight is a good fight, *because fought with the best of issues and results.* No doubt it is a war in which there are tremendous struggles, agonizing conflicts, wounds, bruises, watchings, fastings, fatigue. But still every believer, without exception, is "more than conqueror through Him that loved him" (Rom. 8:37). No soldiers of Christ are ever lost, missing, or left dead on the battlefield. No mourning will ever need to be put on, and no tears to be shed for either private or officer in the army of Christ. The muster roll, when the last evening comes, will be found precisely the same that it was in the morning. The English Guards marched out of London to the Crimean campaign a magnificent body of men; but many of the gallant fellows laid their bones in a foreign grave, and never saw London again. Far different shall be the arrival of the Christian army in "the city which hath foundations, whose builder and maker is God" (Heb. 11:10). Not one shall be found lacking. The words of our great Captain shall be found true: "Of them which Thou hast given Me I have lost none" (John 18:9). Surely this is good!

(e) The Christian's fight is good, *because it does good to the soul of him that fights it.* All other wars have a bad, lowering, and demoralizing tendency. They call forth the worst passions of the human mind. They harden the conscience, and sap the foundations of religion and morality.

The Christian warfare alone tends to call forth the best things that are left in man. It promotes humility and charity, it lessens selfishness and worldliness, it induces men to set their affections on things above. The old, the sick, the dying, are never known to repent of fighting Christ's battles against sin, the world, and the devil. Their only regret is that they did not begin to serve Christ long before. The experience of that eminent saint, Philip Henry, does not stand alone. In his last days he said to his family, "I take you all to record that a life spent in the service of Christ is the happiest life that a man can spend upon earth." Surely this is good!

(f) The Christian's fight is a good fight, *because it does good to the world.* All other wars have a devastating, ravaging, and injurious effect. The march of an army through a land is an awful scourge to the inhabitants. Wherever it goest it impoverishes, wastes, and does harm. Injury to persons, property, feelings, and morals invariably accompanies it. Far different are the effects produced by Christian soldiers. Wherever they live they are a blessing. They raise the standard of religion and morality. They invariably check the progress of drunkenness, Sabbath-breaking, profligacy, and dishonesty. Even their enemies are obliged to respect them. Go where you please, you will rarely find that barracks and garrisons do good to the neighbourhood. But go where you please, you will find that the presence of a few true Christians is a blessing. Surely this is good!

(g) Finally, the Christian's fight is good, *because it ends in a glorious reward for all who fight it.* Who can tell the wages that Christ will pay to all His faithful people? Who can estimate the good things that our Divine Captain has laid up for those who confess Him before men? A grateful country can give to her successful warriors medals, Victoria Crosses, pensions, peerages, honours, and titles. But it can give nothing that will last and endure for ever, nothing that can be carried beyond the grave. Palaces like Blenheim and Strathfieldsay can only be enjoyed for a few years. The bravest generals and soldiers must go down one day before the King of Terrors. Better, far better, is the position of him who fights under Christ's banner against sin, the world, and the devil. He may get little praise of man while he lives, and go down to the grave with little honour; but he shall have that which is far better, because far more enduring. He shall have "a crown of glory that fadeth not away" (1 Pet. 5:4). Surely this is good!

Let us settle it in our minds that the Christian fight is a good fight—really good, truly good, emphatically good. We see only part of it as yet. We see the struggle, but not the end; we see the campaign, but not the reward; we see the cross, but not the crown. We see a few humble, broken-spirited, penitent, praying people, enduring hardships and despised by the world; but we see not the hand of God over them, the face of God smiling on them, the kingdom of glory prepared for them. These things are yet to be revealed. Let us not judge by appearances. There are more good things about the Christian warfare than we see.

And now let me conclude my whole subject with a few words of practical application. Our lot is cast in times when the world seems thinking of little else but battles and fighting. The iron is entering into the soul of more than one nation, and the mirth of many a fair district is clean gone. Surely in times like these a minister may fairly call on men to remember their spiritual warfare. Let me say a few parting words about the great fight of the soul.

(1) It may be *you are struggling hard for the rewards of this world.* Perhaps you are straining every nerve to obtain money, or place, or power, or pleasure. If that be your case, take care. Your sowing will lead to a crop of bitter disappointment. Unless you mind what you are about, your latter end will be to lie down in sorrow.

Thousands have trodden the path you are pursuing, and have awoke too late to find it end in misery and eternal ruin. They have fought hard for wealth, and honour, and office, and promotion, and turned their backs on God, and Christ, and heaven, and the world to come. And what has their end been? Often, far too often, they have found out that their whole life has been a grand mistake. They have tasted by bitter experience the feelings of the dying statesman who cried aloud in his last hours, "The battle is fought: the battle is fought: but the victory is not won."

For your own happiness' sake resolve this day to join the Lord's side. Shake off your past carelessness and unbelief. Come out from the ways of a thoughtless, unreasoning world. Take up the cross, and become a good soldier of Christ. "Fight the good fight of faith," that you may be happy as well as safe.

Think what the children of this world will often do for liberty, without any religious principle. Remember how Greeks, and Romans, and Swiss, and Tyrolese, have endured the loss of all things, and even life itself, rather than bend their necks to a foreign yoke. Let their example provoke you to emulation. If men can do so much for a corruptible crown, how much more should you do for one which is incorruptible! Awake to a sense of the misery of being a slave. For life, and happiness, and liberty, arise and fight.

Fear not to begin and enlist under Christ's banner. The great Captain of your salvation rejects none that come to Him. Like David in the cave of Adullam, He is ready to receive all who apply to Him, however unworthy they may feel themselves. None who repent and believe are too bad to be enrolled in the ranks of Christ's army. All who come to Him by faith are admitted, clothed, armed, trained, and finally led on to complete victory. Fear not to begin this very day. There is yet room for you.

Fear not to go on fighting, if you once enlist. The more thorough and whole-hearted you are as a soldier, the more comfortable will you find your warfare. No doubt you will often meet with trouble, fatigue, and hard fighting, before your warfare is accomplished. But let none of these things move you. Greater is He that is for you than all they that be against you. Everlasting liberty or everlasting captivity are the alternatives before you. Choose liberty, and fight to the last.

(2) *It may be you know something of the Christian warfare,* and are a tried and proved soldier already. If that be your case, accept a parting word of advice and encouragement from a fellow-soldier. Let me speak to myself as well as to you. Let us stir up our minds by way of remembrance. There are some things which we cannot remember too well.

Let us remember that if we would fight successfully we must put on the whole armour of God, and never lay it aside till we die. Not a single piece of the armour can be dispensed with. The girdle of truth, the breastplate of righteousness, the shield of faith, the sword of the Spirit, the helmet of hope—each and all are needful. Not a single day can we dispense with any part of this armour. Well says an old veteran in Christ's army, who died 200 years ago, "In heaven we shall appear, not in armour, but in robes of glory. But here our arms are to be worn night and day. We must walk, work, sleep in them, or else we are not true soldiers of Christ" (Gurnall's *Christian Armour*).

Let us remember the solemn words of an inspired warrior, who went to his rest 1,800 years ago: "No man that warreth entangleth himself with the affairs of this life; that he may please Him who hath chosen him to be a soldier" (2 Tim. 2:4). May we never forget that saying!

Let us remember that some have seemed good soldiers for a little season, and talked loudly of what they would do, and yet turned back disgracefully in the day of battle.

Let us never forget Balaam, and Judas, and Demas, and Lot's wife. Whatever we are, and however weak, let us be real, genuine, true, and sincere.

Let us remember that the eye of our loving Saviour is upon us, morning, noon, and night. He will never suffer us to be tempted above that we are able to bear. He can be touched with the feeling of our infirmities, for He suffered Himself being tempted. He knows what battles and conflicts are, for He Himself was assaulted by the Prince of this world. Having such a High Priest, Jesus the Son of God, let us hold fast our profession (Heb. 4:14).

Let us remember that thousands of soldiers before us have fought the same battle that we are fighting, and come off more than conquerors through Him that loved them. They overcame by the blood of the Lamb; and so also may we. Christ's arm is quite as strong as ever, and Christ's heart is just as loving as ever. He that saved men and women before us is one who never changes. He is "able to save to the uttermost all who come unto God by Him." Then let us cast doubts and fears away. Let us "follow them who through faith and patience inherit the promises," and are waiting for us to join them (Heb. 7:25; 6:12).

Finally, let us remember that the time is short, and the coming of the Lord draweth nigh. A few more battles and the last trumpet shall sound, and the Prince of Peace shall come to reign on a renewed earth. A few more struggles and conflicts, and then we shall bid an eternal good-bye to warfare, and to sin, to sorrow, and to death. Then let us fight on to the last, and never surrender. Thus saith the Captain of our salvation—"He that overcometh shall inherit all things; and I will be his God, and he shall be My son" (Rev. 21:7).

Let me conclude all with the words of John Bunyan, in one of the most beautiful parts of *Pilgrim's Progress*. He is describing the end of one of his best and holiest pilgrims:—

"After this it was noised abroad that Mr. Valiant-for-truth was sent for by a summons, by the same party as the others. And he had this word for a token that the summons was true, 'The pitcher was broken at the fountain' (Eccles. 12:6). When he understood it, he called for his friends, and told them of it. Then said he, 'I am going to my Father's house; and though with great difficulty I have got here, yet now I do not repent me of all the troubles I have been at to arrive where I am. My sword I give to him that shall succeed me in my pilgrimage, and my courage and skill to him that can get it. My marks and scars I carry with me, to be a witness for me that I have fought His battles, who will now be my rewarder.' When the day that he must go home was come, many accompanied him to the river-side, into which, as he went down, he said, 'O death where is thy sting?' And as he went down deeper, he cried, 'O grave, where is thy victory?' So he passed over, and all the trumpets sounded for him on the other side."

May our end be like this! May we never forget that without fighting there can be no holiness while we live, and no crown of glory when we die!

5

THE COST

"Which of you, intending to build a tower, sitteth not down first and counteth the cost?"

The text which heads this page is one of great importance. Few are the people who are not often obliged to ask themselves—"What does it cost?"

In buying property, in building houses, in furnishing rooms, in forming plans, in changing dwellings, in educating children, it is wise and prudent to look forward and consider. Many would save themselves much sorrow and trouble if they would only remember the question—"What does it cost?"

But there is one subject on which it is specially important to "count the cost." That subject is the salvation of our souls. What does it cost to be a true Christian? What does it cost to be a really holy man? This, after all, is the grand question. For want of thought about this, thousands, after seeming to begin well, turn away from the road to heaven, and are lost for ever in hell. Let me try to say a few words which may throw light on the subject.

I. I will show, firstly, *what it costs to be a true Christian.*
II. I will explain, secondly, *why it is of such great importance to count the cost.*
III. I will give, in the last place, *some hints which may help men to count the cost rightly.*

We are living in strange times. Events are hurrying on with singular rapidity. We never know "what a day may bring forth"; how much less do we know what may happen in a year!—We live in a day of great religious profession. Scores of professing Christians in every part of the land are expressing a desire for more holiness and a higher degree of spiritual life. Yet nothing is more common than to see people receiving the Word with joy, and then after two or three years falling away, and going back to their sins. They had not considered "what it costs" to be a really consistent believer and holy Christian. Surely these are times when we ought often to sit down and "count the cost," and to consider the state of our souls. We must mind what we are about. If we desire to be truly holy, it is a good sign. We may thank God for putting the desire into our hearts. But still the cost ought to be counted. No doubt Christ's way to eternal life is a way of pleasantness. But it is folly to shut our eyes to the fact that His way is narrow, and the cross comes before the crown.

I. I have, first, to show *what it costs to be a true Christian.*

Let there be no mistake about my meaning. I am not examining what it costs to save a Christian's soul. I know well that it costs nothing less than the blood of the Son of God to provide an atonement, and to redeem man from hell. The price paid for our redemption was nothing less than the death of Jesus Christ on Calvary. We "are bought with a price." "Christ gave Himself a ransom for all" (1 Cor. 6:20; 1 Tim. 2:6). But all this is wide of the question. The point I want to consider is another one altogether. It is what a man must be *ready to give up* if he wishes to be saved. It is the amount of sacrifice a man must submit to if he intends to serve Christ. It is in this sense that I raise the question, "What does it cost?" And I believe firmly that it is a most important one.

I grant freely that it costs little to be a mere outward Christian. A man has only got to attend a place of worship twice on Sunday, and to be tolerably moral during the week, and he has gone as far as thousands around him ever go in religion. All this is cheap and easy work: it entails no self-denial or self-sacrifice. If this is saving Christianity, and will take us to heaven when we die, we must alter the description of the way of life, and write, "Wide is the gate and broad is the way that leads to heaven!"

But it does cost something to be a real Christian, according to the standard of the Bible. There are enemies to be overcome, battles to be fought, sacrifices to be made, an Egypt to be forsaken, a wilderness to be passed through, a cross to be carried, a race to be run. Conversion is not putting a man in an arm-chair and taking him easily to heaven. It is the beginning of a mighty conflict, in which it costs much to win the victory. Hence arises the unspeakable importance of "counting the cost."

Let me try to show precisely and particularly what it costs to be a true Christian. Let us suppose that a man is disposed to take service with Christ, and feels drawn and inclined to follow Him. Let us suppose that some affliction, or some sudden death, or an awakening sermon, has stirred his conscience, and made him feel the value of his soul and desire to be a true Christian. No doubt there is everything to encourage him. His sins may be freely forgiven, however many and great. His heart may be completely changed, however cold and hard. Christ and the Holy Spirit, mercy and grace, are all ready for him. But still he should count the cost. Let us see particularly, one by one, the things that his religion will cost him.

(1) For one thing, it will cost him *his self-righteousness*. He must cast away all pride and high thoughts, and conceit of his own goodness. He must be content to go to heaven as a poor sinner saved only by free grace, and owing all to the merit and righteousness of another. He must really feel as well as say the Prayer-book words—that he has "erred and gone astray like a lost sheep," that he has "left undone the things he ought to have done, and done the things he ought not to have done, and that there is no health in him." He must be willing to give up all trust in his own morality, respectability, praying, Bible-reading, Church-going, and sacrament-receiving, and to trust in nothing but Jesus Christ.

Now this sounds hard to some. I do not wonder. "Sir," said a godly ploughman to the well-known James Hervey, of Weston Favell, "it is harder to deny proud self than sinful self. But it is absolutely necessary." Let us set down this item first and foremost in our account. To be a true Christian it will cost a man his self-righteousness.

(2) For another thing, it will cost a man *his sins*. He must be willing to give up every habit and practice which is wrong in God's sight. He must set his face against it, quarrel with it, break off from it, fight with it, crucify it, and labour to keep it under, whatever the world around him may say or think. He must do this honestly and fairly. There must be no separate truce with any special sin which he loves. He must count *all* sins as his deadly enemies, and hate every false way. Whether little or great, whether open or secret, all his sins must be thoroughly renounced. They may struggle hard with him every day, and sometimes almost get the mastery over him. But he must never give way to them. He must keep up a perpetual war with his sins. It is written—"Cast away from you all your transgressions."—"Break off thy sins and iniquities."—"Cease to do evil"—(Ezek. 18:31; Dan. 4:27; Isa. 1:16).

This also sounds hard. I do not wonder. Our sins are often as dear to us as our children: we love them, hug them, cleave to them, and delight in them. To part with them is as hard as cutting off a right hand, or plucking out a right eye. But it must be done. The parting must come. "Though wickedness be sweet in the sinner's mouth, though he hide it under his tongue; though he spare it, and forsake it not," yet it must be given up, if he wishes to be saved (Job 20:12-13). He and sin must quarrel, if he and God are to be friends. Christ is willing to receive any sinners. But He will not receive them if they will stick to their sins. Let us set down that item second in our account. To be a Christian it will cost a man his sins.

(3) For another thing, it will cost a man *his love of ease*. He must take pains and trouble, if he means to run a successful race towards heaven. He must daily watch and stand on his guard, like a soldier on enemy's ground. He must take heed to his behaviour every hour of the day, in every company, and in every place, in public as well as in private, among strangers as well as at home. He must be careful over his time, his tongue, his temper, his thoughts, his imaginations, his motives, his conduct in every relation of life. He must be diligent about his prayers, his Bible-reading, and his use of Sundays, with all their means of grace. In attending to these things he may come far short of perfection; but there is none of them that he can safely neglect. "The soul of the sluggard desireth, and hath nothing: but the soul of the diligent shall be made fat" (Prov. 13:4).

This also sounds hard. There is nothing we naturally dislike so much as "trouble" about our religion. We hate trouble. We secretly wish we could have a "vicarious" Christianity, and could be good by proxy, and have everything done for us. Anything that requires exertion and labour is entirely against the grain of our hearts. But the soul can have "no gains without pains." Let us set down that item third in our account. To be a Christian it will cost a man his love of ease.

(4) In the last place, it will cost a man *the favour of the world*. He must be content to be thought ill of by man if he pleases God. He must count it no strange thing to be mocked, ridiculed, slandered, persecuted, and even hated. He must not be surprised to find his opinions and practices in religion despised and held up to scorn. He must submit to be thought by many a fool, an enthusiast, and a fanatic—to have his words perverted and his actions misrepresented. In fact, he must not marvel if some call him mad. The Master says—"Remember the word that I said unto you, The servant is not greater than his lord. If they have persecuted Me, they will also persecute you; if they have kept My saying, they will keep yours also" (John 15:20).

I dare say this also sounds hard. We naturally dislike unjust dealing and false charges, and think it very hard to be accused without cause.

We should not be flesh and blood if we did not wish to have the good opinion of our neighbours. It is always unpleasant to be spoken against, and forsaken, and lied about, and to stand alone. But there is no help for it. The cup which our Master drank must be drunk by His disciples. They must be "despised and rejected of men" (Isa. 53:3). Let us set down that item last in our account. To be a Christian it will cost a man the favour of the world.

Such is the account of what it costs to be a true Christian. I grant the list is a heavy one. But where is the item that could be removed? Bold indeed must that man be who would dare to say that we may keep our self-righteousness, our sins, our laziness, and our love of the world, and yet be saved!

I grant it costs much to be a true Christian. But who in his sound senses can doubt that it is worth any cost to have the soul saved? When the ship is in danger of sinking, the crew think nothing of casting overboard the precious cargo. When a limb is mortified, a man will submit to any severe operation, and even to amputation, to save life. Surely a Christian should be willing to give up anything which stands between him and heaven. A religion that costs nothing is worth nothing! A cheap Christianity, without a cross, will prove in the end a useless Christianity, without a crown.

II. I have now, in the second place, to explain *why "counting the cost" is of such great importance to man's soul.*

I might easily settle this question by laying down the principle, that no duty enjoined by Christ can ever be neglected without damage. I might show how many shut their eyes throughout life to the nature of saving religion, and refuse to consider what it really costs to be a Christian. I might describe how at last, when life is ebbing away, they wake up, and make a few spasmodic efforts to turn to God. I might tell you how they find to their amazement that repentance and conversion are no such easy matters as they had supposed, and that it costs "a great sum" to be a true Christian. They discover that habits of pride and sinful indulgence, and love of ease, and worldliness, are not so easily laid aside as they had dreamed. And so, after a faint struggle, they give up in despair, and leave the world hopeless, graceless, and unfit to meet God! They had flattered themselves all their days that religion would be easy work when they once took it up seriously. But they open their eyes too late, and discover for the first time that they are ruined because they never "counted the cost."

But there is one class of persons to whom especially I wish to address myself in handling this part of my subject. It is a large class—an increasing class—and a class which in these days is in peculiar danger. Let me in a few plain words try to describe this class. It deserves our best attention.

The persons I speak of are not thoughtless about religion: they think a good deal about it. They are not ignorant of religion: they know the outlines of it pretty well. But their great defect is that they are not "rooted and grounded" in their faith. Too often they have picked up their knowledge second-hand, from being in religious families, or from being trained in religious ways, but have never worked it out by their own inward experience. Too often they have hastily taken up a profession of religion under the pressure of circumstances, from sentimental feelings, from animal excitement, or from a vague desire to do like others around them, but without any solid work of grace in their hearts. Persons like these are in a position of immense danger. They are precisely those, if Bible examples are worth anything, who need to be exhorted "to count the cost."

For want of "counting the cost" myriads of the children of Israel perished miserably in the wilderness between Egypt and Canaan. They left Egypt full of zeal and fervour, as if nothing could stop them. But when they found dangers and difficulties in the way, their courage soon cooled down. They had never reckoned on trouble. They had thought the promised land would be all before them in a few days. And so, when enemies, privation, hunger, and thirst began to try them, they murmured against Moses and God, and would fain have gone back to Egypt. In a word, they had "not counted the cost," and so lost everything, and died in their sins.

For want of "counting the cost," many of our Lord Jesus Christ's hearers went back after a time, and "walked no more with Him" (John 6:66). When they first saw His miracles, and heard His preaching, they thought "the kingdom of God would immediately appear." They cast in their lot with His Apostles, and followed Him without thinking of the consequences. But when they found that there were hard doctrines to be believed, and hard work to be done, and hard treatment to be borne, their faith gave way entirely, and proved to be nothing at all. In a word, they had not "counted the cost," and so made shipwreck of their profession.

For want of "counting the cost," King Herod returned to his old sins, and destroyed his soul. He liked to hear John the Baptist preach. He "observed" and honoured him as a just and holy man. He even "did many things" which were right and good. But when he found that he must give up his darling Herodias, his religion entirely broke down. He had not reckoned on this. He had not "counted the cost" (Mark 6:20).

For want of "counting the cost," Demas forsook the company of St.

Paul, forsook the Gospel, forsook Christ, forsook heaven. For a long time he journeyed with the great Apostle of the Gentiles, and was actually a "fellow-labourer." But when he found he could not have the friendship of this world as well as the friendship of God, he gave up his Christianity and clave to the world. "Demas hath forsaken me," says St. Paul, "having loved this present world" (2 Tim. 4:10). He had not "counted the cost."

For want of "counting the cost," the hearers of powerful Evangelical preachers often come to miserable ends. They are stirred and excited into professing what they have not really experienced. They receive the Word with a "joy" so extravagant that it almost startles old Christians. They run for a time with such zeal and fervour that they seem likely to outstrip all others. They talk and work for spiritual objects with such enthusiasm that they make older believers feel ashamed. But when the novelty and freshness of their feelings is gone, a change comes over them. They prove to have been nothing more than stony-ground hearers. The description the great Master gives in the Parable of the Sower is exactly exemplified. "Temptation or persecution arises because of the Word, and they are offended" (Matt. 13:21). Little by little their zeal melts away, and their love becomes cold. By and by their seats are empty in the assembly of God's people, and they are heard of no more among Christians. And why? They had never "counted the cost."

For want of "counting the cost," hundreds of professed converts, under religious revivals, go back to the world after a time, and bring disgrace on religion. They begin with a sadly mistaken notion of what is true Christianity. They fancy it consists in nothing more than a so-called "coming to Christ," and having strong inward feelings of joy and peace. And so, when they find, after a time, that there is a cross to be carried, that our hearts are deceitful, and that there is a busy devil always near us, they cool down in disgust, and return to their old sins. And why? Because they had really never known what Bible Christianity is. They had never learned that we must "count the cost."[1]

For want of "counting the cost," the children of religious parents often turn out ill, and bring disgrace on Christianity. Familiar from their earliest years with the form and theory of the Gospel—taught even from infancy to repeat great leading texts—accustomed every week to be instructed in the Gospel, or to instruct others in Sunday schools—they often grow up professing a religion without knowing why, or without ever having thought seriously about it. And then when the realities of grown-up life begin to press upon them, they often astound every one by dropping all their religion, and plunging right into the world. And why?

They had never thoroughly understood the sacrifices which Christianity entails. They had never been taught to "count the cost."

These are solemn and painful truths. But they are truths. They all help to show the immense importance of the subject I am now considering. They all point out the absolute necessity of pressing the subject of this paper on all who profess a desire for holiness, and of crying aloud in all the Churches—"Count the Cost."

I am bold to say that it would be well if the duty of "counting the cost" were more frequently taught than it is. Impatient hurry is the order of the day with many religionists. Instantaneous conversions, and immediate sensible peace, are the only results they seem to care for from the Gospel. Compared with these all other things are thrown into the shade. To produce them is the grand end and object, apparently, of all their labours. I say without hesitation that such a naked, one-sided mode of teaching Christianity is mischievous in the extreme.

Let no one mistake my meaning. I thoroughly approve of offering men a full, free, present, immediate salvation in Christ Jesus. I thoroughly approve of urging on man the possibility and the duty of immediate instantaneous conversion. In these matters I give place to no one. But I do say that these truths ought not to be set before men nakedly, singly, and alone. They ought to be told honestly what it is they are taking up, if they profess a desire to come out from the world and serve Christ. They ought not to be pressed into the ranks of Christ's army without being told what the warfare entails. In a word, they should be told honestly to "count the cost."

Does any one ask what our Lord Jesus Christ's practice was in this matter? Let him read what St. Luke records. He tells us that on a certain occasion "There went great multitudes with Him: and He turned and said unto them, If any come to Me, and hate not his father, and mother, and wife, and children, and brethren, and sisters, yea, and his own life also, he cannot be My disciple. And whosoever doth not bear his cross and come after Me, cannot be My disciple" (Luke 14:25-27). I must plainly say, that I cannot reconcile this passage with the proceedings of many modern religious teachers. And yet, to my mind, the doctrine of it is as clear as the sun at noon-day. It shows us that we ought not to hurry men into professing discipleship, without warning them plainly to "count the cost."

Does any one ask what the practice of the eminent and best preachers of the Gospel has been in days gone by? I am bold to say that they have all with one mouth borne testimony to the wisdom of our Lord's dealing with the multitudes to which I have just referred. Luther, and Latimer, and Baxter, and Wesley, and Whitfield, and Berridge, and Rowland Hill, were all keenly alive to the deceitfulness of man's heart. They knew full well that all is not gold that glitters, that conviction is not conversion, that feeling is not faith, that sentiment is not grace, that all blossoms do not come to fruit. "Be not deceived," was their constant cry. "Consider well what you do. Do not run before you are called. Count the cost."

If we desire to do good, let us never be ashamed of walking in the steps of our Lord Jesus Christ. Work hard if you will, and have the opportunity, for the souls of others. Press them to consider their ways. Compel them with holy violence to come in, to lay down their arms, and to yield themselves to God. Offer them salvation, ready, free, full, immediate salvation. Press Christ and all His benefits on their acceptance. But in all your work tell the truth, and the whole truth. Be ashamed to use the vulgar arts of a recruiting serjeant. Do not speak only of the uniform, the pay, and the glory; speak also of the enemies, the battle, the armour, the watching, the marching, and the drill. Do not present only one side of Christianity. Do not keep back "the cross" of self-denial that must be carried, when you speak of the cross on which Christ died for our redemption. Explain fully what Christianity entails. Entreat men to repent and come to Christ; but bid them at the same time to "count the cost."

III. The third and last thing which I propose to do, is *to give some hints which may help men to "count the cost" rightly.*

Sorry indeed should I be if I did not say something on this branch of my subject. I have no wish to discourage any one, or to keep any one back from Christ's service. It is my heart's desire to encourage every one to go forward and take up the cross. Let us "count the cost" by all means, and count it carefully. But let us remember, that if we count rightly, and look on all sides, there is nothing that need make us afraid.

Let us mention some things which should always enter into our calculations in counting the cost of true Christianity. Set down honestly and fairly what you will have to give up and go through, if you become Christ's disciple. Leave nothing out. Put it all down. But then set down side by side the following sums which I am going to give you. Do this fairly and correctly, and I am not afraid for the result.

(a) Count up and compare, for one thing, *the profit and the loss,* if you are a true-hearted and holy Christian. You may possibly lose something in this world, but you will gain the salvation of your immortal soul. It is written—"What shall it profit a man, if he shall gain the whole world, and lose his own soul?" (Mark 8:36).

(b) Count up and compare, for another thing, *the praise and the blame,* if you are a true-hearted and holy Christian. You may possibly be blamed by man, but you will have the praise of God the Father, God the Son, and God the Holy Ghost. Your blame will come from the lips of a few erring, blind, fallible men and women. Your praise will come from the King of kings and Judge of all the earth. It is only those whom He blesses who are really blessed. It is written—"Blessed are ye when men shall revile you, and persecute you, and say all manner of evil against you falsely, for My sake. Rejoice and be exceeding glad, for great is your reward in heaven" (Matt. 5:11-12).

(c) Count up and compare, for another thing, *the friends and the enemies,* if you are a true-hearted and holy Christian. On the one side of you is the enmity of the devil and the wicked. On the other, you have the favour and friendship of the Lord Jesus Christ. Your enemies, at most, can only bruise your heel. They may rage loudly, and compass sea and land to work your ruin; but they cannot destroy you. Your Friend is able to save to the uttermost all them that come unto God by Him. None shall ever pluck His sheep out of His hand. It is written—"Be not afraid of them that kill the body, and after that have no more that they can do. But I will forewarn you whom ye shall fear: Fear Him, which after He hath killed hath power to cast into hell; yea, I say unto you, fear Him" (Luke 12:4-5).

(d) Count up and compare, for another thing, *the life that now is and the life to come,* if you are a true-hearted and holy Christian. The time present, no doubt, is not a time of ease. It is a time of watching and praying, fighting and struggling, believing and working. But it is only for a few years. The future time is the season of rest and refreshing. Sin shall be cast out. Satan shall be bound. And, best of all, it shall be a rest for ever. It is written—"Our light affliction, which is but for a moment, worketh for us a far more exceeding and eternal weight of glory; while we look not at the things which are seen, but at the things which are not seen: for the things which are seen are temporal; but the things which are not seen are eternal" (2 Cor. 4:17-18).

(e) Count up and compare, for another thing, *the pleasures of sin and the happiness of God's service,* if you are a true-hearted and holy Christian. The pleasures that the worldly man gets by his ways are hollow, unreal, and unsatisfying. They are like the fire of thorns, flashing and crackling for a few minutes, and then quenched for ever. The happiness that Christ gives to His people is something solid, lasting, and substantial. It is not dependent on health or circumstances. It never leaves a man, even in death. It ends in a crown of glory that fadeth not away. It is written— "The joy of the hypocrite is but for a moment."—"As the crackling of thorns under a pot, so is the laughter of the fool" (Job 20:5; Eccles. 7:6). But it is also written—"Peace I leave with you, My peace give I unto you: not as the world giveth, give I unto you. Let not your heart be troubled, neither let it be afraid" (John 14:27).

(f) Count up and compare, for another thing, *the trouble that true Christianity entails, and the troubles that are in store for the wicked beyond the grave*. Grant for a moment that Bible-reading, and praying, and repenting, and believing, and holy living, require pains and self-denial. It is all nothing compared to that "wrath to come" which is stored up for the impenitent and unbelieving. A single day in hell will be worse than a whole life spent in carrying the cross. The "worm that never dies, and the fire that is not quenched" are things which it passes man's power to conceive fully or describe. It is written—"Son, remember that thou in thy life-time receivedst thy good things, and likewise Lazarus evil things; but now he is comforted and thou art tormented" (Luke 16:25).

(g) Count up and compare, in the last place, *the number of those who turn from sin and the world and serve Christ, and the number of those who forsake Christ and return to the world*. On the one side you will find thousands—on the other you will find none. Multitudes are every year turning out of the broad way and entering the narrow. None who really enter the narrow way grow tired of it and return to the broad. The footsteps in the downward road are often to be seen turning out of it. The footsteps in the road to heaven are all one way. It is written—"The way of the wicked is darkness."—"The way of transgressors is hard" (Prov. 4:19; 13:15). But it is also written—"The path of the just is as the shining light, which shineth more and more unto the perfect day" (Prov. 4:18).

Such sums as these, no doubt, are often not done correctly. Not a few, I am well aware, are ever "halting between two opinions." They cannot make up their minds that it is worth while to serve Christ. The losses and gains, the advantages and disadvantages, the sorrows and the joys, the helps and the hindrances appear to them so nearly balanced that they cannot decide for God. They cannot do this great sum correctly. They cannot make the result so clear as it ought to be. They do not count right.

But what is the secret of their mistakes? It is want of faith. To come to a right conclusion about our souls, we must have some of that mighty principle which St. Paul describes in the 11th chapter of his Epistle to the Hebrews. Let me try to show how that principle operates in the great business of "counting the cost."

How was it that Noah persevered in building the ark? He stood alone amidst a world of sinners and unbelievers. He had to endure scorn, ridicule, and mockery. What was it that nerved his arm, and made him patiently work on and face it all? It was *faith*. He believed in a wrath to come. He believed that there was no safety, excepting in the ark that he was preparing. Believing, he held the world's opinion very cheap. He "counted the cost" by faith, and had no doubt that to build the ark was gain.

How was it that Moses forsook the pleasures of Pharaoh's house, and refused to be called the son of Pharaoh's daughter? How was it that he cast in his lot with a despised people like the Hebrews, and risked everything in this world in carrying out the great work of their deliverance from bondage? To the eye of sense he was losing everything and gaining nothing. What was it that moved him? It was *faith*. He believed that there was One far above Pharaoh, who would carry him safe through all his undertaking. He believed that the "recompense of reward" was far better than all the honours of Egypt. He "counted the cost" by faith, as "seeing Him that is invisible," and was persuaded that to forsake Egypt and go forth into the wilderness was gain.

How was it that Saul the Pharisee could ever make up his mind to become a Christian? The cost and sacrifices of the change were fearfully great. He gave up all his brilliant prospects among his own people. He brought on himself instead of man's favour, man's hatred, man's enmity, and man's persecution, even unto death. What was it that enabled him to face it all? It was *faith*. He believed that Jesus, who met him on the way to Damascus, could give him a hundredfold more than he gave up, and in the world to come everlasting life. By faith he "counted the cost," and saw clearly on which side the balance lay. He believed firmly that to carry the cross of Christ was gain.

Let us mark well these things. That faith which made Noah, Moses, and St. Paul do what they did, that faith is the great secret of coming to a right conclusion about our souls. That same faith must be our helper and ready-reckoner, when we sit down to count the cost of being a true Christian. That same faith is to be had for the asking. "He giveth more grace" (James 4:6). Armed with that faith we shall set things down at their true value. Filled with that faith we shall neither add to the cross nor subtract from the crown. Our conclusions will be all correct. Our sum total will be without error.

(1) In conclusion, let every reader of this paper think seriously, *whether his religion costs him anything at present*. Very likely it costs you nothing. Very probably it neither costs you trouble, nor time, nor thought, nor care, nor pains, nor reading, nor praying, nor self-denial, nor conflict, nor working, nor labour of any kind. Now mark what I say. Such a reli-

gion as this will never save your soul. It will never give you peace while you live, nor hope while you die. It will not support you in the day of affliction, nor cheer you in the hour of death. A religion which costs nothing is worth nothing. Awake before it is too late. Awake and repent. Awake and be converted. Awake and believe. Awake and pray. Rest not till you can give a satisfactory answer to my question, "What does it cost?"

(2) Think, if you want stirring motives for serving God, *what it cost to provide a salvation for your soul.* Think how the Son of God left heaven and became Man, suffered on the cross, and lay in the grave, to pay your debt to God, and work out for you a complete redemption. Think of all this and learn that it is no light matter to posses an immortal soul. It is worth while to take some trouble about one's soul.

Ah, lazy man or woman, is it really come to this, that you will miss heaven for lack of trouble? Are you really determined to make shipwreck for ever, from mere dislike to exertion? Away with the cowardly, unworthy thought. Arise and play the man. Say to yourself, "Whatever it may cost, I will, at any rate, strive to enter in at the strait gate." Look at the cross of Christ, and take fresh courage. Look forward to death, judgment, and eternity, and be in earnest. It may cost much to be a Christian, but you may be sure it pays.

(3) If any reader of this paper really feels that he has counted the cost, and taken up the cross, I bid him *persevere and press on.* I dare say you often feel your heart faint, and are sorely tempted to give up in despair. Your enemies seem so many, your besetting sins so strong, your friends so few, the way so steep and narrow, you hardly know what to do. But still I say, persevere and press on.

The time is very short. A few more years of watching and praying, a few more tossings on the sea of this world, a few more deaths and changes, a few more winters and summers, and all will be over. We shall have fought our last battle, and shall need to fight no more.

The presence and company of Christ will make amends for all we suffer here below. When we see as we have been seen, and look back on the journey of life, we shall wonder at our own faintness of heart. We shall marvel that we made so much of our cross, and thought so little of our crown. We shall marvel that in "counting the cost" we could ever doubt on which side the balance of profit lay. Let us take courage. We are not far from home. IT MAY COST MUCH TO BE A TRUE CHRISTIAN AND A CONSISTENT BELIEVER; BUT IT PAYS.

6

GROWTH

"Grow in grace, and in the knowledge of our Lord and Saviour Jesus Christ."

— 2 PETER 3:18

The subject of the text which heads this page is one which I dare not omit in this volume about Holiness. It is one that ought to be deeply interesting to every true Christian. It naturally raises the questions, Do we grow in grace? Do we get on in our religion? Do we make progress?

To a mere formal Christian I cannot expect the inquiry to seem worth attention. The man who has nothing more than a kind of Sunday religion—whose Christianity is like his Sunday clothes, put on once a week, and then laid aside—such a man cannot, of course, be expected to care about "growth in grace." He knows nothing about such matters. "They are foolishness to him" (1 Cor. 2:14). But to every one who is in downright earnest about his soul, and hungers and thirsts after spiritual life, the question ought to come home with searching power. Do we make progress in our religion? Do we grow?

The question is one that is always useful, but especially so at certain seasons. A Saturday night, a Communion Sunday, the return of a birthday, the end of a year—all these are seasons that ought to set us thinking, and make us look within. Time is fast flying. Life is fast ebbing away. The hour is daily drawing nearer when the reality of our Christianity will be tested, and it will be seen whether we have built on "the rock" or on "the sand." Surely it becomes us from time to time to examine ourselves, and take account of our souls? Do we get on in spiritual things? Do we grow?

The question is one that is of special importance in the present day. Crude and strange opinions are floating in men's minds on some points of doctrine, and among others on the point of "growth in grace," as an essential part of true holiness. By some it is totally denied. By others it is explained away, and pared down to nothing. By thousands it is misunderstood, and consequently neglected. In a day like this it is useful to look fairly in the face the whole subject of Christian growth.

In considering this subject there are three things which I wish to bring forward and establish:—

I. *The reality of religious growth.* There is such a thing as "growth in grace."
II. *The marks of religious growth.* There are marks by which "growth in grace" may be known.
III. *The means of religious growth.* There are means that must be used by those who desire "growth in grace."

I know not who you are, into whose hands this paper may have fallen. But I am not ashamed to ask your best attention to its contents. Believe me, the subject is no mere matter of speculation and controversy. It is intimately and inseparably connected with the whole question of "sanctification." It is a leading mark of true saints that they grow. The spiritual health and prosperity, the spiritual happiness and comfort of every true-hearted and holy Christian, are intimately connected with the subject of spiritual growth.

I. The first point I propose to establish is this: *There is such a thing as growth in grace.*

That any Christian should deny this proposition is at first sight a strange and melancholy thing. But it is fair to remember that man's understanding is fallen no less than his will. Disagreements about doctrines are often nothing more than disagreements about the meaning of words. I try to hope that it is so in the present case. I try to believe that when I speak of "growth in grace" and maintain it, I mean one thing, while my brethren who deny it mean quite another. Let me therefore clear the way by explaining what I mean.

When I speak of "growth in grace," I do not for a moment mean that a believer's interest in Christ can grow. I do not mean that he can grow in safety, acceptance with God, or security. I do not mean that he can ever be more justified, more pardoned, more forgiven, more at peace with God, then he is the first moment that he believes. I hold firmly that the justification of a believer is a finished, perfect, and complete work;

and that the weakest saint, though he may not know and feel it, is as completely justified as the strongest. I hold firmly that our election, calling, and standing in Christ admit of no degrees, increase, or diminution. If any one dreams that by "growth in grace" I mean growth in *justification* he is utterly wide of the mark, and utterly mistaken about the whole point I am considering. I would go to the stake, God helping me, for the glorious truth, that in the matter of justification before God every believer is "complete in Christ" (Col. 2:10). Nothing can be added to his justification from the moment he believes, and nothing taken away.

When I speak of "growth in grace" I only mean increase in the degree, size, strength, vigour, and power of the graces which the Holy Spirit plants in a believer's heart. I hold that every one of those graces admits of growth, progress, and increase. I hold that repentance, faith, hope, love, humility, zeal, courage, and the like, may be little or great, strong or weak, vigorous or feeble, and may vary greatly in the same man at different periods of his life. When I speak of a man "growing in grace," I mean simply this—that his sense of sin is becoming deeper, his faith stronger, his hope brighter, his love more extensive, his spiritual-mindedness more marked. He feels more of it in his life. He is going on from strength to strength, from faith to faith, and from grace to grace. I leave it to others to describe such a man's condition by any words they please. For myself I think the truest and best account of him is this—he is "growing in grace."

One principal ground on which I build this doctrine of "growth in grace," is the plain language of Scripture. If words in the Bible mean anything, there is such a thing as "growth," and believers ought to be exhorted to "grow."—What says St. Paul? "Your faith groweth exceedingly" (2 Thess. 1:3). "We beseech you that ye increase more and more" (1 Thess. 4:10). "Increasing in the knowledge of God" (Col. 1:10). "Having hope, when your faith is increased" (2 Cor. 10:15). "The Lord make you to increase in love" (1 Thess. 3:12). "That ye may grow up into Him in all things" (Eph. 4:15). "I pray that your love may abound more and more" (Phil. 1:9). "We beseech you, as ye have received of us how ye ought to walk and to please God, so ye would abound more and more" (1 Thess. 4:1).—What says St. Peter? "Desire the sincere milk of the Word, that ye may grow thereby" (1 Pet. 2:2). "Grow in grace, and in the knowledge of our Lord and Saviour Jesus Christ" (2 Pet. 3:18). I know not what others think of such texts. To me they seem to establish the doctrine for which I contend, and to be incapable of any other explanation. Growth in grace is taught in the Bible. I might stop here and say no more.

The other ground, however, on which I build the doctrine of "growth in grace," is the ground of fact and experience. I ask any honest reader of the New Testament whether he cannot see degrees of grace in the New Testament saints whose histories are recorded, as plainly as the sun at noon-day?—I ask him whether he cannot see in the very same persons as great a difference between their faith and knowledge at one time and at another, as between the same man's strength when he is an infant and when he is a grown-up man?—I ask him whether the Scripture does not distinctly recognise this in the language it uses, when it speaks of "weak" faith and "strong" faith, and of Christians as "new-born babes," "little children," "young men," and "fathers"? (1 Pet. 2:2; 1 John 2:12-14). I ask him, above all, whether his own observation of believers, now-a-days, does not bring him to the same conclusion?—What true Christian would not confess that there is as much difference between the degree of his own faith and knowledge when he was first converted, and his pres-ent attainments, as there is between a sapling and a full-grown tree? His graces are the same in principle; but they have grown. I know not how these facts strike others: to my eyes they seem to prove, most unanswer-ably, that "growth in grace" is a real thing.

I feel almost ashamed to dwell so long upon this part of my subject. In fact, if any man means to say that the faith, and hope, and knowledge, and holiness of a newly-converted person, are as strong as those of an old-established believer, and need no increase, it is waste of time to argue further. No doubt they are as real, but not so strong—as true, but not so vigorous—as much seeds of the Spirit's planting, but not yet so fruitful. And if any one asks how they are to become stronger, I say it must be by the same process by which all things having life increase—they must grow. And this is what I mean by "growth in grace."[1]

Let us turn away from the things I have been discussing to a more practical view of the great subject before us. I want men to look at "growth in grace" as a thing of infinite importance to the soul. I believe, whatever others may think, that our best interests are concerned in a right view of the question—Do we grow?

(a) Let us know then that "growth in grace" is the best evidence of spiritual *health* and prosperity. In a child, or a flower, or a tree, we are all aware that when there is no growth there is something wrong. Healthy life in an animal or vegetable will always show itself by progress and increase. It is just the same with our souls. If they are progressing and doing well they will grow.[2]

(b) Let us know, furthermore, that "growth in grace" is one way to be *happy* in our religion. God has wisely linked together our comfort and our increase in holiness. He has graciously made it our interest to press on and aim high in our Christianity. There is a vast difference between the amount of sensible enjoyment which one believer has in his religion compared to another. But you may be sure that ordinarily the man who feels the most "joy and peace in believing," and has the clearest witness of the Spirit in his heart, is the man who grows.

(c) Let us know, furthermore, that "growth in grace" is one secret of *usefulness* to others. Our influence on others for good depends greatly on what they see in us. The children of the world measure Christianity quite as much by their eyes as by their ears. The Christian who is always at a standstill, to all appearances the same man, with the same little faults, and weaknesses, and besetting sins, and petty infirmities, is seldom the Christian who does much good. The man who shakes and stirs minds, and sets the world thinking, is the believer who is continually improving and going forward. Men think there is life and reality when they see growth.[3]

(d) Let us know, furthermore, that "growth in grace" *pleases God.* It may seem a wonderful thing, no doubt, that anything done by such creatures as we are can give pleasure to the Most High God. But so it is. The Scripture speaks of walking so as to "please God." The Scripture says there are sacrifices with which "God is well-pleased" (1 Thess. 4:1; Heb. 13:16). The husbandman loves to see the plants on which he has bestowed labour flourishing and bearing fruit. It cannot but disappoint and grieve him to see them stunted and standing still. Now what does our Lord Himself say? "I am the true vine, and My Father is the husbandman."—"Herein is My Father glorified, that ye bear much fruit; so shall ye be My disciples" (John 15:1, 8). The Lord takes pleasure in all His people—but specially in those that grow.

(e) Let us know, above all, that "growth in grace" is not only a thing *possible,* but a thing for which believers are *accountable.* To tell an unconverted man, dead in sins, to "grow in grace" would doubtless be absurd. To tell a believer, who is quickened and alive to God, to grow, is only summoning him to a plain Scriptural duty. He has a new principle within him, and it is a solemn duty not to quench it. Neglect of growth robs him of privileges, grieves the Spirit, and makes the chariot wheels of his soul move heavily. Whose fault is it, I should like to know, if a believer does not grow in grace? The fault, I am sure, cannot be laid on God. He delights to "give more grace"; He "hath pleasure in the prosperity of His servants" (James 4:6; Ps. 35:27). The fault, no doubt, is our own. We ourselves are to blame, and none else, if we do not grow.

II. The second point I propose to establish is this: *There are marks by which growth in grace may be known.*

Let me take it for granted that we do not question the reality of growth in grace and its vast importance.—So far so good. But you now want to know how any one may find out whether he is growing in grace or not? I answer that question, in the first place, by observing that we are very poor judges of our own condition, and that bystanders often know us better than we know ourselves. But I answer further, that there are undoubtedly certain great marks and signs of growth in grace, and that wherever you see these marks you see a "growing" soul. I will now proceed to place some of these marks before you in order.

(a) One mark of "growth in grace" is increased *humility*. The man whose soul is "growing," feels his own sinfulness and unworthiness more every year. He is ready to say with Job, "I am vile,"—and with Abraham, "I am dust and ashes,"—and with Jacob, "I am not worthy of the least of all Thy mercies,"—and with David, "I am a worm,"—and with Isaiah, "I am a man of unclean lips,"—and with Peter, "I am a sinful man, O Lord" (Job 40:4; Gen. 18:27; 32:10; Ps. 22:6; Isa. 6:5; Luke 5:8). The nearer he draws to God, and the more he sees of God's holiness and perfection, the more thoroughly is he sensible of his own countless imperfections. The further he journeys in the way to heaven, the more he understands what St. Paul means when he says, "I am not already perfect,"—"I am not meet to be called an Apostle,"—"I am less than the least of all saints,"—"I am chief of sinners" (Phil. 3:12; 1 Cor. 15:9; Eph. 3:8; 1 Tim. 1:15). The riper he is for glory, the more, like the ripe corn, he hangs down his head. The brighter and clearer is his light, the more he sees of the shortcomings and infirmities of his own heart. When first converted, he would tell you he saw but little of them compared to what he sees now. Would anyone know whether he is growing in grace? Be sure that you look within for increased humility.[4]

(b) Another mark of "growth in grace" is increased *faith and love towards our Lord Jesus Christ.* The man whose soul is "growing," finds more in Christ to rest upon every year, and rejoices more that he has such a Saviour. No doubt he saw much in Him when first he believed. His faith laid hold on the atonement of Christ and gave him hope.—But as he grows in grace he sees a thousand things in Christ of which at first he never dreamed. His love and power—His heart and His intentions—His offices as Substitute, Intercessor, Priest, Advocate, Physician, Shepherd, and Friend, unfold themselves to a growing soul in an unspeakable manner. In short, he discovers a suitableness in Christ to the wants of his soul, of which the half was once not known to him. Would anyone know if he is growing in grace? Then let him look within for increased knowledge of Christ.

(c) Another mark of "growth in grace" is increased *holiness of life and conversation*. The man whose soul is "growing" gets more dominion over sin, the world, and the devil every year. He becomes more careful about his temper, his words, and his actions. He is more watchful over his conduct in every relation of life. He strives more to be conformed to the image of Christ in all things, and to follow Him as his example, as well as to trust in Him as his Saviour. He is not content with old attainments and former grace. He forgets the things that are behind and reaches forth unto those things which are before, making "Higher!" "Upward!" "Forward!" "Onward!" his continual motto (Phil. 3:13). On earth he thirsts and longs to have a will more entirely in unison with God's will. In heaven the chief thing that he looks for, next to the presence of Christ, is complete separation from all sin. Would anyone know if he is growing in grace? Then let him look within for increased holiness.[5]

(d) Another mark of "growth in grace" is increased *spirituality of taste and mind*. The man whose soul is "growing" takes more interest in spiritual things every year. He does not neglect his duty in the world. He discharges faithfully, diligently, and conscientiously every relation of life, whether at home or abroad. But the things he loves best are spiritual things. The ways, and fashions, and amusements, and recreations of the world have a continually decreasing place in his heart. He does not condemn them as downright sinful, nor say that those who have anything to do with them are going to hell. He only feels that they have a constantly diminishing hold on his own affections, and gradually seem smaller and more trifling in his eyes. Spiritual companions, spiritual occupations, spiritual conversation, appear of ever-increasing value to him. Would anyone know if he is growing in grace? Then let him look within for increasing spirituality of taste.[6]

(e) Another mark of "growth in grace" is increase of *charity*. The man whose soul is "growing" is more full of love every year—of love to all men, but especially of love towards the brethren. His love will show itself actively in a growing disposition to do kindnesses, to take trouble for others, to be good-natured to everybody, to be generous, sympathizing, thoughtful, tender-hearted, and considerate. It will show itself passively in a growing disposition to be meek and patient toward all men, to put up with provocation and not stand upon rights, to bear and forbear much rather than quarrel. A growing soul will try to put the best construction on other people's conduct, and to believe all things and hope all things, even to the end. There is no surer mark of backsliding and falling off in grace than an increasing disposition to find fault, pick holes, and see weak points in others. Would anyone know if he is growing in grace? Then let him look within for increasing charity.

(f) One more mark of "growth in grace" is increased *zeal and diligence in trying to do good to souls*. The man who is really "growing" will take greater interest in the salvation of sinners every year. Missions at home and abroad, efforts to increase religious light and diminish religious darkness—all these things will every year have a greater place in his attention. He will not become "weary in well-doing" because he does not see every effort succeed. He will not *care* less for the progress of Christ's cause on earth as he grows older, though he will learn to *expect* less. He will just work on, whatever the result may be—giving, praying, preaching, speaking, visiting, according to his position—and count his work its own reward. One of the surest marks of spiritual decline is a decreased interest about the souls of others and the growth of Christ's kingdom. Would any one know whether he is growing in grace? Then let him look within for increased concern about the salvation of souls.

Such are the most trustworthy marks of growth in grace. Let us examine them carefully, and consider what we know about them. I can well believe that they will not please some professing Christians in the present day. Those high-flying religionists, whose only notion of Christianity is that of a state of perpetual joy and ecstasy—who tell you that they have got far beyond the region of conflict and soul-humiliation—such persons no doubt will regard the marks I have laid down as "legal," "carnal," and "gendering to bondage." I cannot help that. I call no man master in these things. I only wish my statements to be tried in the balance of Scripture. And I firmly believe that what I have said is not only Scriptural, but agreeable to the experience of the most eminent saints in every age. Show me a man in whom the six marks I have mentioned can be found. He is the man who can give a satisfactory answer to the question, DO WE GROW?

III. The third and last thing I propose to consider is this:—*The means that must be used by those who desire to grow in grace*. The words of St. James must never be forgotten: "Every good gift and every perfect gift is from above, and cometh down from the Father of lights" (James 1:17). This is no doubt as true of growth in grace as it is of everything else. It is the "gift of God." But still it must always be kept in mind that God is pleased to work by means. God has ordained means as well as ends. He that would grow in grace must use the means of growth.[7]

This is a point, I fear, which is too much overlooked by believers. Many admire growth in grace in others, and wish that they themselves were like them. But they seem to suppose that those who grow are what they are by some special gift or grant from God, and that as this gift is not bestowed on themselves they must be content to sit still. This is a grievous delusion, and one against which I desire to testify with all my might. I wish it to be distinctly understood that growth in grace is bound up with the use of means within the reach of all believers, and that, as a general rule, growing souls are what they are because they use these means.

Let me ask the special attention of my readers while I try to set forth in order the means of growth. Cast away for ever the vain thought that if a believer does not grow in grace it is not his fault. Settle it in your mind that a believer, a man quickened by the Spirit, is not a mere dead creature, but a being of mighty capacities and responsibilities. Let the words of Solomon sink down into your heart: "The soul of the diligent shall be made fat" (Prov. 13:4).

(a) One thing essential to growth in grace is *diligence in the use of private means of grace.* By these I understand such means as a man must use by himself alone, and no one can use for him. I include under this head private prayer, private reading of the Scriptures, and private meditation and self-examination. The man who does not take pains about these three things must never expect to grow. Here are the roots of true Christianity. Wrong *here,* a man is wrong all the way through! Here is the whole reason why many professing Christians never seem to get on. They are careless and slovenly about their private prayers. They read their Bibles but little, and with very little heartiness of spirit. They give themselves no time for self-inquiry and quiet thought about the state of their souls.

It is useless to conceal from ourselves that the age we live in is full of peculiar dangers. It is an age of great activity, and of much hurry, bustle, and excitement in religion. Many are "running to and fro," no doubt, and "knowledge is increased" (Dan. 12:4). Thousands are ready enough for public meetings, sermon-hearing, or anything else in which there is "sensation." Few appear to remember the absolute necessity of making time to "commune with our hearts, and be still" (Ps. 4:4). But without this there is seldom any deep spiritual prosperity. I suspect that English Christians two hundred years ago read their Bibles more, and were more frequently alone with God, than they are in the present day. Let us remember this point! Private religion must receive our first attention, if we wish our souls to grow.

(b) Another thing which is essential to growth in grace *is carefulness in the use of public means of grace*. By these I understand such means as a man has within his reach as a member of Christ's visible Church. Under this head I include the ordinances of regular Sunday worship, the uniting with God's people in common prayer and praise, the preaching of the Word, and the sacrament of the Lord's Supper. I firmly believe that the *manner* in which these public means of grace are used has much to say to the prosperity of a believer's soul. It is easy to use them in a cold and heartless way. The very familiarity of them is apt to make us careless. The regular return of the same voice, and the same kind of words, and the same ceremonies, is likely to make us sleepy, and callous, and unfeeling. Here is a snare into which too many professing Christians fall. If we would grow we must be on our guard here. Here is a matter in which the Spirit is often grieved and saints take great damage. Let us strive to use the old prayers, and sing the old hymns, and kneel at the old communion-rail, and hear the old truths preached, with as much freshness and appetite as in the year we first believed. It is a sign of bad health when a person loses relish for his food; and it is a sign of spiritual decline when we lose our appetite for means of grace. Whatever we do about public means, let us always do it "with our might" (Eccles. 9:10). This is the way to grow!

(c) Another thing essential to growth in grace is *watchfulness over our conduct in the little matters of everyday life*. Our tempers, our tongues, the discharge of our several relations of life, our employment of time—each and all must be vigilantly attended to if we wish our souls to prosper. Life is made up of days, and days of hours, and the little things of every hour are never so little as to be beneath the care of a Christian. When a tree begins to decay at root or heart, the mischief is first seen at the extreme end of the little branches. "He that despiseth little things," says an uninspired writer, "shall fall by little and little." That witness is true. Let others despise us, if they like, and call us precise and over-careful. Let us patiently hold on our way, remembering that "we serve a precise God," that our Lord's example is to be copied in the least things as well as the greatest, and that we must "take up our cross daily" and hourly, rather than sin. We must aim to have a Christianity which, like the sap of a tree, runs through every twig and leaf of our character, and sanctifies all. This is one way to grow!

(d) Another thing which is essential to growth in grace is *caution about the company we keep and the friendships we form*. Nothing perhaps affects a man's character more than the company he keeps. We catch the ways and tone of those we live and talk with, and unhappily get harm far more easily than good. Disease is infectious, but health is not. Now if a professing Christian deliberately chooses to be intimate with those who are not friends of God and who cling to the world, his soul is sure to take harm. It is hard enough to serve Christ under any circumstances in such a world as this. But it is doubly hard to do it if we are friends of the thoughtless and ungodly. Mistakes in friendship or marriage-engagements are the whole reason why some have entirely ceased to grow. "Evil communications corrupt good manners." "The friendship of the world is enmity with God" (1 Cor. 15:33; James 4:4). Let us seek friends that will stir us up about our prayers, our Bible-reading, and our employment of time—about our souls, our salvation, and a world to come. Who can tell the good that a friend's word in season may do, or the harm that it may stop? This is one way to grow.[8]

(e) There is one more thing which is absolutely essential to growth in grace—and that is *regular and habitual communion with the Lord Jesus.* In saying this, let no one suppose for a minute that I am referring to the Lord's Supper. I mean nothing of the kind. I mean that daily habit of intercourse between the believer and his Saviour, which can only be carried on by faith, prayer, and meditation. It is a habit, I fear, of which many believers know little. A man may be a believer and have his feet on the rock, and yet live far below his privileges. It is possible to have "union" with Christ, and yet to have little if any "communion" with Him. But, for all that, there is such a thing.

The names and offices of Christ, as laid down in Scripture, appear to me to show unmistakably that this "communion" between the saint and his Saviour is not a mere fancy, but a real true thing. Between the "Bridegroom" and his bride—between the "Head" and His members—between the "Physician" and His patients—between the "Advocate" and His clients—between the "Shepherd" and His sheep—between the "Master" and His scholars—there is evidently implied a habit of familiar intercourse, of daily application for things needed, of daily pouring out and unburdening our hearts and minds. Such a habit of dealing with Christ is clearly something more than a vague general trust in the work that Christ did for sinners. It is getting *close* to Him, and laying hold on Him with confidence, as a loving, personal Friend. This is what I mean by communion.

Now I believe that no man will ever grow in grace who does not know something experimentally of the habit of "communion." We must not be content with a general orthodox knowledge that justification is by faith and not by works, and that we put our trust in Christ. We must go further than this. We must seek to have personal intimacy with the Lord Jesus, and to deal with Him as a man deals with a loving friend. We must realize what it is to turn to Him first in every need, to talk to Him about every difficulty, to consult Him about every step, to spread before Him all our sorrows, to get Him to share in all our joys, to do all as in His sight, and to go through every day leaning on and looking to Him. This is the way that St. Paul lived: "The life which I now live in the flesh I live by the faith of the Son of God." "To me to live is Christ" (Gal. 2:20; Phil. 1:21). It is ignorance of this way of living that makes so many see no beauty in the book of Canticles. But it is the man who lives in this way, who keeps up constant communion with Christ—this is the man, I say emphatically, whose soul will grow.

I leave the subject of growth in grace here. Far more might be said about it, if time permitted. But I have said enough, I hope, to convince my readers that the subject is one of vast importance.—Let me wind up all with some practical applications.

(1) This book may fall into the hands of some who *know nothing whatever about growth in grace.* They have little or no concern about religion. A little proper Sunday Church-going or chapel-going makes up the sum and substance of their Christianity. They are without spiritual life, and of course they cannot at present grow. Are you one of these people? If you are, you are in a pitiable condition.

Years are slipping away and time is flying. Graveyards are filling up and families are thinning. Death and judgment are getting nearer to us all. And yet you live like one asleep about your soul! What madness! What folly! What suicide can be worse than this?

Awake before it be too late; awake, and arise from the dead, and live to God. Turn to Him who is sitting at the right hand of God, to be your Saviour and Friend. Turn to Christ, and cry mightily to Him about your soul. There is yet hope! He that called Lazarus from the grave is not changed. He that commanded the widow's son at Nain to arise from his bier can do miracles yet for your soul. Seek Him at once: seek Christ, if you would not be lost for ever. Do not stand still talking, and meaning, and intending, and wishing, and hoping. Seek Christ that you may live, and that living you may grow.

(2) This book may fall into the hands of some who *ought to know something of growth in grace,* but at present know nothing at all. They have made little or no progress since they were first converted. They seem to have "settled on their lees" (Zeph. 1:12). They go on from year to year content with old grace, old experience, old knowledge, old faith, old

measure of attainment, old religious expressions, old set phrases. Like the Gibeonites, their bread is always mouldy, and their shoes are patched and clouted. They never appear to get on. Are you one of these people? If you are, you are living far below your privileges and responsibilities. It is high time to examine yourself.

If you have reason to hope that you are a true believer and yet do not grow in grace, there must be a fault, and a serious fault somewhere. It cannot be the will of God that your soul should stand still. "He giveth more grace." He "takes pleasure in the prosperity of His servants" (James 4:6; Ps. 35:27). It cannot be for your own happiness or usefulness that your soul should stand still. Without growth you will never rejoice in the Lord (Phil. 4:4). Without growth you will never do good to others. Surely this want of growth is a serious matter! It should raise in you great searchings of heart. There must be some "secret thing" (Job 15:11). There must be some cause.

Take the advice I give you. Resolve this very day that you will find out the reason of your standstill condition. Probe with a faithful and firm hand every corner of your soul. Search from one end of the camp to the other, till you find out the Achan who is weakening your hands. Begin with an application to the Lord Jesus Christ, the great Physician of souls, and ask Him to heal the secret ailment within you, whatever it may be. Begin as if you had never applied to Him before, and ask for grace to cut off the right hand and pluck out the right eye. But never, never be content, if your soul does not grow. For your peace sake, for your usefulness sake, for the honour of your Maker's cause, resolve to find out the reason why.

(3) This book may fall into the hands of some who *are really growing in grace,* but are not aware of it, and will not allow it. Their very growth is the reason why they do not see their growth! Their continual increase in humility prevents them feeling that they get on.[9] Like Moses, when he came down from the mount from communing with God, their faces shine. And yet, like Moses, they are not aware of it (Ex. 34:29). Such Christians, I grant freely, are not common. But here and there such are to be found. Like angels' visits, they are few and far between. Happy is the neighbourhood where such growing Christians live! To meet them and see them and be in their company, is like meeting and seeing a bit of "heaven upon earth."

Now what shall I say to such people? What can I say? What ought I to say? Shall I bid them awake to a consciousness of their growth and be pleased with it? I will do nothing of the kind.—Shall I tell them to plume themselves on their own attainments, and look at their own superiority to others? God forbid! I will do nothing of the kind.—To tell them such things would do them no good. To tell them such things, above all, would be useless waste of time. If there is any one feature about a growing soul which specially marks him, it is his deep sense of his own unworthiness. He never sees anything to be praised in himself. He only feels that he is an unprofitable servant and the chief of sinners. It is the righteous, in the picture of the judgment-day, who say, "Lord, when saw we Thee an hungred, and fed Thee?" (Matt. 25:37). Extremes do indeed meet strangely sometimes. The conscience-hardened sinner and the eminent saint are in one respect singularly alike. Neither of them fully realizes his own condition. The one does not see his own sin, nor the other his own grace!

But shall I say nothing to growing Christians? Is there no word of counsel I can address to them? The sum and substance of all that I can say is to be found in two sentences: "Go forward!" "Go on!"

We can never have too much humility, too much faith in Christ, too much holiness, too much spirituality of mind, too much charity, too much zeal in doing good to others. Then let us be continually forgetting the things behind, and reaching forth unto the things before (Phil. 3:13). The best of Christians in these matters is infinitely below the perfect pattern of his Lord. Whatever the world may please to say, we may be sure there is no danger of any of us becoming "too good."

Let us cast to the winds as idle talk the common notion that it is possible to be "extreme" and go "too far" in religion. This is a favourite lie of the devil, and one which he circulates with vast industry. No doubt there are enthusiasts and fanatics to be found who bring evil report upon Christianity by their extravagances and follies. But if any one means to say that a mortal man can be too humbled, too charitable, too holy, or too diligent in doing good, he must either be an infidel or a fool. In serving pleasure and money it is easy to go too far. But in following the things which make up true religion, and in serving Christ there can be no extreme.

Let us never measure our religion by that of others, and think we are doing enough if we have gone beyond our neighbours. This is another snare of the devil. Let us mind our own business. "What is that to thee?" said our master on a certain occasion: "Follow thou Me" (John 21:22). Let us follow on, aiming at nothing short of perfection. Let us follow on, making Christ's life and character our only pattern and example. Let us follow on, remembering daily that at our best we are miserable sinners. Let us follow on, and never forget that it signifies nothing whether we are better than others or not. At our very best we are far worse than we ought to be. There will always be room for improvement in us. We shall be debtors to Christ's mercy and grace to the very last. Then let us leave off looking at others and comparing ourselves with others. We shall find enough to do if we look at our own hearts.

Last, but not least, if we know anything of growth in grace, and desire to know more, let us not be surprised if we have to go through much trial and affliction in this world. I firmly believe it is the experience of nearly all the most eminent saints. Like their blessed Master they have been "men of sorrows, acquainted with grief," and "perfected through sufferings" (Isa. 53:3; Heb. 2:10). It is a striking saying of our Lord, "Every branch in Me that beareth fruit, My Father purgeth it, that it may bring forth more fruit" (John 15:2). It is a melancholy fact, that constant temporal prosperity, as a general rule, is injurious to a believer's soul. We cannot stand it. Sickness, and losses, and crosses, and anxieties, and disappointments seem absolutely needful to keep us humble, watchful, and spiritual-minded. They are as needful as the pruning knife to the vine, and the refiner's furnace to the gold. They are not pleasant to flesh and blood. We do not like them, and often do not see their meaning. "No chastening for the present seemeth to be joyous, but grievous: neverthe-less, *afterward*, it yieldeth the peaceable fruit of righteousness" (Heb. 12:11). We shall find that all worked for our good when we reach heaven. Let these thoughts abide in our minds, if we love growth in grace. When days of darkness come upon us, let us not count it a strange thing. Rather let us remember that lessons are learned on such days which would never have been learned in sunshine. Let us say to ourselves, "This also is for my profit, that I may be a partaker of God's holiness. It is sent in love. I am in God's best school. Correction is instruction. This is meant to make me grow."

I leave the subject of growth in grace here. I trust I have said enough to set some readers thinking about it. All things are growing older: the world is growing old; we ourselves are growing older. A few more sum-mers, a few more winters, a few more sicknesses, a few more sorrows, a few more weddings, a few more funerals, a few more meetings, and a few more partings, and then—what? Why the grass will be growing over our graves!

Now would it not be well to look within, and put to our souls a simple question? In religion, in the things that concern our peace, in the great matter of personal holiness, are we getting on? DO WE GROW?

7

"ASSURANCE"

"I am now ready to be offered, and the time of my departure is at hand. I have fought a good fight, I have finished my course, I have kept the faith: Henceforth there is laid up for me a crown of righteousness, which the Lord, the righteous Judge, shall give me at that day: and not to me only, but unto all them also that love His appearing."

— 2 TIMOTHY 4:6-8

In the words of Scripture which head this page, we see the Apostle Paul looking three ways—downward, backward, forward; downward to the grave—backward to his own ministry—forward to that great day, the day of judgment!

It will do us good to stand by the Apostle's side a few minutes, and mark the words he uses. Happy is that soul who can look where Paul looked, and then speak as Paul spoke!

(a) He looks *downward* to the grave, and he does it without fear. Hear what he says:—

"I am ready to be offered."—I am like an animal brought to the place of sacrifice, and bound with cords to the very horns of the altar. The drink-offering, which generally accompanies the oblation, is already being poured out. The last ceremonies have been gone through. Every preparation has been made. It only remains to receive the death-blow, and then all is over.

"The time of my departure is at hand."—I am like a ship about to unmoor and put to sea. All on board is ready. I only wait to have the moorings cast off that fasten me to the shore, and I shall then set sail, and begin my voyage.

These are remarkable words to come from the lips of a child of Adam like ourselves! Death is a solemn thing, and never so much so as when we see it close at hand. The grave is a chilling, heart-sickening place, and it is vain to pretend it has no terrors. Yet here is a mortal man who can look calmly into the narrow "house appointed for all living," and say, while we stand upon the brink, "I see it all, and am not afraid."

(b) Let us listen to him again. He looks *backward* to his ministerial life, and he does it without shame. Hear what he says:—

"I have fought a good fight."—There he speaks as a soldier. I have fought that good fight with the world, the flesh, and the devil, from which so many shrink and draw back.

"I have finished my course."—There he speaks as one who has run for a prize. I have run the race marked out for me. I have gone over the ground appointed for me, however rough and steep. I have not turned aside because of difficulties, nor been discouraged by the length of the way. I am at last in sight of the goal.

"I have kept the faith."—There he speaks as a steward. I have held fast that glorious Gospel which was committed to my trust. I have not mingled it with man's traditions, nor spoiled its simplicity by adding my own inventions, nor allowed others to adulterate it without withstanding them to the face. "As a soldier—a runner—a steward," he seems to say, "I am not ashamed."

That Christian is happy who, as he quits the world, can leave such testimony behind him. A good conscience will save no man—wash away no sin—nor lift us one hair's breadth toward heaven. Yet a good conscience will be found a pleasant visitor at our bedside in a dying hour. There is a fine passage in *Pilgrim's Progress* which describes Old Honest's passage across the river of death. "The river," says Bunyan, "at that time overflowed its banks in some places; but Mr. Honest in his lifetime had spoken to one Good Conscience to meet him there; the which he also did, and lent him his hand, and so helped him over." We may be sure there is a mine of truth in that passage.

(c) Let us hear the Apostle once more. He looks *forward* to the great day of reckoning, and he does it without doubt. Mark his words:—

"Henceforth there is laid up for me a crown of righteousness, which the Lord, the righteous Judge, shall give me at that day: and not to me only, but unto all them also that love His appearing."—"A glorious reward," he seems to say, "is ready and laid up in store for me—even that crown which is only given to the righteous. In the great day of judgment the Lord shall give this crown to me, and to all beside me who have loved

Him as an unseen Saviour, and longed to see Him face to face. My work on earth is over. This one thing now remains for me to look forward to, and nothing more."

Let us observe that the Apostle speaks without any hesitation or distrust. He regards the crown as a sure thing, as his own already. He declares with unfaltering confidence his firm persuasion that the righteous Judge will give it to him. Paul was no stranger to all the circumstances and accompaniments of that solemn day to which he referred. The great white throne—the assembled world—the open books—the revealing of all secrets—the listening angels—the awful sentence—the eternal separation of the lost and saved—all these were things with which he was well acquainted. But none of these things moved him. His strong faith overleaped them all, and he only saw Jesus, his all-prevailing Advocate, and the blood of sprinkling, and sin washed away. "A crown," he says, "is laid up for me." "The Lord Himself *shall* give it to me." He speaks as if he saw it all with his own eyes.

Such are the main things which these verses contain. Of most of them I shall not speak, because I want to confine myself to the special subject of this paper. I shall only try to consider one point in the passage. That point is the strong "assurance of hope," with which the Apostle looks forward to his own prospects in the day of judgment.

I shall do this the more readily, because of the great importance which attaches to the subject of assurance, and the great neglect with which, I humbly conceive, it is often treated in this day.

But I shall do it at the same time with fear and trembling. I feel that I am treading on very difficult ground, and that it is easy to speak rashly and unscripturally in this matter. The road between truth and error is here especially a narrow pass; and if I shall be enabled to do good to some without doing harm to others, I shall be very thankful.

There are four things I wish to bring forward in speaking of the subject of assurance, and it may clear our way if I name them at once.

I. First, then, I will try to show *that an assured hope, such as Paul here expresses, is a true and Scriptural thing.*

II. Secondly, I will make this broad concession—*that a man may never arrive at this assured hope, and yet be saved.*

III. Thirdly, I will give some reasons why *an assured hope is exceedingly to be desired.*

IV. Lastly, I will try to point out some causes *why an assured hope is so seldom attained.*

I ask special attention of all who take an interest in the great subject of this volume. If I am not greatly mistaken, there is a very close connection between true holiness and assurance. Before I close this paper I hope to show my readers the nature of that connection. At present, I content myself with saying, that where there is the most holiness, there is generally the most assurance.

I. First, then, I will try to show that *an assured hope is a true and Scriptural thing.*

Assurance, such as Paul expresses in the verses which head this paper, is not a mere fancy or feeling. It is not the result of high animal spirits, or a sanguine temperament of body. It is a positive gift of the Holy Ghost, bestowed without reference to men's bodily frames or constitutions, and a gift which *every believer* in Christ ought to aim at and seek after.

In matters like these, the first question is this—What saith the Scripture? I answer that question without the least hesitation. The Word of God appears to me to teach distinctly that a believer may arrive at an assured confidence with regard to his own salvation.

I lay it down fully and broadly, as God's truth, that a true Christian, a converted man, may reach such a comfortable degree of faith in Christ, that in general he shall feel entirely confident as to the pardon and safety of his soul—shall seldom be troubled with doubts—seldom be distracted with fears—seldom be distressed by anxious questionings—and, in short, though vexed by many an inward conflict with sin, shall look forward to death without trembling, and to judgment without dismay.[1] This, I say, is the doctrine of the Bible.

Such is my account of assurance. I will ask my readers to mark it well. I say neither less nor more than I have here laid down.

Now such a statement as this is often disputed and denied. Many cannot see the truth of it at all.

The Church of Rome denounces assurance in the most unmeasured terms. The Council of Trent declares roundly that a "believer's assurance of the pardon of his sins is a vain and ungodly confidence"; and Cardinal Bellarmine, the well-known champion of Romanism, calls it "a prime error of heretics."

The vast majority of the worldly and thoughtless Christians among ourselves oppose the doctrine of assurance. It offends and annoys them to hear of it. They do not like others to feel comfortable and sure, because they never feel so themselves. Ask them whether their sins are forgiven, and they will probably tell you they do not know! That *they* cannot receive the doctrine of assurance is certainly no marvel.

But there are also some true believers who reject assurance, or shrink from it as a doctrine fraught with danger. They consider it borders on presumption. They seem to think it a proper humility never to feel sure, never to be confident, and to live in a certain degree of doubt and suspense about their souls. This is to be regretted, and does much harm.

I frankly allow there are some *presumptuous* persons who profess to feel a confidence for which they have no Scriptural warrant. There are always some people who think well of themselves when God thinks ill, just as there are some who think ill of themselves when God thinks well. There always will be such. There never yet was a Scriptural truth without abuses and counterfeits. God's election—man's impotence—salvation by grace—all are alike abused. There will be fanatics and enthusiasts as long as the world stands. But, for all this, assurance is a reality and a true thing; and God's children must not let themselves be driven from the use of a truth, merely because it is abused.[2]

My answer to all who deny the existence of real, well-grounded assurance, is simply this—What saith the Scripture? If assurance be not there, I have not another word to say.

But does not Job say, "I *know* that my Redeemer liveth, and that he shall stand at the latter day upon the earth; and though after my skin worms destroy this body, yet in my flesh shall I see God"? (Job 19:25-26).

Does not David say, "Though I walk through the valley of the shadow of death, *I will fear no evil:* for Thou art with me; Thy rod and Thy staff they comfort me"? (Ps. 23:4).

Does not Isaiah say, "Thou wilt keep him in *perfect peace* whose mind is stayed on Thee, because he trusteth in Thee"? (Isa. 26:3).

And again, "The work of righteousness shall be peace; and the effect of righteousness quietness, and *assurance* for ever" (Isa. 32:17).

Does not Paul say to the Romans, "I am *persuaded* that neither death, nor life, nor angels, nor principalities, nor powers, nor things present, nor things to come, nor height, nor depth, nor any other creature, shall be able to separate us from the love of God, which is in Christ Jesus our Lord"? (Rom. 8:38-39).

Does he not say to the Corinthians, "We *know* that if our earthly house of this tabernacle were dissolved, we have a building of God, an house not made with hands, eternal in the heavens"? (2 Cor. 5:1).

And again, "We are always *confident,* knowing that, whilst we are at home in the body, we are absent from the Lord"? (2 Cor. 5:6).

Does he not say to Timothy, "I know whom I have believed, and am *persuaded* that He is able to keep that which I have committed to Him"? (2 Tim. 1:12).

And does he not speak to the Colossians of "the full assurance of understanding" (Col. 2:2), and to the Hebrews of the "full assurance of faith," and the "full assurance of hope"? (Heb. 6:11; 10:22).

Does not Peter say expressly, "Give diligence to make your calling and election *sure*"? (2 Pet. 1:10).

Does not John say, "We *know* that we have passed from death unto life"? (1 John 3:14).

And again, "These things have I written unto you that believe on the name of the Son of God, that ye may *know* that ye have eternal life" (1 John 5:13).

And again, "We *know* that we are of God" (1 John 5:19).

What shall we say to these things? I desire to speak with all humility on any controverted point. I feel that I am only a poor fallible child of Adam myself. But I must say that in the passages I have just quoted I see something far higher than the mere "hopes" and "trusts," with which so many believers appear content in this day. I see the language of persuasion, confidence, knowledge—nay, I may almost say, of certainty. And I feel, for my own part, if I may take these Scriptures in their plain obvious meaning, *the doctrine of assurance is true.*

But my answer, furthermore, to all who dislike the doctrine of assurance, as bordering on presumption, is this:—It can hardly be presumption to tread in the steps of Peter and Paul, of Job and of John. They were all eminently humble and lowly-minded men, if ever any were; and yet they all speak of their own state with an assured hope. Surely this should teach us that deep humility and strong assurance are perfectly compatible, and that there is not any necessary connection between spiritual confidence and pride.[3]

My answer, furthermore, is that many have attained to such an assured hope as our text expresses, even in modern times. I will not concede for a moment that it was a peculiar privilege confined to the Apostolic day. There have been in our own land many believers, who have appeared to walk in almost uninterrupted fellowship with the Father and the Son—who have seemed to enjoy an almost unceasing sense of the light of God's reconciled countenance shining down upon them, and have left their experience on record. I could mention well-known names, if space permitted. The thing has been, and is—and that is enough.

My answer, lastly, is, It cannot be wrong to feel confidently in a matter where God speaks unconditionally—to believe decidedly when God promises decidedly—to have a sure persuasion of pardon and peace when we rest on the word and oath of Him that never changes. It is an utter mistake to suppose that the believer who feels assurance is resting on anything he sees in himself. He simply leans on the Mediator of the New Covenant, and the Scripture of truth. He believes the Lord Jesus means what He says, and *takes Him at His word*. Assurance after all is no more than a *full-grown faith;* a masculine faith that grasps Christ's promise with both hands—a faith that argues like the good centurion, If the Lord "speak the word only," I am healed. Wherefore then should I doubt? (Matt. 8:8).[4]

We may be sure that Paul was the last man in the world to build his assurance on anything of his own. He who could write himself down "chief of sinners" (1 Tim. 1:15), had a deep sense of his guilt and corruption. But then he had a still deeper sense of the length and breadth of Christ's righteousness imputed to him.—He who could cry, "O wretched man that I am" (Rom. 7:24), had a clear view of the fountain of evil within his heart. But then he had a still clearer view of that other Fountain which can remove "all sin and uncleanness." He who thought himself "less than the least of all saints" (Eph. 3:8), had a lively and abiding feeling of his own weakness. But he had a still livelier feeling that Christ's promise, "My sheep shall never perish" (John 10:28), could not be broken.—Paul knew, if ever man did, that he was a poor, frail bark, floating on a stormy ocean. He saw, if any did, the rolling waves and roaring tempest by which he was surrounded. But then he looked away from self to Jesus, and was not afraid. He remembered that anchor within the veil, which is both "sure and steadfast" (Heb. 6:19). He remembered the word, and work, and constant intercession of Him that loved him and gave Himself for him. And this it was, and nothing else, that enabled him to say so boldly, "A crown is laid up for me, and the Lord shall give it to me"; and to conclude so surely, "The Lord will preserve me; I shall never be confounded."[5]

I may not dwell longer on this part of the subject. I think it will be allowed I have shown some good ground for the assertion I made, that assurance is a true thing.

II. I pass on to the second thing I spoke of. I said, *a believer may never arrive at this assured hope, which Paul expresses, and yet be saved.*

I grant this most freely. I do not dispute it for a moment. I would not desire to make one contrite heart sad that God has not made sad, or to discourage one fainting child of God, or to leave the impression that men have no part or lot in Christ, except they feel assurance.

A person may have saving faith in Christ, and yet never enjoy an assured hope, such as the Apostle Paul enjoyed. To believe and have a glimmering hope of acceptance is one thing; to have "joy and peace" in our believing, and abound in hope, is quite another. All God's children have faith; not all have assurance. I think this ought never to be forgotten.

I know some great and good men have held a different opinion. I believe that many excellent ministers of the Gospel, at whose feet I would gladly sit, do not allow the distinction I have stated. But I desire to call no man master. I dread as much as any one the idea of healing the wounds of conscience slightly; but I should think any other view than that I have given, a most uncomfortable Gospel to preach, and one very likely to keep souls back a long time from the gate of life.[6]

I do not shrink from saying that by grace a man may have sufficient faith to flee to Christ; sufficient faith really to lay hold on Him—really to trust in Him—really to be a child of God—really to be saved; and yet to his last day be never free from much anxiety, doubt, and fear.

"A letter," says an old writer, "may be written, which is not sealed; so grace may be written in the heart, yet the Spirit may not set the seal of assurance to it."

A child may be born heir to a great fortune, and yet never be aware of his riches; may live childish, die childish, and never know the greatness of his possessions. And so also a man may be a babe in Christ's family, think as a babe, speak as a babe, and, though saved, never enjoy a lively hope, or know the real privileges of his inheritance.

Let no man mistake my meaning when I dwell strongly on the reality, privilege, and importance of assurance. Do not do me the injustice to say, I teach that none are saved except such as can say with Paul, "I know and am persuaded—there is a crown laid up for me." I do not say so. I teach nothing of the kind.

Faith in the Lord Jesus Christ a man *must* have, beyond all question, if he is to be saved. I know no other way of access to the Father. I see no intimation of mercy, excepting through Christ. A man *must* feel his sins and lost estate—*must* come to Jesus for pardon and salvation—*must* rest his hope on Him, and on Him alone. But if he only has faith to do this, however weak and feeble that faith may be, I will engage, from Scripture warrants, he shall not miss heaven.

Never, never let us curtail the freeness of the glorious Gospel, or clip its fair proportions. Never let us make the gate more strait and the way more narrow than pride and the love of sin have made it already. The Lord Jesus is very pitiful, and of tender mercy. He does not regard the *quantity* of faith, but the *quality:* He does not measure its degree, but its truth. He will not break any bruised reed, nor quench any smoking flax. He will never let it be said that any perished at the foot of the cross. "Him that cometh unto Me," He says, "I will in no wise cast out" (John 6:37).[7]

Yes! Though a man's faith be no bigger than a grain of mustard seed, if it only brings him to Christ, and enables him to touch the hem of His garment, he shall be saved—saved as surely as the oldest saint in paradise—saved as completely and eternally as Peter, or John, or Paul. There are degrees in our sanctification. In our justification there are none. What is written, is written, and shall never fail: "Whosoever believeth on Him,"—not whosoever has a strong and mighty faith—"Whosoever *believeth* on Him shall not be ashamed" (Rom. 10:11).

But all this time, be it remembered, the poor believing soul may have no full assurance of his pardon and acceptance with God. He may be troubled with fear upon fear, and doubt upon doubt. He may have many an inward question, and many an anxiety—many a struggle, and many a misgiving—clouds and darkness—storm and tempest to the very end.

I will engage, I repeat, that bare simple faith in Christ shall save a man, though he may never attain to assurance; but I will not engage it shall bring him to heaven with strong and abounding consolations. I will engage it shall land him safe in harbour; but I will not engage he shall enter the harbour in full sail, confident and rejoicing. I shall not be surprised if he reaches his desired haven weather-beaten and tempest-tossed, scarcely realizing his own safety, till he opens his eyes in glory.

I believe it is of great importance to keep in view this distinction between faith and assurance. It explains things which an inquirer in religion sometimes finds it hard to understand.

Faith, let us remember, is the root, and assurance is the flower. Doubtless you can never have the flower without the root; but it is no less certain you may have the root and not the flower.

Faith is that poor trembling woman who came behind Jesus in the press, and touched the hem of His garment (Mark 5:27). Assurance is Stephen standing calmly in the midst of his murderers, and saying, "I see the heavens opened, and the Son of man standing on the right hand of God" (Acts 7:56).

Faith is the penitent thief, crying, "Lord, remember me" (Luke 23:42). Assurance is Job, sitting in the dust, covered with sores, saying, "I know that my Redeemer liveth" (Job 19:25); "Though He slay me, yet will I trust Him" (Job 13:15).

Faith is Peter's drowning cry, as he began to sink: "Lord, save me!"

(Matt. 14:30). Assurance is that same Peter declaring before the Council in after times, "This is the stone which was set at nought of your builders, which is become the head of the corner. Neither is there salvation in any other: for there is none other name under heaven given among men, whereby we must be saved" (Acts 4:11, 12).

Faith is the anxious, trembling voice, "Lord, I believe: help Thou my unbelief" (Mark 9:24). Assurance is the confident challenge, "Who shall lay anything to the charge of God's elect? Who is he that condemneth?" (Rom. 8:33, 34). Faith is Saul praying in the house of Judas at Damascus, sorrowful, blind, and alone (Acts 9:11). Assurance is Paul, the aged prisoner, looking calmly into the grave, and saying, "I know whom I have believed. There is a crown laid up for me" (2 Tim. 1:12; 4:8).

Faith is *life*. How great the blessing! Who can describe or realize the gulf between life and death? "A living dog is better than a dead lion" (Eccles. 9:4). And yet life may be weak, sickly, unhealthy, painful, trying, anxious, weary, burdensome, joyless, smileless to the very end. Assurance is *more than life*. It is health, strength, power, vigour, activity, energy, manliness, beauty.

It is not a question of "saved or not saved," that lies before us, but of "privilege or no privilege."—It is not a question of peace or no peace, but of great peace or little peace.—It is not a question between the wanderers of this world and the school of Christ; it is one that belongs only to the school: it is between the first form and the last.

He that has faith does *well*. Happy should I be, if I thought all readers of this paper had it. Blessed, thrice blessed are they that believe! They are safe. They are washed. They are justified. They are beyond the power of hell. Satan, with all his malice, shall never pluck them out of Christ's hand. But he that has assurance does *far better*—sees more, feels more, knows more, enjoys more, has more days like those spoken of in Deuteronomy, even "the days of heaven upon the earth" (Deut. 11:21).[8]

III. I pass on to the third thing of which I spoke. I will give *some reasons why an assured hope is exceedingly to be desired*.

I ask special attention to this point. I heartily wish that assurance was more sought after than it is. Too many among those who believe begin doubting and go on doubting, live doubting and die doubting, and go to heaven in a kind of mist.

It would ill become me to speak in a slighting way of "hopes" and "trusts." But I fear many of us sit down content with them, and go no further. I should like to see fewer "peradventurers" in the Lord's family, and more who could say, "I know and am persuaded." Oh, that all believers would covet the best gifts, and not be content with less! Many miss the full tide of blessedness the Gospel was meant to convey. Many keep themselves in a low and starved condition of soul, while their Lord is saying, "Eat and drink abundantly, O beloved." "Ask and receive, that your joy may be full" (Song 5:1; John 16:24).

(1) Let us remember then, for one thing, that assurance is to be desired, because of the *present comfort and peace it affords.*

Doubts and fears have power to spoil much of the happiness of a true believer in Christ. Uncertainty and suspense are bad enough in any condition—in the matter of our health, our property, our families, our affections, our earthly callings—but never so bad as in the affairs of our souls. And so long as a believer cannot get beyond "I hope," and "I trust," he manifestly feels a degree of uncertainty about his spiritual state. The very words imply as much. He says "I hope," because he dares not say, "I know."

Now assurance goes far to set a child of God free from this painful kind of bondage, and thus ministers mightily to his comfort. It enables him to feel that the great business of life is a settled business, the great debt a paid debt, the great disease a healed disease, and the great work a finished work; and all other business, diseases, debts, and works, are then by comparison small. In this way assurance makes him patient in tribulation, calm under bereavements, unmoved in sorrow, not afraid of evil tidings, in every condition content, for it gives him a fixedness of heart. It sweetens his bitter cups; it lessens the burden of his crosses; it smooths the rough places over which he travels; it lightens the valley of the shadow of death. It makes him always feel that he has something solid beneath his feet and something firm under his hands—a sure friend by the way, and a sure home at the end.[9]

Assurance will help a man to bear poverty and loss. It will teach him to say, "I know that I have in heaven a better and more enduring substance. Silver and gold have I none, but grace and glory are mine, and these can never make themselves wings and flee away. Though the fig tree shall not blossom, yet I will rejoice in the Lord" (Hab. 3:17, 18).

Assurance will support a child of God under the heaviest bereavements, and assist him to feel "It is well." An assured soul will say, "Though beloved ones are taken from me, yet Jesus is the same, and is alive for evermore. Christ, being raised from the dead, dieth no more. Though my house be not as flesh and blood could wish, yet I have an everlasting covenant, ordered in all things and sure" (2 Kings 4:26; Heb. 13:8; Rom. 6:9; 2 Sam. 23:5).

Assurance will enable a man to praise God, and be thankful, even in prison, like Paul and Silas at Philippi. It can give a believer songs even in the darkest night, and joy when all things seem going against him[10] (Job 35:10; Ps. 42:8).

Assurance will enable a man to sleep with the full prospect of death on the morrow, like Peter in Herod's dungeon. It will teach him to say, "I will both lay me down in peace and sleep, for Thou, Lord, only makest me to dwell in safety" (Ps. 4:8).

Assurance can make a man rejoice to suffer shame for Christ's sake, as the Apostles did when put in prison at Jerusalem (Acts 5:41). It will remind him that he may "rejoice and be exceeding glad" (Matt. 5:12), and that there is in heaven an exceeding weight of glory that shall make amends for all (2 Cor. 4:17).

Assurance will enable a believer to meet a violent and painful death without fear, as Stephen did in the beginning of Christ's Church, and as Cranmer, Ridley, Hooper, Latimer, Rogers, and Taylor did in our own land. It will bring to his heart the texts, "Be not afraid of them which kill the body, and after that have no more that they can do" (Luke 12:4). "Lord Jesus, receive my spirit" (Acts 7:59).[11]

Assurance will support a man in pain and sickness, make all his bed, and smooth down his dying pillow. It will enable him to say, "If my earthly house fail, I have a building of God" (2 Cor. 5:1). "I desire to depart and be with Christ" (Phil. 1:23). "My flesh and my heart may fail, but God is the strength of my heart, and my portion for ever"[12] (Ps. 73:26).

The strong consolation which assurance can give in the hour of death is a point of great importance. We may depend on it, we shall never think assurance so precious as when our turn comes to die. In that awful hour there are few believers who do not find out the value and privilege of an "assured hope," whatever they may have thought about it during their lives. General "hopes" and "trusts" are all very well to live upon while the sun shines and the body is strong; but when we come to die, we shall want to be able to say, "I *know*" and "I *feel.*" The river of death is a cold stream, and we have to cross it alone. No earthly friend can help us. The last enemy, the king of terrors, is a strong foe. When our souls are departing, there is no cordial like the strong wine of assurance.

There is a beautiful expression in the Prayer-book service for the Visitation of the Sick: "The Almighty Lord, who is a most strong tower to all them that put their trust in Him, be now and evermore thy defence, and make thee *know* and *feel* that there is none other name under heaven, through whom thou mayest receive health and salvation, but only the name of our Lord Jesus Christ." The compilers of that service showed great wisdom there. They saw that when the eyes grow dim, and the heart grows faint, and the spirit is on the eve of departing, there must then be *knowing* and *feeling* what Christ has done for us, or else there cannot be perfect peace.[13]

(2) Let us remember, for another thing, that assurance is to be desired, because *it tends to make a Christian an active working Christian.*

None, generally speaking, do so much for Christ on earth as those who enjoy the fullest confidence of a free entrance into heaven, and trust not in their own works, but in the finished work of Christ. That sounds wonderful, I dare say, but it is true.

A believer who lacks an assured hope, will spend much of his time in inward searchings of heart about his own state. Like a nervous, hypochondriacal person, he will be full of his own ailments, his own doubtings and questionings, his own conflicts and corruptions. In short, you will often find he is so taken up with his internal warfare that he has little leisure for other things, and little time to work for God.

But a believer who has, like Paul, an assured hope, is free from these harassing distractions. He does not vex his soul with doubts about his own pardon and acceptance. He looks at the everlasting covenant sealed with blood, at the finished work and never-broken word of his Lord and Saviour, and therefore counts his salvation a *settled thing*. And thus he is able to give an undivided attention to the work of the Lord, and so in the long run to do more.[14]

Take, for an illustration of this, two English emigrants, and suppose them set down side by side in New Zealand or Australia. Give each of them a piece of land to clear and cultivate. Let the portions allotted to them be the same both in quantity and quality. Secure that land to them by every needful legal instrument; let it be conveyed as freehold to them and theirs for ever; let the conveyance be publicly registered, and the property made sure to them by every deed and security that man's ingenuity can devise.

Suppose then that one of them shall set to work to clear his land and bring it into cultivation, and labour at it day after day without intermission or cessation.

Suppose in the meanwhile that the other shall be continually leaving his work, and going repeatedly to the public registry to ask whether the land really is his own—whether there is not some mistake—whether after all there is not some flaw in the legal instruments which conveyed it to him.

The one shall never doubt his title, but just work diligently on. The other shall hardly ever feel sure of his title, and spend half his time in going to Sydney or Melbourne or Auckland, with needless inquiries about it.

Which now of these two men will have made most progress in a year's time? Who will have done the most for his land, got the greatest breadth of soil under tillage, have the best crops to show, be altogether the most prosperous?

Any one of common sense can answer that question. I need not supply an answer. There can only be one reply. Undivided attention will always attain the greatest success.

It is much the same in the matter of our title to "mansions in the skies." None will do so much for the Lord who bought him as the believer who sees his title clear, and is not distracted by unbelieving doubts, questionings, and hesitations. The joy of the Lord will be that man's strength. "Restore unto me," says David, "the joy of Thy salvation; *then* will I teach transgressors Thy ways" (Ps. 51:12-13).

Never were there such working Christians as the Apostles. They seemed to live to labour. Christ's work was truly their meat and drink. The counted not their lives dear to themselves. They spent and were spent. They laid down ease, health, worldly comfort, at the foot of the cross. And one grand cause of this, I believe, was their assured hope. They were men who could say, "We *know* that we are of God, and the whole world lieth in wickedness" (1 John 5:19).

(3) Let us remember, for another thing, that assurance is to be desired, because *it tends to make a Christian a decided Christian.*

Indecision and doubt about our own state in God's sight is a grievous evil, and the mother of many evils. It often produces a wavering and unstable walk in following the Lord. Assurance helps to cut many a knot, and to make the path of Christian duty clear and plain.

Many of whom we feel hopes that they are God's children, and have true grace, however weak, are continually perplexed with doubts in points of practice. "Should we do such and such a thing? Shall we give up this family custom? Ought we to go into that company? How shall we draw the line about visiting? What is to be the measure of our dressing and our entertainments? Are we never, under any circumstances, to dance, never to touch a card, never to attain parties of pleasure?" These are a kind of questions which seem to give them constant trouble. And often, very often, the simple root of their perplexity is, that they do not feel assured they are themselves children of God. They have not yet settled the point, which side of the gate they are on. They do not know whether they are inside the ark or not.

That a child of God ought to act in a certain decided way, they quite feel; but the grand question is, "Are they children of God themselves?" If they only felt they were so, they would go straight-forward, and take a decided line. But not feeling sure about it, their conscience is for ever hesitating and coming to a deadlock. The devil whispers, "Perhaps after all you are only a hypocrite: what right have you to take a decided course? Wait till you are really a Christian." And this whisper too often turns the scale, and leads on to some miserable compromise or wretched conformity to the world!

I believe we have here one chief reason why so many in this day are inconsistent, trimming, unsatisfactory, and half-hearted in their conduct about the world. Their faith fails. They feel no assurance that they are Christ's, and so feel a hesitancy about breaking with the world. They shrink from laying aside all the ways of the old man, because they are not quite confident they have put on the new. In short, I have little doubt that one secret cause of "halting between two opinions" is want of assurance. When people can say decidedly, "The Lord, He is the God," their course becomes very clear (1 Kings 18:39).

(4) Let us remember, finally, that assurance is to be desired, because *it tends to make the holiest Christians.*

This, too, sounds wonderful and strange, and yet it is true. It is one of the paradoxes of the Gospel, contrary at first sight to reason and common sense, and yet it is a fact. Cardinal Bellarmine was seldom more wide of the truth than when he said, "Assurance tends to carelessness and sloth." He that is freely forgiven by Christ will always do much for Christ's glory, and he that enjoys the fullest assurance of this forgiveness will ordinarily keep up the closest walk with God. It is a faithful saying and worthy to be remembered by all believers, "He that hath this hope in Him purifieth himself, even as He is pure" (1 John 3:3). A hope that does not purify is a mockery, a delusion, and a snare.[15]

None are so likely to maintain a watchful guard over their own hearts and lives as those who know the comfort of living in close communion with God. They feel their privilege, and will fear losing it. They will dread falling from the high estate, and marring their own comforts, by bringing clouds between themselves and Christ. He that goes on a journey with little money about him takes little thought of danger, and cares little how late he travels. He, on the contrary, that carries gold and jewels will be a cautious traveller. He will look well to his roads, his lodgings, and his company, and run no risks. It is an old saying, however unscientific it may be, that the fixed stars are those which tremble most. The man that most fully enjoys the light of God's reconciled countenance, will be a man tremblingly afraid of losing its blessed consolations, and jealously fearful of doing anything to grieve the Holy Ghost.

I commend these four points to the serious consideration of all professing Christians. Would you like to feel the Everlasting Arms around you, and to hear the voice of Jesus daily drawing nigh to your soul, and saying, "I am thy salvation"?—Would you like to be a useful labourer in the vineyard in your day and generation?—Would you be known of all men as a bold, firm, decided, single-eyed, uncompromising follower of Christ?—Would you be eminently spiritually-minded and holy?—I doubt not some readers will say, "These are the very things our hearts desire. We long for them. We pant after them: but they seem far from us."

Now, has it never struck you that your neglect of assurance may possibly be the main secret of all your failures—that the low measure of faith which satisfies you may be the cause of your low degree of peace? Can you think it a strange thing that your graces are faint and languishing, when faith, the root and mother of them all, is allowed to remain feeble and weak?

Take my advice this day. Seek an increase of faith. Seek an assured hope of salvation like the Apostle Paul's. Seek to obtain a simple, childlike confidence in God's promises. Seek to be able to say with Paul, "I know whom I have believed: I am persuaded that He is mine, and I am His."

You have very likely tried other ways and methods and completely failed. Change your plan. Go upon another tack. Lay aside your doubts. Lean more entirely on the Lord's arm. Begin with implicit trusting. Cast aside your faithless backwardness to take the Lord at His word. Come and roll yourself, your soul, and your sins, upon your gracious Saviour. Begin with simple believing, and all other things shall soon be added to you.[16]

IV. I come now to the last thing of which I spoke. I promised to point out *some probable causes why an assured hope is so seldom attained*. I will do it very shortly.

This is a very serious question, and ought to raise in all of us great searchings of heart. Few, certainly, of Christ's people seem to reach up to this blessed spirit of assurance. Many comparatively believe, but few are persuaded. Many comparatively have saving faith, but few that glorious confidence which shines forth in the language of St. Paul. That such is the case, I think we must all allow.

Now, why is this so?—Why is a thing which two Apostles have strongly enjoined us to seek after, a thing of which few believers have any experimental knowledge in these latter days? Why is an assured hope so rare?

I desire to offer a few suggestions on this point, with all humility. I know that many have never attained assurance, at whose feet I would gladly sit both in earth and heaven. *Perhaps* the Lord sees something in the natural temperament of some of His children, which makes assurance not good for them. *Perhaps,* in order to be kept in spiritual health, they need to be kept very low. God only knows. Still, after every allowance, I fear there are many believers without an assured hope, whose case may too often be explained by causes such as these.

(1) One most common cause, I suspect, is a *defective view of the doctrine of justification.*

I am inclined to think that justification and sanctification are insensibly confused together in the minds of many believers. They receive the Gospel truth—that there must be something done in us, as well as something done for us, if we are true members of Christ: and so far they are right. But then, without being aware of it, perhaps, they seem to imbibe the idea that their justification is, in some degree, affected by something within themselves. They do not clearly see that Christ's work, not their own work—either in whole or in part, either directly or indirectly—is alone the ground of our acceptance with God; that justification is a thing entirely without us, for which nothing whatever is needful on our part but simple faith—and that the weakest believer is as fully and completely justified as the strongest.[17]

Many appear to forget that we are saved and justified as sinners, and only sinners; and that we never can attain to anything higher, if we live to the age of Methuselah. *Redeemed* sinners, *justified* sinners, and *renewed* sinners doubtless we must be—but sinners, sinners, sinners, we shall be always to the very last. They do not seem to comprehend that there is a wide difference between our justification and our sanctification. Our justification is a perfect finished work, and admits of no degrees. Our sanctification is imperfect and incomplete, and will be so to the last hour of our life. They appear to expect that a believer may at some period of his life be in a measure free from corruption, and attain to a kind of inward perfection. And not finding this angelic state of things in their own hearts, they at once conclude there must be something very wrong in their state. And so they go mourning all their days—oppressed with fears that they have no part or lot in Christ, and refusing to be comforted.

Let us weigh this point well. If any believing soul desires assurance, and has not got it, let him ask himself, first of all, if he is quite sure he is sound in the faith, if he knows how to distinguish things that differ, and if his eyes are thoroughly clear in the matter of justification. He must know what it is simply to *believe* and to be justified by faith before he can expect to feel assured.

In this matter, as well as in many others, the old Galatian heresy is the most fertile source of error, both in doctrine and in practice. People ought to seek clearer views of Christ, and what Christ has done for them. Happy is the man who really understands "justification by faith without the deeds of the law."

(2) Another common cause of the absence of assurance is, *slothfulness about growth in grace.*

I suspect many true believers hold dangerous and unscriptural views on this point; I do not of course mean intentionally, but they do hold them. Many appear to think that, once converted, they have little more to attend to, and that a state of salvation is a kind of easy chair, in which they may just sit still, lie back, and be happy. They seem to fancy that grace is given them that they may enjoy it, and they forget that it is given, like a talent, to be used, employed, and improved. Such persons lose sight of the many direct injunctions "to increase—to grow—to abound more and more—to add to our faith," and the like; and in this little-doing condition, this sitting-still state of mind, I never marvel that they miss assurance.

I believe it ought to be our continual aim and desire to go forward, and our watchword on every returning birthday, and at the beginning of every year, should be, "More and more" (1 Thess. 4:1): more knowledge—more faith—more obedience—more love. If we have brought forth thirtyfold, we should seek to bring forth sixty; and if we have brought forth sixty, we should strive to bring forth a hundred. The will of the Lord is our sanctification, and it ought to be our will too (Matt. 13:23; 1 Thess. 4:3).

One thing, at all events, we may depend upon—there is an inseparable connection between diligence and assurance. "Give *diligence*," says Peter, "to make your calling and election sure" (2 Pet. 1:10). "We desire," says Paul, "that every one of you do show the same *diligence* to the full assurance of hope unto the end" (Heb. 6:11). "The soul of the *diligent*," says Solomon, "shall be made fat" (Prov. 13:4). There is much truth in the old maxim of the Puritans: "Faith of adherence comes by hearing, but faith of assurance comes not without *doing.*"

Is any reader of this paper one of those who desires assurance, but has not got it? Mark my words. You will never get it without diligence, however much you may desire it. There are no gains without pains in spiritual things, any more than in temporal. "The soul of the sluggard desireth and hath nothing" (Prov. 13:4).[18]

(3) Another common cause of a want of assurance is *an inconsistent walk in life.*

With grief and sorrow I feel constrained to say that I fear nothing more frequently prevents men attaining an assured hope than this. The stream of professing Christianity in this day is far wider than it formerly was, and I am afraid we must admit at the same time it is much less deep.

Inconsistency of life is utterly destructive of peace of conscience. The two things are incompatible. They cannot and they will not go together. If you will have your besetting sins, and cannot make up your minds to give them up—if you will shrink from cutting off the right hand and plucking out the right eye when occasion requires it—I will engage you will have no assurance.

A vacillating walk—a backwardness to take a bold and decided line—a readiness to conform to the world—a hesitating witness for Christ—a lingering tone of religion—a flinching from a high standard of holiness and spiritual life—all these make up a sure receipt for bringing a blight upon the garden of your soul.

It is vain to suppose you will feel assured and persuaded of your own pardon and acceptance with God, unless you count *all* God's commandments concerning *all* things to be right, and hate every sin, whether great or small (Ps. 119:128). One Achan allowed in the camp of your heart will weaken your hands and lay your consolations low in the dust. You must be daily sowing to the Spirit, if you are to reap the witness of the Spirit. You will not find and feel that all the Lord's ways are ways of pleasantness, unless you labour in all your ways to please the Lord.[19]

I bless God that our salvation in no wise depends on our own works. By grace we are saved—not by works of righteousness—through faith—without the deeds of the law. But I never would have any believer for a moment forget that our sense of salvation depends much on the manner of our living. Inconsistency will dim our eyes, and bring clouds between us and the sun. The sun is the same behind the clouds, but you will not be able to see its brightness or enjoy its warmth, and your soul will be gloomy and cold. It is in the path of well doing that the day-spring of assurance will visit you, and shine down upon your heart.

"The secret of the Lord," says David, "is with them that fear Him, and He will show them His covenant" (Ps. 25:14).

"To him that ordereth his conversation aright, will I show the salvation of God" (Ps. 50:23).

"Great peace have they which love Thy law, and nothing shall offend them" (Ps. 119:165).

"If we walk in the light, as He is in the light, we have fellowship one with another" (1 John 1:7).

"Let us not love in word, neither in tongue; but in deed and in truth; and hereby we *know* that we are of the truth, and shall assure our hearts before Him" (1 John 3:18-19).

"Hereby we do know that we know Him, if we keep His commandments" (1 John 2:3).

Paul was a man who exercised himself to have always a conscience void of offence toward God and toward man (Acts 24:16). He could say with boldness, "I have fought the good fight, I have kept the faith." I do not therefore wonder that the Lord enabled him to add with confidence, "Henceforth there is a crown laid up for me, and the Lord shall give it me at that day."

If any believer in the Lord Jesus desires assurance, and has not got it, let him think over this point also. Let him look at his own heart, look at his own conscience, look at his own life, look at his own ways, look at his own home. And perhaps when he has done that, he will be able to say, "There is a *cause* why I have no assured hope."

I leave the three matters I have just mentioned to the private consideration of every reader of this paper. I am sure they are worth examining. May we examine them honestly. And may the Lord give us understanding in all things.

(1) And now in closing this important inquiry, let me speak first to those readers who have not yet given themselves to the Lord, who have not yet come out from the world, chosen the good part, and followed Christ.

I ask you then to learn from this subject, the *privileges and comforts of a true Christian.*

I would not have you judge of the Lord Jesus Christ by His people. The best of servants can give you but a faint idea of that glorious Master. Neither would I have you judge of the privileges of His kingdom, by the measure of comfort to which many of His people attain. Alas, we are most of us poor creatures! We come short, very short, of the blessedness we might enjoy. But, depend upon it, there are glorious things in the city of our God, which they who have an assured hope taste, even in their lifetime. There are lengths and breadths of peace and consolation there, which it has not entered into your heart to conceive. There is bread enough and to spare in our Father's house, though many of us certainly eat but little of it, and continue weak. But the fault must not be laid to our Master's charge: it is all our own.

And, after all, the weakest child of God has a mine of comforts within him, of which you know nothing. You see the conflicts and tossings of the surface of his heart, but you see not the pearls of great price which are hidden in the depths below. The feeblest member of Christ would not change conditions with you. The believer who possesses the least assurance is far better off than you are. He has a hope, however faint, but you have none at all. He has a portion that will never be taken from him, a Saviour that will never be taken from him, a Saviour that will never forsake him, a treasure that fadeth not away, however little he may realize it all at present. But, as for you, if you die as you are, your expectations will all perish. Oh, that you were wise! Oh, that you understood these things! Oh, that you would consider your latter end!

I feel deeply for you in these latter days of the world, if I ever did. I feel deeply for those whose treasure is all on earth, and whose hopes are all on this side of the grave. Yes! When I see old kingdoms and dynasties shaking to the very foundation—when I see, as we all saw a few years ago, kings and princes and rich men and great men fleeing for their lives, and scarce knowing where to hide their heads—when I see property dependent on public confidence melting like snow in the spring, and the public stocks and funds losing their value—when I see these things, I feel deeply for those who have no better portion than this world can give them, and no place in that kingdom which cannot be removed.[20]

Take advice of a minister of Christ this very day. Seek durable riches—a treasure that cannot be taken from you—a city which hath lasting foundations. Do as the Apostle Paul did. Give yourself to the Lord Jesus Christ, and seek that incorruptible crown He is ready to bestow. Take His yoke upon you, and learn of Him. Come away from a world which will never really satisfy you, and from sin which will bite like a serpent, if you cleave to it, at last. Come to the Lord Jesus as lowly sinners, and He will receive you, pardon you, give you His renewing Spirit, fill you with peace. This shall give you more real comfort than the world has ever done. There is a gulf in your heart which nothing but the peace of Christ can fill. Enter in and share our privileges. Come with us, and sit down by our side.

(2) Lastly, let me turn to all believers who read these pages, and speak to them a few words of brotherly counsel.

The main thing that I urge upon you is this—*if you have not got an assured hope of your own acceptance in Christ, resolve this day to seek it.* Labour for it. Strive after it. Pray for it. Give the Lord no rest till you "know whom you have believed."

I feel, indeed, that the small amount of assurance in this day, among those who are reckoned God's children, is a shame and a reproach. "It is a thing to be heavily bewailed," says old Traill, "that many Christians have lived twenty or forty years since Christ called them by His grace, yet *doubting* in their life." Let us call to mind the earnest "desire" Paul expresses, that "every one" of the Hebrews should seek after full assurance; and let us endeavour, by God's blessing, to roll this reproach away (Heb. 6:11).

Believing reader, do you really mean to say that you have no desire to exchange hope for confidence, trust for persuasion, uncertainty for knowledge? Because weak faith will save you, will you therefore rest content with it? Because assurance is not essential to your entrance into heaven, will you therefore be satisfied without it upon earth? Alas, this is not a healthy state of soul to be in; this is not the mind of the Apostolic day! Arise at once and go forward. Stick not at the foundations of religion: go on to perfection. Be not content with a day of small things. Never despise it in others, but never be content with it yourself.

Believe me, believe me, assurance is worth the seeking. You forsake your own mercies when you rest content without it. The things I speak are for your peace. If it is good to be sure in earthly things, how much better is it to be sure in heavenly things! Your salvation is a fixed and certain thing. God knows it. Why should not you seek to know it too? There is nothing unscriptural in this. Paul never saw the Book of Life, and yet Paul says, "I know and am persuaded."

Make it then your daily prayer that you may have an increase of faith. According to your faith will be your peace. Cultivate that blessed root more, and sooner or later, by God's blessing, you may hope to have the flower. You may not perhaps attain to full assurance all at once. It is good sometimes to be kept waiting: we do not value things which we get without trouble. But though it tarry, wait for it. Seek on, and expect to find.

There is one thing, however, of which I would not have you ignorant:—*You must not be surprised if you have occasional doubts,* after you have got assurance. You must not forget you are on earth, and not in heaven. You are still in the body, and have indwelling sin: the flesh will lust against the spirit to the very end. The leprosy will never be out of the walls of the old house till death takes it down. And there is a devil, too, and a strong devil: a devil who tempted the Lord Jesus, and gave Peter a fall; and he will take care you know it. Some doubts there always will be. He that never doubts has nothing to lose. He that never fears possesses nothing truly valuable. He that is never jealous knows little of deep love. Be not discouraged: you shall be more than conqueror through Him that loved you.[21]

Finally, do not forget that assurance is a thing which *may be lost for a season,* even by the brightest Christians, unless they take care.

Assurance is a most delicate plant. It needs daily, hourly watching, watering, tending, cherishing. So watch and pray the more when you have got it. As Rutherford says, "Make much of assurance." Be always upon your guard. When Christian slept in the arbour, in *Pilgrim's Progress,* he lost his certificate. Keep that in mind.

David lost assurance for many months by falling into transgression. Peter lost it when he denied his Lord. Each found it again undoubtedly, but not till after bitter tears. Spiritual darkness comes on horseback, and goes away on foot. It is upon us before we know that it is coming. It leaves us slowly, gradually, and not till after many days. It is easy to run down hill. It is hard work to climb up. So remember my caution—when you have the joy of the Lord, watch and pray.

Above all, grieve not the Spirit. Quench not the Spirit. Vex not the Spirit. Drive Him not to a distance, by tampering with small bad habits and little sins. Little jarrings between husbands and wives make unhappy homes, and petty inconsistencies, known and allowed, will bring in a strangeness between you and the Spirit.

Hear the conclusion of the whole matter.

The man who walks with God in Christ most closely will generally be kept in the greatest peace.

The believer who follows the Lord most fully and aims at the highest degree of holiness will ordinarily enjoy the most assured hope, and have the clearest persuasion of his own salvation.

Special Note on Chapter 7

(Referred to in note 6 for chapter 7)

Extracts from English Divines, showing that there is a difference between faith and assurance—that a believer may be justified and accepted with God, and yet not enjoy a comfortable knowledge and persuasion of his own safety—and that the weakest faith in Christ, if it be true, will save a man as surely as the strongest.

(1) "The mercy of God is greater than all the sins in the world. But we sometimes are in such a case, that we think we have no faith at all; or if we have any, it is very feeble and weak. And therefore these are two things: to have faith, and to have the feeling of faith. For some men would fain have the feeling of faith, but they cannot attain unto it; and yet they must not despair, but go forward in calling upon God, and it will come at the length: God will open their hearts, and let them feel His goodness."— *Bishop Latimer's Sermons.* 1552.

(2) "Weak faith may fail in the applying, or in the apprehension and appropriating of Christ's benefits to a man's own self. This is to be seen in ordinary experience. For many a man there is of humble and contrite heart, that serveth God in spirit and truth, yet is not able to say, without great doubtings and waverings, I know and am fully assured that my sins are pardoned. Now shall we say that all such are without faith? God forbid.

"This weak faith will as truly apprehend God's merciful promises for the pardon of sin as strong faith, though not so soundly. Even as a man with a palsied hand can stretch it out as well to receive a gift at the hand of a king as he that is more sound, though it may be not so firmly and steadfastly."—*Exposition of the Creed, by William Perkins, Minister of Christ in the University of Cambridge. 1612.*

(3) "This certainty of our salvation, spoken of by Paul, rehearsed by Peter, and mentioned by David (Ps. 4:7), is that special fruit of faith, which breedeth spiritual joy and inward peace, which passeth all under-standing. True it is, all God's children have it not. One thing is the tree, and another thing is the fruit of the tree: one thing is faith, and another thing is the fruit of faith. And that remnant of God's elect which feel the want of this faith, have notwithstanding faith."—*Sermons by Richard Greenham, Minister and Preacher of the Word of God. 1612.*

(4) "Some think they have no faith at all, because they have no full assurance. Yet the fairest fire that can be will have some smoke."—*The Bruised Reed, by Richard Sibbes, Master of Catherine Hall, Cambridge, and Preacher of Gray's Inn, London. 1630.*

(5) "The act of faith is to apply Christ to the soul; and this the weakest faith can do as well as the strongest, if it be true. A child can hold a staff as well, though not so strongly, as a man. The prisoner through a hole sees the sun, though not so perfectly as they in the open air. They that saw the brazen serpent, though a great way off, yet were healed.

"The least faith is as precious to the believer's soul as Peter's or Paul's faith was to themselves; for it lays hold upon Christ and brings eternal salvation."—*An Exposition of the Second Epistle General of Peter, by the Rev. Thomas Adams, Rector of St. Gregory's, London. 1633.*

(6) "Weak faith is true faith—as precious, though not so great as strong faith: the same Holy Ghost the author, the same Gospel the instrument.

"If it never proves great, yet weak faith shall save; for it interests us in Christ, and makes Him and all His benefits ours. For it is not the strength of our faith that saves, but the truth of our faith—not the weakness of our faith that condemns, but the want of faith; for the least faith layeth hold on Christ, and so will save us. Neither are we saved by the worth or quantity of our faith, but by Christ, who is laid hold on by a weak faith as well as a strong. Just as a weak hand that can put meat into the mouth shall feed and nourish the body as well as if it were a strong hand; seeing the body is not nourished by the strength of the hand, but by the goodness of the meat."—*The Doctrine of Faith, by John Rogers, Preacher of God's Word, at Dedham, in Essex. 1634.*

(7) "It is one thing to have a thing surely, another thing to know I have it surely. We seek many things that we have in our hands, and we have many things that we think we have lost. So a believer, who hath a sure belief, yet doth not always know that he so believeth. Faith is necessary to salvation: but full assurance that I do believe is not of like necessity."— *Ball on Faith*. 1637.

(8) "There is a weak faith, which yet is true; and although it be weak, yet, because it is true, it shall not be rejected of Christ.

"Faith is not created perfect at the first, as Adam was; but is like a man in the ordinary course of nature, who is first an infant, then a child, then a youth, then a man.

"Some utterly reject all weak ones, and tax all weakness in faith with hypocrisy. Certainly these are either proud or cruel men.

"Some comfort and establish those who are weak, saying, 'Be quiet. Thou hast faith and grace enough, and are good enough: thou needest no more, neither must thou be too righteous.' (Eccles. 7:16). These are soft, but not safe, cushions: these are fawning flatterers, and not faithful friends.

"Some comfort and exhort, saying, 'Be of good cheer: He who hath begun a good work will also finish it in you; therefore pray that His grace may abound in you; yea, do not sit still, but go forward, and march on in the way of the Lord.' (Heb. 6:1). Now this is the safest and best course."—*Questions, Observations, etc., upon the Gospel According to St. Matthew, by Richard Ward, Sometime Student at Cambridge, and Preacher of the Gospel in London*. 1640.

(9) "A man may be in the favour of God, in the state of grace, a justified man before God, and yet want the sensible assurance of His salvation, and of the favour of God in Christ.

"A man may have saving grace in him, and not perceive it himself; a man may have true justifying faith in him, and not have the use and operation of it, so far as to work in him a comfortable assurance of his reconciliation with God. Nay, I will say more: a man may be in the state of grace, and have true justifying faith in him, and yet be so far from sensible assurance of it in himself, as in his own sense and feeling he may seem to be assured of the contrary. Job was certainly in this case when he cried unto God, 'Wherefore hidest Thou Thy face and holdest me for Thine enemy?' (Job 13:24).

"The weakest faith will justify. If thou canst receive Christ and rest upon Him, even with the weakest faith, it will serve thy turn. Take heed thou think not it is the strength of thy faith that justifieth thee. No, no: it is Christ and His perfect righteousness which thy faith receiveth and resteth upon, that doth it. He that hath the feeblest and weakest hand may receive an alms and apply a sovereign plaster to his wound, as well as he that hath the strongest, and receive as much good by it too."—*Lectures upon the 51st Psalm, Preached at Ashby-de-la-Zouch, by Arthur Hildersam, Minister of Jesus Christ. 1642.*

(10) "Though your grace be never so weak, if ye have truth of grace, you have as great a share in the righteousness of Christ for your justification as the strong Christian hath. You have as much of Christ imputed to you as any other."—*Sermons by William Bridge, Formerly Fellow of Emmanuel College, Cambridge, and Pastor of the Church of Christ, in Great Yarmouth. 1648.*

(11) "There are some who are true believers, and yet weak in faith. They do indeed receive Christ and free grace, but it is with a shaking hand; they have, as divines say, the faith of adherence; they will stick to Christ, as theirs. But they want the faith of evidence; they cannot see themselves as His. They are believers, but of little faith; they hope that Christ will not cast them off, but are not sure that He will take them up."—*Sips of Sweetness, or Consolation for Weak Believers, by John Durant, Preacher in Canterbury Cathedral. 1649.*

(12) "I know, thou sayest, that Jesus Christ came into the world to save sinners: and that 'Whosoever believeth in Him shall not perish, but have eternal life' (John 3:15). Neither can I know but that, in a sense of my own sinful condition, I do cast myself in some measure upon my Saviour, and lay some hold upon His all-sufficient redemption: but, alas, my apprehensions of Him are so feeble, as that they can afford no sound comfort to my soul!

"Courage, my son. Were it that thou lookedst to be justified, and saved by the power of the very act of thy faith, thou hadst reason to be disheartened with the conscience of the weakness thereof; but now that the virtue and efficacy of this happy work is in the object apprehended by thee, which is the infinite merits and mercy of thy God and Saviour, which cannot be abated by thine infirmities, thou hast cause to take heart to thyself, and cheerfully to expect His salvation.

"Understand thy case aright. Here is a double hand, that helps us up toward Heaven. Our hand of faith lays hold upon our Saviour; our Saviour's hand of mercy and plenteous redemption lays hold on us. Our hold of Him is feeble and easily loosed; His hold of us is strong and irresistible.

"If work were stood upon, a strength of hand were necessary; but now that only taking and receiving of a precious gift is required, why may not a weak hand do that as well as a strong? As well, though not as forcibly."—*Bishop Hall's "Balm of Gilead."* 1650.

(13) "I find not salvation put upon the strength of faith, but the truth of faith—not upon the brightest degree, but upon any degree of faith. It is not said, If you have such a degree of faith you shall be justified and saved; but simply believing is required. The lowest degree of true faith will do it; as Romans 10:9, 'If thou shalt confess with thy mouth the Lord Jesus, and shalt believe in thine heart that God hath raised Him from the dead, thou shalt be saved.' The thief upon the cross had not attained to such high degrees of faith: he by one act, and that of a weak faith, was justified and saved (Luke 23:42)."—*Exposition of the Prophet Ezekiel, by William Greenhill, Rector of Stepney, London, and Chaplain to the Dukes of York and Gloucester.* 1650.

(14) "A man may have true grace that hath not the assurance of the love and favour of God, or the remission of his sins, and salvation of his soul. A man may be God's, and yet he not know it; his estate may be good, and yet he not see it; he may be in a safe condition, when he is not in a comfortable position. All may be well with him in the court of glory, when he would give a thousand worlds that all were but well in the court of conscience.

"Assurance is requisite to the well-being of a Christian, but not to the being; it is requisite to the consolation of a Christian, but not to the salvation of a Christian; it is requisite to the well-being of grace, but not to the mere being of grace. Though a man cannot be saved without faith, yet he may be saved without assurance. God hath in many places of the Scripture declared that without faith there is no salvation; but God hath not in any one place of Scripture declared that without assurance there is no salvation."—*Heaven on Earth, by Thomas Brooks, Preacher of the Gospel, at St. Margaret's, Fish Street Hill, London.* 1654.

(15) "You that can clear this to your own hearts that you have faith, though it be weak, be not discouraged, be not troubled. Consider that the smallest degree of faith is true, is saving faith as well as the greatest. A spark of fire is as true fire as any is in the element of fire. A drop of water

is as true water as any is in the ocean. So the least grain of faith is as true faith, and as saving as the greatest faith in the world.

"The least bud draws sap from the root as well as the greatest bough. So the weakest measure of faith doth as truly ingraft thee into Christ, and by that draw life from Christ, as well as the strongest. The weakest faith hath communion with the merits and blood of Christ as well as the strongest.

"The least faith marries the soul to Christ. The weakest faith hath as equal a share in God's love as the strongest. We are beloved in Christ, and the least measure of faith makes us members of Christ. The least faith hath equal right to the promises as the strongest. And therefore let not our souls be discouraged for weakness."—*Nature and Royalties of Faith, by Samuel Bolton, D. D., of Christ's College, Cambridge. 1657.*

(16) "Some are afraid they have no faith at all, because they have not the highest degree of faith, which is full assurance, or because they want the comfort which others attain to, even joy unspeakable and full of glory. But for the rolling of this stone out of the way, we must remember there are several degrees of faith. It is possible thou mayest have faith, though not the highest degree of faith, and so joy in the Spirit. That is rather a point of faith than faith itself. It is indeed rather a living by sense than a living by faith, when we are cheered up with continual cordials. A stronger faith is required to live upon God without comfort, than when God shines in on our spirit with abundance of joy."—*Matthew Lawrence, Preacher at Ipswich, on Faith. 1657.*

(17) "If any person abroad have thought that a special and full persuasion of the pardon of their sin was of the essence of faith, let them answer for it. Our divines at home generally are of another judgment. Bishop Davenant and Bishop Prideaux, and others, have shown the great difference between recumbence and assurance, and they all do account and call assurance, a daughter, fruit, and consequent of faith. And the late learned Arrowsmith tells us, that God seldom bestows assurance upon believers till they are grown in grace: for, says he, there is the same difference between faith of recumbence and faith of assurance, as is between reason and learning. Reason is the foundation of learning; so, as there can be no learning if reason be wanting (as in beasts), in like manner there can be no assurance where there is no faith of adherence. Again: as reason well exercised in the study of arts and sciences arises to learning, so faith being well exercised on its proper object, and by its proper

fruits, arises to assurance. Further, as by negligence, non-attendance, or some violent disease, learning may be lost, while reason doth abide; so by temptation, or by spiritual sloth, assurance may be lost, while saving faith may abide. Lastly, as all men have reason, but all men are not learned, so all regenerate persons have faith to comply savingly with the gospel method of salvation, but all true believers have not assurance."—*Sermon by R. Fairclough, Fellow of Immanuel College, Cambridge, in the Morning Exercises, Preached at Southwark.* 1660.

(18) "We must distinguish between weakness of faith and nullity. A weak faith is true. The bruised reed is but weak, yet it is such as Christ will not break. Though thy faith be but weak, yet be not discouraged. A weak faith may receive a strong Christ; a weak hand can tie the knot in marriage as well as a strong; a weak eye might have seen the brazen serpent. The promise is not made to strong faith, but to true. The promise doth not say, Whosoever hath a giant faith that can remove mountains, that can stop the mouth of lions, shall be saved; but whosoever believes, be his faith never so small.

"You may have the water of the Spirit poured on you in sanctification, though not the oil of gladness in assurance: there may be faith of adherence, and not of evidence; there may be life in the root where there is no fruit in the branches, and faith in the heart where no fruit of assurance."—*A Body of Divinity, by Thomas Watson, formerly Minister of St. Stephen's, Walbrook, London.* 1660.

(19) "Many of God's dear children for a long time may remain very doubtful as to their present and eternal condition, and know not what to conclude, whether they shall be damned or whether they shall be saved. There are believers of several growths in the Church of God,—fathers, young men, children, and babes; and as in most families there are more babes and children than grown men, so in the Church of God there are more weak, doubting Christians than strong ones, grown up to a full assurance. A babe may be born, and yet not know it; so a man may be born again, and yet not be sure of it.

"We make a difference betwixt saving faith, as such, and a full persuasion of the heart. Some of those that shall be saved may not be certain that they shall be saved; for the promise is made to the grace of faith, and not to the evidence of it—to faith as true, and not to faith as strong. They may be sure of heaven, and yet in their own sense not assured of heaven."—*Sermon by Rev. Thomas Doolittle, of Pembroke*

Hall, Cambridge, and Sometime Rector of St. Alphege, London, in the Morning Exercises, at Cripplegate. 1661.

(20) "Is it not necessary to justification to be assured that my sins are pardoned, and that I am justified? No: that is no act of faith as it justifieth, but an effect and fruit that followeth after justification.

"It is one thing for a man to have his salvation certain, another thing to be certain that it is certain.

"Even as a man fallen into a river, and like to be drowned, as he is carried down with the flood, espies the bough of a tree hanging over the river, which he catcheth at, and clings unto with all his might to save him, and seeing no other way of succour but that, ventures his life upon it. This man, so soon as he has fastened on this bough, is in a safe condition, though all troubles, fears, and terrors are not presently out of his mind, until he comes to himself, and sees himself quite out of danger. Then he is sure he is safe; but he was safe before he was sure. Even so it is with a believer. Faith is but the espying of Christ as the only means to save, and the reaching out of the heart to lay hold upon Him. God hath spoke the word, and made the promise to His Son; I believe Him to be the only Saviour, and remit my soul to Him to be saved by His mediation. So soon as the soul can do this, God imputeth the righteousness of His Son unto it, and it is actually justified in the court of heaven, though it is not presently quieted and pacified in the court of conscience. That is done afterwards: in some sooner, in some later, by the fruits and effects of justification."—*Archbishop Usher's "Body of Divinity." 1670.*

(21) "There are those who doubt, because they doubt, and multiply distrust upon itself, concluding that they have no faith, because they find so much and so frequent doubting within them. But this is a great mistake. Some doubtings there may be, where there is even much faith; and a little faith there may be, where there is much doubting.

"Our Saviour requires, and delights in a strong, firm believing on Him, though the least and weakest He rejects not."—*Archbishop Leighton's Lectures on the First Nine Chapters of St. Matthew's Gospel. 1670.*

(22) "Many formerly, and those of the highest remark and eminency, have placed true faith in no lower degree than assurance, or the secure persuasion of the pardon of their sins, the acceptation of their persons, and their future salvation.

"But this, as it is very sad and uncomfortable for thousands of doubting and deserted souls, concluding all those to fall short of grace who fall short of certainty, so hath it given the Papists too great advantage.

"Faith is not assurance. But this doth sometimes crown and reward a strong, vigorous and heroic faith; the Spirit of God breaking in upon the soul with an evidencing light, and scattering all that darkness, and those fears and doubts which before beclouded it."—*Bishop Hopkins on the Covenants.* 1680.

(23) "A want of assurance is not unbelief. Drooping spirits may be believers. There is a manifest distinction made between faith in Christ, and the comfort of that faith—between believing to eternal life, and knowing we have eternal life. There is a difference between a child's having a right to an estate, and his full knowledge of the title.

"The character of faith may be written in the heart, as letters engraven upon a seal, yet filled with so much dust as not to be distinguished. The dust hinders the reading of the letters, yet doth not raze them out."—*Discourses by Stephen Charnock, of Emmanuel College, Cambridge.* 1680.

(24) "Some rob themselves of their own comfort by placing saving faith in full assurance. Faith, and sense of faith, are two distinct and separable mercies; you may have truly received Christ, and not receive the knowledge or assurance of it. Some there be that say, 'Thou art our God,' of whom God never said, 'You are my people'; these have no authority to be called the sons of God. Others there are, of whom God saith, 'These are my people,' yet they dare not call God 'their God'; these have authority to be called the sons of God, yet know it not. They have received Christ, that is their safety; but they have not yet received the knowledge and assurance of it, that is their trouble. . . . The father owns his child in the cradle, who yet knows him not to be his father."—*Method of Grace, by John Flavel, Minister of the Gospel at Dartmouth, Devon.* 1680.

(25) "It is confessed weak faith hath as much peace with God, through Christ, as another hath by strong faith, but not so much bosom peace.

"Weak faith will as surely land the Christian in heaven as strong faith, for it is impossible the least dram of true grace should perish, being all incorruptible seed; but the weak, doubting Christian is not like to have so pleasant a voyage thither as another with strong faith. Though all in the ship come safe to shore, yet he that is all the way sea-sick hath not so comfortable a voyage as he that is strong and healthful."—*The*

Christian in Complete Armour, by William Gurnall, Sometime Rector of Lavenham, Suffolk. 1680.

(26) "Be not discouraged if it doth not yet appear to you that you were given by the Father to the Son. It may be, though you do not see it. Many of the given do not for a long time know it; yea, I see no great danger in saying that not a few of the given to the Son may be in darkness, and doubts, and fears about it, till the last and brightest day declare it, and till the last sentence proclaims it.

"If, therefore, any of you be in the dark about your own election, be not discouraged: it may be, though you do not know it."—*Sermons on the Lord's Prayer, by Robert Traill, Minister of the Gospel, in London, and Sometime at Cranbrook, Kent.* 1690.

(27) "Assurance is not essential to the being of faith. It is a strong faith; but we read likewise of a weak faith, little faith, faith like a grain of mustard seed. True saving faith in Jesus Christ is only distinguishable by its different degrees; but in every degree and in every subject, it is universally of the same kind."—*Sermons, by the Rev. John Newton, Sometimes Vicar of Olney, and Rector of St. Mary, Woolnoth, London.* 1776.

(28) "There is no reason why weak believers should conclude against themselves. Weak faith unites as really with Christ as strong faith—as the least bud in the vine is drawing sap and life from the root, no less than the strongest branch. Weak believers, therefore, have abundant cause to be thankful; and while they reach after growth in grace, ought not to overlook what they have already received."—*Letter of Rev. Henry Venn.* 1784.

(29) "The faith necessary and sufficient for our salvation is not assurance. Its tendency doubtless is to produce that lively expectation of the Divine favour which will issue in a full confidence. But the confidence is not itself the faith of which we speak, nor is it necessarily included in it: nay, it is a totally distinct thing.

"Assurance will generally accompany a high degree of faith. But there are sincere persons who are endued with only small measures of grace, or in whom the exercise of that grace may be greatly obstructed. When such defects or hindrances prevail, many fears and distresses may be expected to arise."—*The Christian System, by the Rev. Thomas Robinson, Vicar of St. Mary's, Leicester.* 1795.

(30) "Salvation, and the joy of salvation, are not always contemporaneous; the latter does not always accompany the former in present experience.

"A sick man may be under a process of recovery, and yet be in doubt concerning the restoration of his health. Pain and weakness may cause him to hesitate. A child may be heir to his estate or kingdom, and yet derive no joy from the prospect of his future inheritance. He may be unable to trace his genealogy, or to read his title-deeds, and the testament of his father; or with a capacity of reading them he may be unable to understand their import, and his guardian may for a time deem it right to suffer him to remain in ignorance. But his ignorance does not affect the validity of his title.

"Personal assurance of salvation is not necessarily connected with faith. They are not essentially the same. Every believer might indeed infer, from the effect produced in his own heart, his own safety and privileges; but many who truly believe are unskillful in the word of righteousness, and fail of drawing the conclusion from Scriptural premises which they would be justified in drawing."—*Lectures on the 51st Psalm, by the Rev. Thomas Biddulph, Minister of St. James's, Bristol.* 1830.

EXTRACTS FROM OLD WRITERS

Robert Traill, Thomas Brooks

The passages I append from Traill and Brooks on the subject of Holiness appear to me so valuable that I make no apology for introducing them.

They are the product of an age when, I am obliged to say, experimental religion was more deeply studied and far better understood than it is now.

(1) Reverend Robert Traill, *Sometime Minister of Cranbrook, Kent.* 1696:

"Concerning sanctification, there are three things that I would speak to:

"I. What sanctification is.
"II. Wherein it agrees with justification.
"III. Wherein it differs from justification.

"I. *What is sanctification?* It is a great deal better to feel it than to express it.

"Sanctification is the same with regeneration; the same with the renovation of the whole man. Sanctification is the forming and the framing of the new creature; it is the implanting and engraving the image of Christ upon the poor soul. It is what the Apostle breathed after—'That Christ might be formed in them' (Gal. 4:19); That they might 'bear the image of the heavenly' (1 Cor. 15:49).

"There are but two men only that all the world is like; and so will it fare with them, as they are like the one, or like the other: the first Adam, and the second Adam. Every man by nature is like the first Adam and like the devil: for the devil and the first fallen Adam were like one another. 'Ye are of your father the devil,' saith our Lord (John 8:44), and he was 'a murderer from the beginning.' All the children of the first Adam are the devil's children, there is no difference here. And all the children of the other sort are like to Jesus Christ, the second Adam; and when His image shall be perfected in them, then they shall be perfectly happy. 'As we have borne the image of the earthly, so shall we also bear the image of the heavenly' (1 Cor. 15:49). Pray observe; we bear the image of the earthly by being born in sin and misery; we bear the image of the earthly by living in sin and misery; and we bear the image of the earthly by dying in sin and misery; and we bear the image of the earthly in the rottenness of the grave; and we bear the image of the heavenly Adam when we are sanctified by His Spirit. This image increases in us according to our growth in sanctification: and we perfectly bear the image of the heavenly Adam when we are just like the Man Christ, both in soul and body, perfectly happy, and perfectly holy; when we have overcome death by His grace, as he overcame it by His own strength. It will never be known how like believers are to Jesus Christ, till they are risen again: when they shall arise from their graves, like so many little suns shining in glory and brightness. Oh, how like will they be to Jesus Christ, though His personal transcendent glory will be His property and prerogative to all eternity.

"II. *Wherein are justification and sanctification alike?* I answer, in many things.

"1st. They are like one another as they are the same in their author; it is God that justifieth, and it is God that sanctifies. 'Who shall lay anything to the charge of God's elect? It is God that justifieth' (Rom. 8:33). "I am the Lord that doth sanctify you," is a common word in the Old Testament (Ex. 31:13; Lev. 20:8).

"2ndly. They are alike and the same in their rise, being both of free grace; justification is an act of free grace, and sanctification is the same. 'Not by works of righteousness which we have done, but according to His mercy, He saved us by the washing of regeneration, and the renewing of the Holy Ghost' (Titus 3:5). They are both of grace.

"3rdly. They are alike in that they are both towards the same persons. Never a man is justified but he is also sanctified; and never a man is sanctified but he is also justified; all the elect of God, all the redeemed, have both these blessings passing upon them.

"4thly. They are alike as to the time, they are the same in time. It is a hard matter for us to talk or think of time when we are speaking of the works of God: these saving works of His are always done at the same time; a man is not justified before he is sanctified, though it may be conceived so in order of nature, yet at the same time the same grace works both. 'Such were some of you,' saith the Apostle, 'but ye are washed, but ye are sanctified, but ye are justified in the name of the Lord Jesus, and by the Spirit of our God' (1 Cor. 6:11).

"5thly. They are the same as to the operation of them by the same means, that is, by the Word of God: we are justified by the Word, sentencing us to eternal life by the promise; and we are also sanctified by the power of the same Word. 'Now ye are clean,' saith our Lord, 'through the Word that I have spoken unto you' (John 15:3). 'That He might sanctify and cleanse His Church,' saith the Apostle, 'with the washing of water by the Word' (Eph. 5:26).

"6th and lastly. They are the same as to their equal necessity to eternal life. I do not say as to their equal order, but as to their equal necessity: that is, as it is determined that no man who is not justified shall be saved, so it is determined that no man who is not sanctified shall be saved: no unjustified man can be saved, and no unsanctified man can be saved. They are of equal necessity in order to the possessing of eternal life.

"III. *Wherein do justification and sanctification differ?* This is a matter of great concernment for people's practice and daily exercise: wherein they differ. They agree in many things, as has just now been declared, but they likewise differ vastly.

"1st. Justification is an act of God about the *state* of a man's person; but sanctification is the work of God about the *nature* of a man: and these two are very different, as I shall illustrate by a similitude. Justification is an act of God as a judge about a delinquent, absolving him from a sentence of death; but sanctification is an act of God about us, as a physician, in curing us of a mortal disease. There is a criminal that comes to the bar, and is arraigned for high treason; the same criminal has a mortal disease, that he may die of, though there was no judge on the bench to pass the sentence of death upon him for his crime. It is an act of grace which absolves the man from the sentence of the law, that he shall not suffer death for his treason—*that* saves the man's life. But notwithstanding this, unless his disease be cured, he may die quickly after, for all the judge's pardon. Therefore, I say, justification is an act of God as a gracious Judge, sanctification is a work of God as a merciful Physician. David joins them both together (Ps. 103:3): 'Who forgiveth all thine iniquities, who healeth all thy diseases.' It is promised that, 'iniquity shall not be your ruin' (Ezek. 18:30), in the *guilt* of it; that is justification. And it shall not be your ruin, in the power of it; there lies sanctification.

"2ndly. Justification is an act of God's grace upon the account of the righteousness of another, but sanctification is a work of God, infusing a righteousness into us. Now there is a great difference between these two: for the one is by imputation, the other by infusion.

"In justification, the sentence of God proceeds this way: the righteousness that Christ wrought out by His life and death, and the obedience that He paid to the law of God, is reckoned to the guilty sinner for his absolution; so that when a sinner comes to stand at God's bar, when the question is asked, Hath not this man broken the law of God? Yes, saith God; yes, saith the conscience of the poor sinner, I have broken it in innumerable ways. And doth not the law condemn thee to die for thy transgression? Yes, saith the man; yes, saith the law of God, the law knows nothing more but this: 'the soul that sinneth must die.' Well, then, but is there no hope in this case? Yes, and Gospel grace reveals this hope. There is One that took sin on Him, and died for our sins, and His righteousness is reckoned for the poor sinner's justification; and thus we are absolved. We are absolved in justification by God's reckoning on our account, on our behalf, and for our advantage, what Christ hath done and suffered for us.

"In sanctification the Spirit of God infuses a holiness into the soul. I do not say He infuses a righteousness; for I would fain have these words, righteousness and holiness, better distinguished than generally they are. Righteousness and holiness are, in this case, to be kept vastly asunder. Our righteousness is without us; our holiness is within us, it is our own; the Apostle plainly makes that distinction. 'Not having mine own righteousness' (Phil. 3:9). It is our own, not originally, but our own inherently; not our own so as to be of our own working, but our own because it is indwelling in us. But our righteousness is neither our own originally nor inherently; it is neither wrought out by us, nor doth it dwell in us; but it is wrought out by Jesus Christ, and it eternally dwells in Him, and is only to be pleaded by faith, by a poor creature. But our holiness, though it be not our own originally, yet it is our own inherently, it dwells in us: this is the distinction that the Apostle makes. 'That I may be found in Him, not having my own righteousness, which is of the law, but that which is through the faith of Christ, the righteousness which is of God by faith' (Phil. 3:9).

"3rdly. Justification is perfect, but sanctification is imperfect; and here lies a great difference between them. Justification, I say, is perfect, and admits of no degrees; admits of no decays, admits of no intermission, nor of any interruption; but sanctification admits of all these. When I say justification is perfect, I mean, that every justified man is equally and perfectly justified. The poorest believer that is this day in the world, is justified as much as ever the Apostle Paul was; and every true believer is as much justified now as he will be a thousand years hence. Justification is perfect in all them that are partakers of it, and to all eternity; it admits of no degrees. And the plain reason of it is this—the ground of it is the perfect righteousness of Jesus Christ, and the entitling us to it is by an act of God the gracious Judge, and that act stands for ever; and if God justifies, who is he that shall condemn? (Rom. 8:33). But sanctification is an imperfect, incomplete, changeable thing. One believer is more sanctified than another. I am apt to believe that the Apostle Paul was more sanctified the first hour of his conversion, than any man this day in the world.

"Sanctification differs greatly as to the persons that are partakers of it; and it differs greatly too as to the same man; for a true believer, a truly sanctified man, may be more holy and sanctified at one time than at another. There is a work required of us—to be perfecting *holiness* in the fear of God (2 Cor. 7:1). But we are nowhere required to be perfecting *righteousness* in the sight of God; for God hath brought in a perfect righteousness, in which we stand; but we are to take care, and to give diligence to perfect holiness in the fear of God. A saint in glory is more sanctified than ever he was, for he is perfectly so; but he is not more justified than he was. Nay, a saint in heaven is not more justified than a believer on earth is: only they know it better, and the glory of that light in which they see it, discovers it more brightly and more clearly to them."

—From *Traill's Sermons, upon 1 Pet. 1:1-3,* vol. 4, p. 71.
Edinburgh edition of Traill's Works. 1810.

(2) Rev. Thomas Brooks, *Rector of St. Margaret, Fish Street Hill, London.* 1662.

"Consider the necessity of holiness. It is impossible that ever you should be happy, except you are holy. No holiness here, no happiness hereafter. The Scripture speaks of three bodily inhabitants of heaven—Enoch, before the law; Elijah, under the law; and Jesus Christ, under the Gospel: all three eminent in holiness, to teach us, that even in an ordinary course there is no going to heaven without holiness. There are many thousand thousands now in heaven, but not one unholy one among them all; there is not one sinner among all those saints; not one goat among all those sheep; not one weed among all those flowers; not one thorn or prickle among all those roses; not one pebble among all those glistering diamonds. There is not one Cain among all those Abels; nor one Ishmael among all those Isaacs; nor one Esau among all those Jacobs in heaven. There is not one Ham among all the patriarchs; not one Saul among all the prophets; nor one Judas among all the apostles; nor one Demas among all the preachers; nor one Simon Magus among all the professors.

"Heaven is only for the holy man, and the holy man is only for heaven: heaven is a garment of glory, that is only suited to him that is holy. God, who is truth itself, and cannot lie, hath said it, that without holiness no man shall see the Lord. Mark that word 'no man.' Without holiness the rich man shall not see the Lord; without holiness the poor man shall not see the Lord; without holiness the nobleman shall not see the Lord; without holiness the mean man shall not see the Lord; without holiness the prince shall not see the Lord; without holiness the ruler shall not see the Lord; without holiness the ruled shall not see the Lord; without holiness the learned man shall not see the Lord; without holiness the ignorant man shall not see the Lord; without holiness the husband shall not see the Lord; without holiness the wife shall not see the Lord; without holiness the father shall not see the Lord; without holiness the child shall not see the Lord; without holiness the master shall not see the Lord; without holiness the servant shall not see the Lord. 'For faithful and strong is the Lord of hosts that hath spoken it' (Josh. 23:14).

"In this day some cry up one form, some another; some cry up one Church state, some another; some cry up one way, some another; but certainly the way of holiness is the good old way (Jer. 6:16); it is the King of kings' highway to heaven and happiness: 'And a highway shall be there, and a way, and it shall be called The way of holiness; the unclean shall not pass over it; but it shall be for those: the wayfaring men, though fools, shall not err therein' (Isa. 35:8). Some men say, Lo, here is the way; other men say, Lo, there is the way; but certainly the way of holiness is the surest, the safest, the easiest, the noblest, and the shortest way to happiness.

"Among the heathen, no man could enter into the temple of honour, but must first enter the temple of virtue. There is no entering the temple of happiness, except you enter into the temple of holiness. Holiness must first enter into you, before you can enter into God's holy hill. As Samson cried out, 'Give me water, or I die'; or as Rachel cried out, 'Give me children, or I die'; so all unsanctified souls may well cry out, "Lord, give me holiness, or I die: give me holiness or I eternally die." If the angels, those princes of glory, fall once from their holiness, they shall be for ever excluded from everlasting happiness and blessedness. If Adam in paradise fall from his purity, he shall quickly be driven out from the presence of

Divine glory. Augustine would not be a wicked man, an unholy man, one hour for all the world, because he did not know but that he might die that hour; and should he die in an unholy estate, he knew he should be for ever separated from the presence of the Lord and the glory of His power.

"O, sirs, do not deceive your own souls; holiness is of absolute necessity; without it you shall never see the Lord (2 Thess. 1:8-10). It is not absolutely necessary that you should be great or rich in the world; but it is absolutely necessary that you should be holy: it is not absolutely necessary that you should enjoy health, strength, friends, liberty, life; but it is absolutely necessary that you should be holy. A man may see the Lord without worldly prosperity, but he can never see the Lord except he be holy. A man may to heaven, to happiness, without honour or worldly glory, but he can never to heaven, to happiness, without holiness. Without holiness here, no heaven hereafter. 'And there shall in no wise enter into it anything that defileth' (Rev. 21:27). God will at last shut the gates of glory against every person that is without heart-purity.

"Ah, sirs, holiness is a flower that grows not in Nature's garden. Men are not born with holiness in their hearts, as they are born with tongues in their mouths: holiness is of a Divine offspring: it is a pearl of price, that is to be found in no nature but a renewed nature, in no bosom but a sancti- fied bosom. There is not the least beam or spark of holiness in any natural man in the world. 'Every imagination of the thoughts of man's heart is only evil continually' (Gen. 6:5). 'How can man be clean that is born of a woman?' (Job 25:4). The interrogation carries in it a strong negation, 'How can man be clean?' that is, man cannot be clean that is born of a woman: a man that is born of a woman is born in sin, and born both under wrath and under the curse. 'And who can bring a clean thing out of an unclean?' 'But we are all as an unclean thing, and all our righteous- nesses are as filthy rags' (Job 14:4; Isa. 64:6). 'There is none righteous, no not one; there is none that understandeth, there is none that seeketh after God' (Rom. 3:10-11). Every man that comes into this world comes with his face towards sin and hell, and with his back upon God and holiness.

"Such is the corruption of our nature, that, propound any Divine good to it, it is entertained as fire by water, or wet wood, with hissing. Propound any evil, then it is like fire to straw; it is like the foolish satyr that made haste to kiss the fire; it is like that unctuous matter which, the naturalists say, sucks and snatches the fire to it, with which it is consumed. All men are born sinners, and there is nothing but an infinite power than can make them saints. All men would be happy, and yet they naturally loathe to be holy. By all which you may clearly see that food is not more necessary for the preservation of natural life, than holiness is necessary for the preservation and salvation of the soul. If a man had the wisdom of Solomon, the strength of Samson, the courage of Joshua, the policy of Ahithophel, the dignities of Haman, the power of Ahasuerus, and the eloquence of Apollos, yet all those without holiness would never save him. The days and times wherein we live call aloud for holiness. If you look upon them as days and times of grace, what greater and higher engagements to holiness were ever put upon a people, than those that God hath put upon us, who enjoy so many ways, means, and helps to make us holy? Oh, the pains, the care, the cost, the charge, that God hath been at, and that God is daily at, to make us holy! Hath He not sent, and doth He not still send His messengers, rising up early, and going to bed late, and all to provoke you to be holy? Have not many of them spent their time, and spent their strength, and spent their spirits, and spent their lives to make you holy? O, sirs, what do holy ordinances call for, but holy hearts and holy lives? What do days of light call for, but walking in the light, and casting off the deeds of darkness? What is the voice of all the means of grace, but this, 'Oh, labour to be gracious'? And what is the voice of the Holy Spirit, but this, 'Oh, labour to be holy'? And what is the voice of all the miracles of mercy that God hath wrought in the midst of you, but this, 'Be ye holy, be ye holy'? O, sirs, what could the Lord have done that He hath not done to make you holy? Hath He not lifted you up to heaven in respect of holy helps? Hath He not to this very day followed you close with holy offers, and holy entreaties, and holy counsels, and holy encouragements, and all to make you holy? And will you be loose still, and proud still, and worldly still, and malicious still, and envious still, and contentious still, and unholy still? Oh, what is this, but to provoke the Lord to put out all the lights of heaven, to drive your teachers into corners, to remove your candlesticks, and to send His everlasting Gospel, that hath stood long a tip-toe, among a people that may more highly prize it, and dearly love it, and stoutly defend it, and conscientiously practise it, than you have done to this very day? (Rev. 2:4-5; Isa. 42:25). I suppose there is nothing more evident than that the times and seasons wherein we live call aloud upon every one to look after holiness, and to labour for holiness. Never complain of the times, but cease to do evil, and labour to do well, and all will be well; get but better hearts and better lives, and you will quickly see better times (Isa. 1:16-19)."

—From Brooks's *"Crown and Glory of Christianity; or, Holiness the Only Way to Happiness."*—Brooks's *Works*, vol. 4, pp. 151-153, 187-188.—Grosart's edition. 1866.

NOTES

Faithfulness and Holiness (Packer)

CHAPTER 1: A GREAT MAN

1. Richard Hobson, *What Hath God Wrought*, 2nd ed. (London: Thynne, 1907), 327-328. Ryle had made Hobson's Church, St. Nathanael's, Windsor, his and his family's spiritual home. At his first visit to St. Nathanael's, a year into his episcopate, having helped Hobson administer Holy Communion to some four hundred people, Ryle told him: "I make much of hands, and I conclude that five out of every six of your communicants are working people. St. Nathanael's is an answer to those who say the Church of England is not suited to working people. . . . I wish to preach in this Church every six months" (cited from ibid., 145).

CHAPTER 2: A GREAT VICTORIAN

1. This appears when in 1873 Ryle writes of a certain Mrs. Bradley ("a wonderful person"), "considering she had been only ladies-maid to Mr. Bradley's sister, and he had run away with her, it would be vain to say she was a thorough lady"; and of his own three marriages: "the great thing I always desired to find was *a woman who was a real Christian, who was a real lady, and who was not a fool*" (J. C. Ryle, *J. C. Ryle: A Self-Portrait*, ed. Peter Toon [Swengel, Pa.: Reiner, 1976], 64, 73). So, too, when in 1882 his son got engaged to a woman he had not yet met, he wrote, in a letter to an unidentified addressee, "Herbert is a reasonable fellow, and I do not think he would choose a fool—or an unbeliever or a papist—or one who was not a lady" (cited from Maurice H. Fitzgerald, *A Memoir of Herbert Edward Ryle* [London: Macmillan, 1928], 50).

2. Thus, when Joseph Arch came to Suffolk to recruit for the Agricultural Labourers' Union, Ryle went no further than publicly admonishing farmers to treat others as they would wish to be treated themselves, and labourers to accept their lot, since there would always be rich and poor, as there would always be sorrow and pain (Peter Toon and Michael Smout, *John Charles Ryle, Evangelical Bishop* [Cambridge: James Clarke; and Swengel, Pa.: Reiner, 1976], 55). At the Croydon Church Congress in 1877 he said: ". . . in the matter of the Unions my sentence is that the clergy had better not interfere with them. Let them mind their own business and remember that business is to preach and live the gospel" (cited from ibid., 56). His point was that if the clergy took sides between class and class in temporal affairs, it would distract and alienate from their proper ministry. In 1895, however, speaking in the urban context of Liverpool rather than the rural context of Suffolk, he told his Diocesan Conference: " . . . the gulf between masters and men is much wider than it was in the days of our grandfathers, and the relations between employers and employees have gradually become less friendly. . . . Under these circumstances, you cannot find fault with the formation of Trade Unions . . . the working class must not be blamed if they co-operate, combine, and endeavor to protect their interests and defend their rights in every legal way. . . . We in Lancashire . . . ought to help forward all efforts to bridge the gulf between employers and employees, and to promote friendly relations between them" (J. C. Ryle, *Charges and Addresses* [Edinburgh: Banner of Truth, 1978], 293). To suggest that Ryle lacked a social conscience would be a major mistake.

CHAPTER 3: A GREAT SUFFERER

1. J. C. Ryle, *J. C. Ryle: A Self-Portrait,* ed. Peter Toon, (Swengel, Pa.: Reiner, 1975), 21.

2. Ibid., 55.

3. See J. I. Packer, *A Quest for Godliness* (Wheaton, Ill.: Crossway, 1990), 22-23. Also published as *Among God's Giants* (Eastbourne, UK: Kingsway, 1991), 24-25.

4. Ibid., 22-23.

5. The original manuscript, which passed into the hands of Ryle's son, Bishop Herbert E. Ryle, and was used by Maurice H. Fitzgerald in *A Memoir of Herbert Edward Ryle* (London: Macmillan, 1928), has not survived. M. Guthrie Clark, *John Charles Ryle* (London: Church Book Room, 1947) evidently used a copy of it, though it does not appear in his bibliography. Peter Toon published it as *J. C. Ryle: A Self-Portrait* from a copy in the library of Latimer House, Oxford.

6. Ryle, *A Self-Portrait,* 3. His children's ages in 1873 were Georgina (27), Isabella (Jessie) (22), Reginald (19), Herbert (17), Arthur (16).

7. Ibid., 53-56.

8. This began with Henri Nouwen, *The Wounded Healer* (Garden City, N.Y.: Doubleday, 1972).

9. See, for example, the sermons "Without Clouds," *The Upper Room* (Edinburgh: Banner of Truth, 1970), 255ff.; "Ruler of the Waves," *Holiness* (Welwyn, UK: Evangelical Press, 1979), 191ff.; "Happiness," *Practical Religion,* new ed. (London: Charles Murray, 1900), 230ff.

10. Ryle, *A Self-Portrait,* 59-60. Ordained before the days of theological colleges, Ryle's theological formation at this time had come from his study of the Thirty-nine Articles for the Newcastle scholarship at Eton and for his Oxford degree exam, and from reading "the books that helped me most" as a Christian: William Wilberforce's *Practical View of Christianity* (full title, *A Practical View of the Prevailing Religious System of Professed Christians in the Higher and Middle Classes in this Country, Contrasted with Real Christianity*); John Angell James's *The Christian Professor* (a book on discipleship by a Congregationalist evangelical); Thomas Scott's *Reply to Bishop Tomline* (establishing the Reformed cast of defined Anglican doctrine); John Newton's *Cardiphonia* (letters on Christian experience); and Edward Bickersteth's *The Christian Student,* which set out a curriculum for would-be evangelical clergy that included "Hebrew, Greek, the Fathers, the Reformers, dissenting and Anglican writers, Biblical criticism, historical, controversial, and pastoral theology. He provided a 100-page reading list" (W. Clyde Ervine, in ed. D. M. Lewis, *Dictionary of Evangelical Biography 1730–1860* [Oxford: Blackwell, 1995], I.92). See Ryle, *A Self-Portrait,* 40-41.

11. Ryle's rather grim sense of humor appears as he describes his Exbury experience: "The district was a very wild and dreary one. . . . Drunkenness and sin of every kind abounded. . . . My house was reputed to be haunted. . . . I had one maid servant, one boy, one dog, one cat, and one pig. The maid servant turned out a bad character and though she was thirty years of age she married the boy who was in his seventeenth year. The cat died of bleeding of the nose, the pig died of string belt. . . . The maid servant for some time received the money for paying the bills for me, but she did not pay them. . . . The yachting man [a wealthy local resident] quarrelled with me and complained to the bishop because I spoke against cricket matches late on Saturday night. Altogether my residence . . . was not a very cheerful one" (Ryle, *A Self-Portrait,* 61).

12. Ibid., 64.

13. Ibid., 64-65.

14. See note 1 of chapter 2. His first wife was the daughter of an evangelical M.P., Matilda Plumptre, whom he married in 1845, and who died in 1847. His second wife was Jessie Walker, whom he married in 1850, and who died in 1860. Henrietta Legh-Clowes, whom he married in 1861, lived till 1889.

15. Ibid., 81. Five years earlier, in 1868, he had written of Henry Venn of Huddersfield, whose wife died in 1767 leaving him with five young children, as follows: "She was in fact her husband's right hand. When she died such a load of care and anxiety was accumulated on his head that his health gave way. . . . Those who have had this cross

to carry can testify that there is no position in this world so trying to body and soul as that of a minister who is left a widower, with a young family and a large congregation. There are anxieties in such cases which no one knows but he who has gone through them; anxieties which can crush the strongest spirit and wear out the strongest constitution" (J. C. Ryle, *Christian Leaders of the Eighteenth Century* [Edinburgh: Banner of Truth, 1997], 280). One senses deep empathy here.

16. Ryle, *A Self-Portrait,* 57-58.

17. Clark, *John Charles Ryle,* 9.

CHAPTER 4: A GREAT CHANGE

1. In the *viva voce* part of the exam Ryle "came off with flying colours" and "received the public thanks of the examiners for my brilliant answers in moral philosophy and divinity" (J. C. Ryle, *J. C. Ryle: A Self-Portrait,* ed. Peter Toon [Swengel, Pa.: Reiner, 1975], 33).

2. Ibid., 35.

3. Ibid., 38-39.

4. Ibid., 39.

5. Ibid., 41-43.

6. Ibid., 44.

CHAPTER 5: A GREAT EVANGELICAL

1. J. C. Ryle, *Knots Untied,* 10th ed. (London: Thynne, 1898), 2-7.

2. Ibid., 10, 11.

3. Ibid., IV., "The Thirty-nine Articles," 62-86; J. C. Ryle, *Principles for Churchmen* (London: William Hunt, 1884), "The Church's Distinctive Principles," 1-30; etc. "It is a burning shame that the Articles are not made an essential part of the system of every school connected with the Church of England. . . . I do not say this without reason. It is a simple fact, that the beginning of any clear doctrinal views I have ever attained myself, was reading up the Articles at Eton, for the Newcastle Scholarship, and attending a lecture, at Christ Church, Oxford, on the Articles, by a college tutor. I shall always thank God for what I learned then. Before that time I really knew nothing systematically of Christianity. . . . I had a religion without order in my head. What I found good myself I commend to others. If you love young people's souls . . . teach them not only the Catechism, but also the Articles" (26-27).

4. See Ryle, *Principles for Churchmen,* II., "The Church's Comprehensiveness," III., "How Far May Churchmen Differ?" IV., "Can There Be More Unity Among Churchmen?" V., "The Importance of Dogma," 31-110.

CHAPTER 6: A GREAT PURITAN

1. J. C. Ryle, *Light from Old Times* (London: Thynne, 1902), 235.

2. Samuel Ward, William Gurnall, and Richard Baxter. The essays on Ward and Gurnall were written to introduce reprints of their writings; that on Baxter was originally a YMCA lecture delivered in 1853.

3. Ryle, *Light from Old Times,* xiv-xviii.

4. J. C. Ryle, *Holiness* (Welwyn, UK: Evangelical Press, 1979), 317.

CHAPTER 7: A GREAT AGENDA

1. Socinianism, spread by Faustus Socinus in Poland at the end of the sixteenth century, was a form of unitarian teaching that denied the divinity of Jesus and the significance of his death as a penal sacrifice for sins. It also denied original sin and the immortality of man as such.

2. J. C. Ryle, *Knots Untied,* 10th ed. (London: Thynne, 1898), 328-335.

3. Cited partly from Peter Toon and Michael Smout, *John Charles Ryle, Evangelical Bishop* (Cambridge: James Clarke; and Swengel, Pa.: Reiner, 1976), 77; and partly

from G. W. Hart, *Bishop J. C. Ryle—Man of Granite* (London: Falcon Booklets, 1963), 15. Ryle liked to quote the dictum of "good old Berridge": "God washes all our hearts on earth, and in heaven he will also wash our brains" (J. C. Ryle, *Principles for Churchmen* [London: William Hunt, 1884], 71).

4. For details, see Toon and Smout, *John Charles Ryle,* 79-80.

5. "I do not particularly like Congresses. I never expect them to do very much for the Church, or to add much to our stock of knowledge. I have attended them purely as a matter of duty. I have advised others to attend them for the same reason. . . . They help Churchmen to understand one another, and in this way they are useful" (Ryle, *Principles for Churchmen,* 78).

6. Marcus Loane, *John Charles Ryle* (London: James Clarke, 1953), 36-37. On the Act of Uniformity, see J. C. Ryle, *Light from Old Times* (London: Thynne, 1902), 385, where Ryle discusses the conformity in 1662 of the Puritan William Gurnall. "I thoroughly disapprove the Act of Uniformity, although personally I feel no difficulty about its requirements. . . . But while I protest against the Act of Uniformity as an unjust, unwise, impolitic, unstatesmanlike, and hard measure, I do not for a moment admit that no good man could possibly submit to its requirements." With regard to Wesley, Ryle's address at the Hull Church Congress of 1890 contains the following sentences on what we would call every-member ministry in the body of Christ: "I should like every parochial incumbent to make a point of teaching every communicant that he is an integral part of the Church of England, and is bound to do all that he can for its welfare—to visit, to teach, to warn, to exhort, to edify, to help, to advise, to comfort, to support, to evangelize. . . . He should educate his people to see that they must give up the lazy modern plan of leaving everything to the parson, and must be active agents instead of sleeping partners. On this point I believe John Wesley was the first man who understood the wants of this country in the last [eighteenth] century. The old Methodists beat Churchmen hollow. With them every new member was a new home missionary . . . and the first question asked . . . was 'What are you going to do?' The blind stupidity with which John Wesley was treated was a disaster to our Church" (J. C. Ryle, *Charges and Addresses* [Edinburgh: Banner of Truth, 1978], 243).

7. Ryle, *Principles for Churchmen,* 309.

8. J. C. Ryle, *Holiness,* Preface to Second Edition (Welwyn, UK: Evangelical Press, 1979), xiii.

9. J. C. Ryle, *Practical Religion,* Preface, new ed. (London: Charles Murray, 1900), vi.

CHAPTER 8: A GREAT ANGLICAN

1. J. C. Ryle, *Principles for Churchmen* (London: William Hunt, 1884), 135.

2. Ibid., 413.

3. Ibid., 418-420. Ryle was describing Richard Hobson's parish of St. Nathanael's, Windsor.

4. Ibid., 421.

5. Ibid., 357-385.

6. Ibid., 135.

7. Ibid., 136.

8. J. C. Ryle, *The Upper Room* (Edinburgh: Banner of Truth, 1970), 334.

9. Ibid., 338.

10. Ryle's argument on this is fully set out in *Principles for Churchmen,* XIV., 313-353.

11. Ibid., 304. "We never will admit that the acts and doings of any Bishops . . . are to be received as infallible. . . . We cannot forget that erring Bishops ruined the Church of England in the days of Charles the First, almost ruined it again in 1662, when they cast out the Puritans, and nearly ruined it once more . . . when they shut out the Methodists" (J. C. Ryle, *Knots Untied,* 10th ed. [London: Thynne, 1898], 13).

12. Ryle, *Principles for Churchmen,* 303. Ryle's friendliness to the local Methodists during his episcopate led to him being called "the nonconformist Bishop of Liverpool" (Eric Russell, *Not a Dead See* [Southport, UK: Eric Russell, 1996], 14).

CHAPTER 9: A GREAT BISHOP

1. Peter Toon and Michael Smout, *John Charles Ryle, Evangelical Bishop* (Cambridge: James Clarke; and Swengel, Pa.: Reiner, 1976), 57.

    A letter from Ryle to "My dear Friend" (unidentified), dated 5 March 1880, of which the owner, the Rev. Simon Manchester, has given me a facsimile copy, reveals the depth of Ryle's reluctance to move to Salisbury: "Flesh and blood were utterly against it. But *almost* every one of 16 men I consulted said, 'You ought certainly to go for the sake of Christ's cause in the Ch. of E.'—So who was I that I could withstand? I had prayed for light and signs of God's will, and this was all I got. If three men had said 'refuse,' I would have refused. Cathedral music is not *congenial* to me.

    "I go into a nest of hornets, and shall stand alone. . . .

    "I have little heart for any move except into heaven. The last 20 years have swept away nearly all I knew and loved best and I feel sadly alone [a reference apparently to the advance of ritualism].

    "But after all the time is short. I am a soldier. The Captain of my salvation seems to say, 'these are your marching orders.' I have nothing to do but to *obey.*

    "Pray for me. My heart is very heavy."

2. Ibid., 72. The dialogue reflects the way Ryle himself subsequently told the story.

3. Cited from James Jones, "Ryle for the Third Millennium," *Churchman* 114:2 (Summer 2000), 114. "Large-minded" here is evidently a code word for openness to doubts about and alternatives to historic Christian orthodoxy.

4. Richard Hobson, *What Hath God Wrought,* 2nd ed. (London: Thynne, 1907), 139. Hobson continues: "For alike by his telling Gospel tracts, his controversial books, and his convincing sermons, Dr. Ryle had long since vindicated the evangelical character of the Church in England as settled at the Reformation; and by his consistent godly life had both commended to others the religion which he himself professed, and accentuated the great Gospel truths which he had so striven to set before the whole Church of God."

5. Cited from Toon and Smout, *John Charles Ryle,* 74.

6. Ibid., 57.

7. J. C. Ryle, *Knots Untied,* Preface to Tenth Edition (London: Thynne, 1898), iii.

8. As reported in *The Guardian,* April 28, 1880.

9. They are collected in J. C. Ryle, *Charges and Addresses* (Edinburgh: Banner of Truth, 1978).

10. Ibid., 62, 64.

11. Ibid., 69.

12. Ibid., 70.

13. Ibid., 71-72.

14. Cited from Toon and Smout, *John Charles Ryle,* 86.

15. At least one of Ryle's contemporaries agreed, and put his money where his mouth was: William Groves gave ten thousand pounds for building new churches rather than to a cathedral fund because he held "it was more important to provide pastoral superintendence and spiritual instruction to those perishing multitudes than to erect a material building, however splendid, to justify the tastes and wishes of a few" (*Liverpool Mercury,* November 10, 14, 1882; cited from Toon and Smout, *John Charles Ryle,* 86).

16. "Ordinary Church discipline" meant, in the first instance, episcopal admonitions, but: "A clergyman has only got to tell his Bishop . . . that his monitions are not 'lawful and honest,' and the unfortunate Bishop is checkmated, brought to a dead standstill, and can do no more" (Ryle, *Charges and Addresses,* 134).

17. Ibid., 185. For more details on the Bell Cox case, see Toon and Smout, *John Charles Ryle,* 87-90; Ian D. Farley, *J. C. Ryle, First Bishop of Liverpool* (Carlisle, UK: Paternoster, 2000), 205-228; and Eric Russell, *That Man of Granite with the Heart of a Child* (Fearn, UK: Christian Focus, 2001), 163-168.

18. Ryle, *Charges and Addresses,* 196-197.

19. Ibid., 368.

20. J. C. Ryle, *Principles for Churchmen* (London: William Hunt, 1884), xxiv.

21. Though viewed by some as mentally aloof and offhand to the last with those whose views did not match his own, Ryle as diocesan leader was warm, relaxed, and mellow. He is on record as telling his diocesan conference after they had voted against him on some issue that he was "a big man getting on for sixteen stone and he could not help treading on people's toes" (Eric Russell, *Not a Dead See* [Southport, UK: Eric Russell, 1996], 8). Ryle's annual parties at St. Nathanael's, Windsor, held till 1899 for all the clergy he had ordained, were distinctly jolly occasions. Of them Richard Hobson wrote: "As it was my privilege to be present on these interesting occasions, I am able to testify to their value in keeping the young presbyters on evangelical lines, and in building them up in the true faith. Nothing could be more delightful than the genial, loving manner of the Bishop, or more helpful than his wise, fatherly counsel" (Hobson, *What Hath God Wrought,* 193). On his eightieth birthday the clergy presented Ryle with an illuminated address stating "warm appreciation of your Lordship's personal work, your kindly feeling with and for us in times of sorrow and joy alike" (Toon and Smout, *John Charles Ryle,* 95). On Ryle's death, Hobson wrote: "There was, as usual, the general chorus of lamentation, joined in, forsooth, even by certain portions of the religious press which had so maligned that great and good man. . . . The head and front of his offending was his able championship of thorough Protestant evangelical principles. Bold as a lion for the truth, he was yet tender, even to those who could not see anything good in him, in his work as a Bishop. . . . It was clear that towards the end of his episcopate some of those who had shown him scanty respect began to understand him. One of them, a Canon [one of Ryle's own appointees, therefore], said to me, 'Though we differ from him we have learned to love him'" (Hobson, *What Hath God Wrought,* 293-294).

22. Cited from Marcus Loane, *John Charles Ryle* (London: James Clarke, 1953), 58-59.

23. Ryle, *Charges and Addresses,* 367. On the "many difficulties," see Farley, *J. C. Ryle.*

24. It should be noted that as Toon and Smout (*John Charles Ryle*) declare in their Preface that they are offering "a much fuller life of Ryle than has previously been available," they comment that "due to soaring production costs the size of the total work was restricted to 50,000 words," indicating that they would like to have written at greater length [5].

25. Michael Smout, in his biographical postscript appended to J. C. Ryle, *J. C. Ryle: A Self-Portrait,* ed. Peter Toon (Swengel, Pa.: Reiner, 1975), 101.

CHAPTER 10: A GREAT PREACHER

1. Compare this, from Hobson: "The Bishop . . . made his mark among the working people of the city by his terse, homely style of speaking, and the practical nature of his strong, sound, commonsense utterances: indeed he might well have been styled the working man's bishop" (Richard Hobson, *What Hath God Wrought,* 2nd ed. [London: Thynne, 1907], 166).

2. J. C. Ryle, *The Upper Room* (Edinburgh: Banner of Truth, 1970), 52-53. Works by Traill, Flavel, Charnock, Baxter, and Watson have been made available in recent years by Banner of Truth publishers, and works by Baxter and Watson have been made available by Soli Deo Gloria publishers (Morgan, Pa.).

3. Ryle, *Upper Room,* 42.

4. Ibid., 54.

5. J. C. Ryle, *Expository Thoughts on the Gospel of John* (Ipswich, UK: William Hunt, 1865), I. 358-361.

6. J. C. Ryle, *J. C. Ryle: A Self-Portrait,* ed. Peter Toon (Swengel, Pa.: Reiner, 1975), 80.

7. I have seen this holograph letter (written in a steady, sprawling hand with a quill pen) by courtesy of the Rev. Arthur Benjamin Turton, who owns it.

8. J. C. Ryle, *Light from Old Times* (London: Thynne, 1902), 249-250.

CHAPTER 11: A GREAT LEGACY

1. J. C. Ryle, *J. C. Ryle: A Self-Portrait*, ed. Peter Toon (Swengel, Pa.: Reiner, 1975), 43, 47, 49.

2. Denied institution to the living of Brampford Speke, Devon, by the Bishop of Exeter for not believing in baptismal regeneration, George Cornelius Gorham secured from the Judicial Committee of the Privy Council, the highest English court of appeal, the verdict that this belief was not mandatory for Anglican clergymen. Evangelicals rejoiced, High Churchmen were disgusted, and the Episcopal Church of Scotland repudiated the decision. Holidaying in Scotland where he worshiped in the Presbyterian Church of Scotland, as being the national church, Ryle once told an Episcopalian vicar that "so long as the synodial Declaration of your Church . . . regarding the Gorham judgment is not withdrawn or cancelled" he would find "the difficulty in worshipping in the Scottish Episcopal Church insuperable" (Peter Toon and Michael Smout, *John Charles Ryle, Evangelical Bishop* [Cambridge: James Clarke; and Swengel, Pa.: Reiner, 1976], 96).

3. Ryle was a vice president of the Association from its foundation, but resigned on becoming a bishop, though his personal support continued. See Toon and Smout, *John Charles Ryle*, 67. He frequently spoke at Church Association meetings.

4. J. C. Ryle, *Coming Events and Present Duties* (Ipswich, UK: William Hunt, 1867), ix. Ryle's sentence continued: ". . . although I think it highly probable that a more complete development of anti-Christ will yet be exhibited to the world."

5. See Toon and Smout, *John Charles Ryle*, 61, 94; and J. C. Ryle, *Old Paths* (Ipswich, UK: William Hunt, 1878), I: "Inspiration"; also published in slightly expanded form as *Is All Scripture Inspired?* (London: William Hunt, 1892); *Charges and Addresses* (Edinburgh: Banner of Truth, 1978), 253-267 (a Diocesan Conference address of 1892); and *Practical Religion*, new ed. (London: Charles Murray, 1900), V: "Bible-Reading."

6. Maurice H. Fitzgerald, *Herbert Edward Ryle* (London: Macmillan, 1928), 364.

7. For evidence of the strength of Ryle's belief in providence as it affects believers, and as it had affected him personally, see pp. 23-24.

8. Herbert Ryle, cited from Fitzgerald, *Herbert Edward Ryle*, 134-135. The differences centered on higher criticism of the Pentateuch, which the son embraced and the father rejected and spoke and wrote against.

9. Ibid., 11.

10. Ryle, *A Self-Portrait*, 61.

11. Ibid., 9. A private memorandum, "The Late Bishop of Liverpool as an Eton boy," by H. E. Ryle (n.d.), a copy of which is in my possession, says that the dog measured five feet ten and a half inches from nose to tip of tail, and its shoulder was two feet seven and a half inches off the ground, so "huge" is well justified. Descended from a guard dog that distinguished itself at Agincourt in 1415, the Lyme Hall mastiff breed always needed human contact and bonded closely with affectionate owners.

12. Ryle, *A Self-Portrait*, 56.

13. When preparing to move into the house in Abercromby Square that had been bought as the Bishop's Palace, Ryle wrote: "Mine is a large and important Library of Protestant Theology and whether it will be necessary to convert the stables, for which I have no further use, into a Library, I do not know" (cited from M. Guthrie Clark, *John Charles Ryle* [London: Church Book Room, 1947], 30). (Ryle had had a gig at Helmingham and a carriage at Stradbroke, but sold the latter to finance his sons at Cambridge, and apparently never had any carriage of his own thereafter.) He willed his library to be moved to Church House for use by diocesan clergy. Both house and library were destroyed by a bomb in 1941, but a printed catalogue of the library is kept in both Liverpool's University Library and City Central Library.

14. When Ryle's degree result became known, "I believe I might have had a studentship [i.e., fellowship] at Christ Church or a fellowship at Brasenose or Balliol, at once if I had liked; but I declined every offer to be a candidate for such positions. In my foolish-

ness I thought that I had a very different line of life before me and left Oxford as soon as I could, never to return" (Ryle, *A self-Portrait,* 34).

15. J. C. Ryle, *Light from Old Times* (London: Thynne, 1902), 409.

16. J. C. Ryle, *Principles for Churchmen* (London: William Hunt, 1884), 97-98. "The Importance of Dogma," the chapter from which the quotation comes, began life as the annual CPAS sermon for 1882, and before that these paragraphs had appeared, almost word for word, in Ryle's first visitation charge at Wigan, October 20, 1881: see Ryle, *Charges and Addresses,* 52-53.

17. The following are examples: *Holiness: Its Nature, Hindrances, Difficulties, and Roots. Being a Series of Papers on the Subject; Practical Religion: Being Plain Papers on the Daily Duties, Experience, Dangers, and Privileges of Professing Christians; Old Paths: Being Plain Statements on Some of the Weightier Matters of Christianity; Knots Untied: Being Plain Statements on Disputed Points in Religion, from the Standpoint of an Evangelical Churchman;* etc.

18. Clark, *John Charles Ryle,* 22-25. The seven heads are taken from Ryle's own *Christian Leaders of the Eighteenth Century* (Edinburgh: Banner of Truth, 1997), 26-28, where Ryle describes the message of the evangelists a century before his time; but the heads focus his own message as well as theirs.

19. Ryle, *Practical Religion,* 183-185.

20. J. C. Ryle, *Holiness* (Welwyn, UK: Evangelical Press, 1979), 230-231.

21. The eleven are: George Whitefield, John Wesley, William Grimshaw, William Romaine, Daniel Rowlands, John Berridge, Henry Venn, Samuel Walker, James Hervey, Augustus Toplady, and John Fletcher.

22. Cited from J. B. Lancelot, *Francis James Chavasse* (Oxford: Blackwell, 1929), 143, 147.

23. Ryle's *Old Paths* (see note 5, above) is a presentation of "the leading truths of Christianity which are 'necessary to salvation,'" in a set of papers written over a period of twenty years, covering "the immortality of the soul, the sinfulness of human nature, the work of Christ for us as our Redeemer, the work of the Holy Ghost in us, forgiveness, justification, conversion, faith, repentance, the marks of a right heart, Christ's invitations, Christ's intercession, and the like" (Preface, v-vi).

CHAPTER 12: THE GREAT TRADITION

1. J. C. Ryle, *Old Paths* (Ipswich, UK: William Hunt, 1878), vii-viii.

2. J. C. Ryle, *Light from Old Times* (London: Thynne, 1902), 293.

NOTES

Holiness (Ryle)

INTRODUCTION

1. "There is a double justification by God: the one authoritative, the other declarative or demonstrative."—The first is St. Paul's scope, when he speaks of justification by faith without the deeds of the law. The second is St. James's scope, where he speaks of justification by works."—*T. Goodwin on Gospel Holiness. Works,* vol. vii., p. 181.

2. Those who care to go into the subject will find it fully discussed in the Commentaries of Willet, Elton, Chalmers, and Haldane, and in Owen on *Indwelling Sin,* and in the work of Stafford on the *Seventh of Romans.*

3. Old Sibbes's Sermon on "Victorious Violence" deserves the attention of all who have his works.—Vol. vii., p. 30.

CHAPTER 1: SIN

1. Hooker's "Learned Discourse of Justification."

CHAPTER 2: SANCTIFICATION

1. "There is mention in the Scripture of a twofold sanctification, and consequently of a twofold holiness. The first is common unto persons and things, consisting of the peculiar dedication, consecration, or separation of them unto the service of God, by His own appointment, whereby they become holy. Thus the priests and Levites of old, the ark, the altar, the tabernacle, and the temple, were sanctified and made holy; and indeed, in all holiness whatever, there is a peculiar dedication and separation unto God. But in the sense mentioned, this was solitary and alone. No more belonged unto it but this sacred separation, nor was there any other effect of this sanctification. But, secondly, there is another kind of sanctification and holiness, wherein this separation to God is not the first thing done or intended, but a consequent and effect thereof. This is real and internal, by the communicating of a principle of holiness unto our natures, attended with its exercise in acts and duties of holy obedience unto God. This is that which we inquire after."—*John Owen on the Holy Spirit.* Vol. iii, p. 370, Works, Goold's edition.

2. "The devil's war is better than the devil's peace. Suspect dumb holiness. When the dog is kept out of doors he howls to be let in again."—"Contraries meeting, such as fire and water, conflict one with another.—When Satan findeth a sanctified heart, he tempteth with much importunity. Where there is much of God and of Christ, there are strong injections and firebrands cast in at the windows, so that some of much faith have been tempted to doubt."—*Rutherford's Trial of Faith,* p. 403.

3. "There is no imagination wherewith man is besotted, more foolish, none so pernicious, as this,—that persons not purified, not sanctified, not made holy in their life, should afterwards be taken into that state of blessedness which consists in the enjoyment of God. Neither can such persons enjoy God, nor would God be a reward to them.—Holiness indeed is perfected in heaven: but the beginning of it is invariably confined to this world."—*Owen on Holy Spirit,* p. 575. Goold's edition.

4. "Christ in the Gospel is proposed to us as our pattern and example of holiness; and as it is a cursed imagination that this was the whole end of his life and death: namely, to exemplify and confirm the doctrine of holiness which He taught—so to neglect His being our example, in considering Him by faith to that end, and labouring after conformity to Him, is evil and pernicious. Wherefore let us be much in the contemplation of what He was, and what He did, and how in all duties and trials He carried Himself, until an image or idea of His perfect holiness is implanted in our minds, and we are made like unto Him thereby."—*Owen on the Holy Ghost*, p. 513. Goold's edition.

CHAPTER 5: THE COST

1. I should be very sorry indeed if the language I have used above about *revivals* was misunderstood. To prevent this I will offer a few remarks by way of explanation.

   For true revivals of religion no one can be more deeply thankful than I am. Wherever they may take place, and by whatever agents they may be effected, I desire to bless God for them, with all my heart. "If Christ is preached," I rejoice, whoever may be the preacher. If souls are saved, I rejoice, by whatever section of the Church the word of life has been ministered.

   But it is a melancholy fact that, in a world like this, you cannot have good without evil. I have no hesitation in saying, that one consequence of the revival movement [of 1859, and thereafter] has been the rise of a theological system which I feel obliged to call defective and mischievous in the extreme.

   The leading feature of the theological system I refer to, is this: an extravagant and disproportionate magnifying of three points in religion,—viz., instantaneous conversion—the invitation of unconverted sinners to come to Christ,—and the possession of inward joy and peace as a test of conversion. I repeat that these three grand truths (for truths they are) are so incessantly and exclusively brought forward, in some quarters, that great harm is done.

   Instantaneous conversion, no doubt, ought to be pressed on people. But surely they ought not to be led to suppose that there is no other sort of conversion, and that unless they are suddenly and powerfully converted to God, they are not converted at all.

   The duty of coming to Christ at once, "just as we are," should be pressed on all hearers. It is the very corner-stone of Gospel preaching. But surely men ought to be told to repent as well as to believe. They should be told why they are to come to Christ, and what they are to come for, and whence their need arises.

   The nearness of peace and comfort in Christ should be proclaimed to men. But surely they should be taught that the possession of strong inward joys and high frames of mind is not essential to justification, and that there may be true faith and true peace without such very triumphant feelings. Joy alone is no certain evidence of grace.

   The defects of the theological system I have in view appear to me to be these: (1) The work of the Holy Ghost in converting sinners is far too much narrowed and confined to one single way. Not all true converts are converted instantaneously, like Saul and the Philippian jailor. (2) Sinners are not sufficiently instructed about the holiness of God's law, the depth of their sinfulness, and the real guilt of sin. To be incessantly telling a sinner to "come to Christ" is of little use, unless you tell him why he needs to come, and show him fully his sins. (3) Faith is not properly explained. In some cases people are taught that mere feeling is faith. In others they are taught that if they believe that Christ died for sinners they have faith! At this rate the very devils are believers! (4) The possession of inward joy and assurance is made essential to believing. Yet assurance is certainly not of the essence of saving faith. There may be faith when there is no assurance. To insist on all believers at once "rejoicing," as soon as they believe, is most unsafe. Some, I am quite sure, will rejoice without believing, while others will believe who cannot at once rejoice. (5) Last, but not least, the sovereignty of God in saving sinners, and the absolute necessity of preventing [i.e., prevenient] grace, are far too much overlooked. Many talk as if conversions could be manufactured at man's pleasure, and as if there were no such text as this, "It is not of him that willeth, nor of him that runneth, but of God that showeth mercy" (Rom. 9:16).

   The mischief done by the theological system I refer to is, I am persuaded, very great. On the one hand, many humble-minded Christians are totally discouraged and daunted. They fancy they have no grace because they cannot reach up to the high frames and feelings which are pressed on their attention. On the other side, many graceless people are deluded into thinking they are "converted," because under the pressure of animal excitement and temporary feelings they are led to profess themselves Christians. And all this time the thoughtless and ungodly look on with contempt, and find fresh reasons for neglecting religion altogether.

The antidotes to the state of things I deplore are plain and few. (1) Let "all the counsel of God be taught" in Scriptural proportion; and let not two or three precious doctrines of the Gospel be allowed to overshadow all other truths. (2) Let repentance be taught fully as well as faith, and not thrust completely into the background. Our Lord Jesus Christ and St. Paul always taught both. (3) Let the variety of the Holy Ghost's works be honestly stated and admitted; and while instantaneous conversion is pressed on men, let it not be taught as a necessity. (4) Let those who profess to have found immediate sensible peace be plainly warned to try themselves well, and to remember that feeling is not faith, and that "patient continuance in well-doing" is the great proof that faith is true (John 8:31). (5) Let the great duty of "counting the cost" be constantly urged on all who are disposed to make a religious profession, and let them be honestly and fairly told that there is warfare as well as peace, a cross as well as a crown, in Christ's service.

I am sure that unhealthy excitement is above all things to be dreaded in religion, because it often ends in fatal, soul-ruining reaction and utter deadness. And when multitudes are suddenly brought under the power of religious impressions, unhealthy excitement is almost sure to follow.

I have not much faith in the soundness of conversions when they are said to take place in masses and wholesale. It does not seem to me in harmony with God's general dealings in this dispensation. To my eyes it appears that God's ordinary plan is to call in individuals one by one. Therefore, when I hear of large numbers being suddenly converted all at one time, I hear of it with less hope than some. The healthiest and most enduring success in mission fields is certainly not where natives have come over to Christianity in a mass. The most satisfactory and firmest work at home does not always appear to me to be the work done in revivals.

There are two passages of Scripture which I should like to have frequently and fully expounded in the present day by all who preach the Gospel, and specially by those who have anything to do with revivals. One passage is the parable of the sower. That parable is not recorded three times over without good reason and a deep meaning.—The other passage is our Lord's teaching about "counting the cost," and the words which He spoke to the "great multitudes" whom He saw following Him. It is very noteworthy that He did not on that occasion say anything to flatter these volunteers or encourage them to follow Him. No: He saw what their case needed. He told them to stand still and "count the cost" (Luke 14:25, etc). I am not sure that some modern preachers would have adopted this course of treatment.

CHAPTER 6: GROWTH

1. "True grace is progressive, of a spreading, growing nature. It is with grace as it is with light: first, there is the day-break; then it shines brighter to the full noon-day. The saints are not only compared to stars for their light, but to trees for their growth (Isa. 61:3; Hos. 14:5). A good Christian is not like Hezekiah's sun that went backwards, nor Joshua's sun that stood still, but is always advancing in holiness, and increasing with the increase of God."—*Thomas Watson, Minister of St. Stephen's Walbrook,* 1660. (*Body of Divinity*)

2. "The growth of grace is the best evidence of the truth of grace. Things that have not life will not grow. A picture will not grow. A stake in a hedge will not grow. But a plant that hath vegetative life will grow. The growing of grace shows it to be alive in the soul."—*T. Watson.* 1660.

3. "Christian, as ever you would stir up others to exalt the God of grace, look to the exercise and improvement of your own graces. When poor servants live in a family, and see the faith, and love, and wisdom, and patience, and humility of a master, shining like the stars in heaven, it draws forth their hearts to bless the Lord that ever they came into such a family.—When men's graces shine as Moses' face did, when their life, as one speaketh of Joseph's life, is a very heaven, sparkling with virtues as so many bright

stars, how much others are stirred up to glorify God, and cry, 'These are Christians indeed! These are an honour to their God, a crown to their Christ, and a credit to their Gospel! Oh, if they were all such, we would be Christians too!'"—*T. Brooks.* 1661. (*Unsearchable Riches*)

4. "The right manner of growth is to grow less in one's own eyes. 'I am a worm and no man,' (Ps. 22:6). The sight of corruption and ignorance makes a Christian grow into a dislike of himself. He doth vanish in his own eyes. Job abhorred himself in the dust (Job 42:6). This is good, to grow out of conceit with oneself."—*T. Watson.* 1660.

5. "It is a sign of not growing in grace, when we are less troubled about sin. Time was when the least sin did grieve us (as the least hair makes the eye weep), but now we can digest sin without remorse. Time was when a Christian was troubled if he neglected closet prayer; now he can omit family prayer. Time was when vain thoughts did not trouble him; now he is not troubled for loose practices. There is a sad declension in religion; and grace is so far from growing that we can hardly perceive its pulse to beat."—*T. Watson.* 1660.

6. "If now you would be rich in graces, look to your walking. It is not the knowing soul, nor the talking soul, but the close-walking soul, the obedient soul, that is rich. Others may be rich in notions, but none so rich in spiritual experience, and in all holy and heavenly graces, as close-walking Christians."—*T. Brooks.* 1661.

"It is a sign of not growing in grace, when we grow more worldly. Perhaps once we were mounted into higher orbits, we did set our hearts on things above, and speak the language of Canaan. But now our minds are taken off heaven, we dig our comforts out of those lower mines, and with Satan compass the earth. It is a sign we are going down hill apace, and our grace is in a consumption. It is observable when nature decays, and people are near dying, they grow more stooping. And truly when men's hearts grow more stooping to the earth, and they can hardly lift up themselves to an heavenly thought, if grace be not dead, yet it is ready to die."—*T. Watson.* 1660.

7. "Experience will tell every Christian that the more strictly, and closely, and constantly he walketh with God, the stronger he groweth in duty. Infused habits are advantaged by exercise. As the fire that kindled the wood for sacrifices upon the altar first came down from heaven, but then was to be kept alive by the care and labour of the priests, so the habits of spiritual grace are indeed infused from God, and must be maintained by daily influences from God, yet with a concurrence also of our own labours, in waiting upon God, and exercising ourselves with godliness; and the more a Christian doth so exercise himself, the more strong he shall grow."—*Collinges on Providence.* 1678.

8. "Let them be thy choicest companions, that have made Christ their chiefest companion. Do not so much eye the outsides of men as their inside: look most to their internal worth. Many persons have their eyes upon the external garb of a professor. But give me a Christian that minds the internal worth of persons, that makes such as are most filled with the fulness of God his choicest and chiefest companions."—*T. Brooks.* 1661.

9. "Christians may be growing when they think they do not grow. 'There is that maketh himself poor, yet he is rich.' (Prov. 13:7). The sight that Christians have of their defects in grace, and their thirst after greater measures of grace, makes them think they do not grow. He who covets a great estate, because he hath not so much as he desires, thinks himself poor."—*T. Watson.* 1660.

"Souls may be rich in grace, and yet not know it, not perceive it. The child is heir to a crown or a great estate, but knows it not. Moses' face did shine, and others saw it, but he perceived it not. So many a precious soul is rich in grace, and others see it, and know it, and bless God for it, and yet the poor soul perceives it not.—Sometimes this arises from the soul's strong desires of spiritual riches. The strength of the soul's desires after spiritual riches doth often take away the very sense of growing spiritually rich. Many covetous men's desires are so strongly carried forth after earthly riches, that though they do grow rich, yet they cannot perceive it, they cannot believe it. It is just so with many a precious Christian: his desires after spiritual riches are so strong, that they take away the very sense of his growing rich in spirituals. Many Christians have much worth within them, but they see it not. It was a good man that said, 'The Lord was in this place and I knew it not.'—Again, this ariseth sometimes from men neglecting to cast up their accounts. Many men thrive and grow rich, and yet, by neglecting to cast up their accounts, they cannot tell whether they go forward or backward. It is so with many precious souls. Again, this ariseth sometimes from the soul's too frequent casting up of its accounts. If a man should cast up his accounts once a week, or once a month, he may not be able to discern that he doth grow rich, and yet he may grow rich. But let him compare one year with another, and he shall clearly see that he doth grow rich.—Again, this sometimes ariseth from the soul's mistakes in casting up its accounts. The soul many times mistakes: it is in a hurry, and then it puts down ten for a hundred, and a hundred for a thousand. Look, as hypocrites put down their counters for gold, their pence for pounds, and always prize themselves above the market, so sincere souls do often put down their pounds for pence, their thousands for hundreds, and still prize themselves below the market."—*Thomas Brooks. 1661. (Unsearchable Riches)*

Chapter 7: "Assurance"

1. "Full assurance that Christ hath delivered Paul from condemnation, yea, so full and real as produceth thanksgiving and triumphing in Christ, may and doth consist with complaints and outcries of a wretched condition for the indwelling of the body of sin."—*Rutherford's Triumph of Faith.* 1645.

2. "We do not vindicate every vain pretender to 'the witness of the spirit'; we are aware that there are those in whose professions of religion we can see nothing but their forwardness and confidence to recommend them. But let us not reject any doctrine of revelation through an over-anxious fear of consequences."—*Robinson's Christian System.* 1795.

    "True assurance is built upon a Scripture basis: presumption hath no Scripture to show for its warrant; it is like a will without seal and witnesses, which is null and void in law. Presumption wants both the witness of the Word and the seal of the Spirit. Assurance always keeps the heart in a lowly posture; but presumption is bred of pride. Feathers fly up, but gold descends; he who hath this golden assurance, his heart descends in humility."—*Watson's Body of Divinity.* 1650.

    "Presumption is joined with looseness of life; persuasion with a tender conscience; *that* dares sin because it is sure, *this* dares not for fear of losing assurance. Persuasion will not sin, because it cost her Saviour so dear; presumption will sin, because grace doth abound. Humility is the way to heaven. They that are proudly secure of their going to heaven do not so often come thither as they that are afraid of going to hell."—*Adams on Second Epistle of Peter.* 1633.

3. "They are quite mistaken that think faith and humility are inconsistent; they not only agree well together, but they cannot be parted."—*Traill.*

4. "To be assured of our salvation," Augustine saith, "is no arrogant stoutness; it is our faith. It is no pride; it is devotion. It is no presumption; it is God's promise."—*Bishop Jewell's Defence of the Apology.* 1570.

    "If the ground of our assurance rested in and on ourselves, it might justly be called presumption; but the Lord and the power of His might being the ground thereof, they either know not what is the might of His power, or else too lightly esteem it, who account assured confidence thereon presumption."—*Gouge's Whole Armour of God.* 1647.

    "Upon what ground is this certainty built? Surely not upon anything that is in us. Our assurance of perseverance is grounded wholly upon God. If we look upon ourselves, we see cause of fear and doubting; but if we look up to God, we shall find cause enough for assurance."—*Hildersam on John 4.* 1632.

    "Our hope is not hung upon such an untwisted thread as, 'I imagine so,' or 'It is likely'; but the cable, the strong rope of our fastened anchor, is the oath and promise of Him who is eternal verity. Our salvation is fastened with God's own hand, and Christ's own strength, to the strong state of God's unchangeable nature."—*Rutherford's Letters.* 1637.

5. "Never did a believer in Jesus Christ die or drown in his voyage to heaven. They will all be found safe and sound with the Lamb on Mount Zion. Christ loseth none of them; yea, nothing of them (John 6:39). Not a bone of a believer is to be seen in

the field of battle. They are all more than conquerors through Him that loved them" (Rom. 8:37).—*Traill.*

6. The reader who would like to hear more about this point is referred to "Special Note on Chapter 7," at the end of this paper [see pages 227-237, above], in which he will find extracts from several well-known English Divines, supporting the view here maintained. The extracts are too long for insertion in this page.

7. "He that believeth on Jesus shall never be confounded. Never was any; neither shall you, if you believe. It was a great word of faith spoken by a dying man, who had been converted in a singular way, betwixt his condemnation and execution: his last words were these, spoken with a mighty shout: 'Never man perished with his face towards Christ Jesus.'"—*Traill.*

8. "The greatest thing that we can desire, next to the glory of God, is our own salvation; and the sweetest thing we can desire is the assurance of our salvation. In this life we cannot get higher than to be assured of that which in the next life is to be enjoyed. All saints shall enjoy a heaven when they leave this earth; some saints enjoy a heaven while they are here on earth."—*Joseph Caryl. 1633.*

9. "It was a saying of Bishop Latimer to Ridley, 'When I live in a settled and steadfast assurance about the state of my soul, methinks then I am as bold as a lion. I can laugh at all trouble: no affliction daunts me. But when I am eclipsed in my comforts, I am of so fearful a spirit that I could run into a very mouse-hole.'"—*Quoted by Christopher Love. 1653.*

"Assurance will assist us in all duties: it will arm us against all temptations; it will answer all objections; it will sustain us in all conditions into which the saddest of times can bring us. 'If God be for us, who can be against us?'"—*Bishop Reynolds on Hosea xiv. 1642.*

"We cannot come amiss to him that hath assurance. God is his. Hath he lost a friend?—his father lives. Hath he lost an only child?—God hath given him His only Son. Hath he scarcity of bread?—God hath given him the finest of the wheat, the bread of life. Are his comforts gone?—he hath a Comforter. Doth he meet with storms?—he knows where to put in for harbour. God is his Portion, and heaven is his haven."—*Thomas Watson. 1662.*

10. These were John Bradford's words in prison, shortly before his execution: "I have no request to make. If Queen Mary gives me my life, I will thank her; if she will banish me, I will thank her; if she will burn me, I will thank her; if she will condemn me to perpetual imprisonment, I will thank her."

This was Rutherford's experience when banished to Aberdeen: "How blind are my adversaries, who sent me to a banqueting house, and not to a prison or a place of exile." "My prison is a palace to me, and Christ's banqueting house."—*Letters.*

11. These were the last words of Hugh Mackail on the scaffold, at Edinburgh, 1666: "Now I begin my intercourse with God, which shall never be broken off. Farewell, father and mother, friends and relations; farewell, the world and all its delights; farewell, meat and drinks; farewell, sun, moon and stars. Welcome, God and Father; welcome, sweet Lord Jesus, the Mediator of the new covenant; welcome, blessed Spirit of grace, and God of all consolation; welcome, glory; welcome, eternal life; welcome, death. O Lord, into Thy hands I commit my spirit; for Thou hast redeemed my soul, O Lord God of truth!"

12. These were Rutherford's words on his death-bed: "O that all my brethren did know what a Master I have served, and what peace I have this day! I shall sleep in Christ, and when I awake I shall be satisfied with His likeness." 1661.

These were Baxter's words on his death-bed: "I bless God I have a well-grounded assurance of my eternal happiness, and great peace and comfort within." Towards the close he was asked how he did. The answer was, "Almost well." 1691.

13. "The least degree of faith takes away the sting of death, because it takes away guilt; but the full assurance of faith breaks the very teeth and jaws of death, by taking away the fear and dread of it."—*Fairclough's Sermon in the Morning Exercises. 1660.*

14. "Assurance would make us active and lively in God's service: it would excite prayer, quicken obedience. Faith would make us walk, but assurance would make us run—we

should think we could never do enough for God. Assurance would be as wings to the bird, as weights to the clock, to set all the wheels of obedience a-running."—*Thomas Watson.*

"Assurance will make a man fervent, constant, and abundant in the work of the Lord. When the assured Christian hath done one work, he is calling out for another.— What is next, Lord, says the assured soul, what is next? An assured Christian will put his hand to any work, he will put his neck in any yoke for Christ—he never thinks he hath done enough, he always thinks he had done too little; and when he hath done all he can, he sits down, saying, I am an unprofitable servant."—*Thomas Brooks.*

15. "The true assurance of salvation which the Spirit of God hath wrought in any heart hath that force to restrain a man from looseness of life, and to knit his heart in love and obedience to God, as nothing else hath in all the world. It is certainly either the want of faith and assurance of God's love, or a false and carnal assurance of it, that is the true cause of all the licentiousness that reigns in the world."—*Hildersam on 51st Psalm.*

"None walk so evenly with God, as they who are assured of the love of God. Faith is the mother of obedience, and sureness of trust makes way for strictness of life. When men are loose from Christ, they are loose in point of duty, and their floating belief is soon discovered in their inconstancy and unevenness of walking. We do not, with alacrity, engage in that of the success of which we are doubtful; and, therefore, when we know not whether God will accept us or not, when we are off and on in point of trust, we are just so in the course of our lives, and serve God by fits and starts. It is the slander of the world to think assurance an idle doctrine."—*Manton's Exposition of James.* 1660.

"Who is more obliged, or who feels the obligation to observance more cogently— the son who knows his near relation, and knows his father loves him, or the servant that hath great reason to doubt it? Fear is a weak and impotent principle, in comparison of love. Terrors may awaken: love enlivens. Terrors may 'almost persuade': love over-persuades. Sure am I that a believer's knowledge that his Beloved is his, and he is his Beloved's (Song 6:3), is found by experience to lay the most strong and cogent obligations upon him to loyalty and faithfulness to the Lord Jesus. For as to him that believes Christ is precious (1 Pet. 2:7), so to him that knows he believes Christ is so much the more precious, even the 'chiefest of ten thousand'" (Song 5:10).—*Fairclough's Sermon in Morning Exercises.* 1660.

"Is it necessary that men should be kept in continual dread of damnation, in order to render them circumspect and ensure their attention to duty? Will not the well-grounded expectation of heaven prove far more efficacious? Love is the noblest and strongest principle of obedience; nor can it be but that a sense of God's love to us will increase our desire to please Him."—*Robinson's Christian System.* 1795.

16. "That which breeds so much perplexity is, that we would invert God's order. 'If I knew,' say some, 'that the promise belonged to me, and Christ was a Saviour to me, I could believe': that is to say, I would first see and then believe. But the true method is just the contrary: 'I had fainted,' says David, 'unless I had believed to see the goodness of the Lord.' He believed it first, and saw it afterwards."—*Archbishop Leighton.*

"It is a weak and ignorant, but common thought of Christians, that they ought not to look for heaven, nor trust Christ for eternal glory, till they be well advanced in holiness and meetness for it. But as the first sanctification of our natures flows from our *faith and trust* in Christ for acceptance, so our further sanctification and meetness for glory flows from the renewed and repeated exercise of *faith in Him.*"—*Traill.*

17. The Westminster Confession of Faith gives an admirable account of justification: "Those whom God effectually calleth, He also freely justifieth—not by infusing righteousness into them, but by pardoning their sins, and by accounting and accepting their persons as righteous; not for anything wrought in them or done by them, but for Christ's sake alone; not by imputing faith itself, the act of believing, or any other evangelical obedience, to them, as their righteousness; but by imputing the obedience and righteousness of Christ unto them, they receiving and resting on Him and His righteousness by faith."

18. "Whose fault is it that thy interest in Christ is not put out of question? Were Christians more in self-examination, more close in walking with God, and if they had more

near communion with God and were more in acting of faith, this shameful darkness and doubting would quickly vanish."—*Traill*.

"A lazy Christian shall always want four things: viz., comfort, content, confidence, and assurance. God hath made a separation between joy and idleness, between assurance and laziness; and, therefore, it is impossible for thee to bring these together that God hath put so far asunder."—*Thomas Brooks*.

"Are you in depths and doubts, staggering and uncertain, not knowing what is your condition, nor whether you have any interest in the forgiveness that is of God? Are you tossed up and down between hopes and fears, and want peace, consolation, and establishment? Why lie you upon your faces? Get up: watch, pray, fast, meditate, offer violence to your lusts and corruptions; fear not, startle not at their crying to be spared; press unto the throne of grace by prayer, supplications, importunities, restless requests—this is the way to take the kingdom of God. These things are not peace, are not assurance; but they are part of the means God hath appointed for the attainment of them."—*Owen on the 130th Psalm*.

19. "Would'st thou have thy hope strong? Then keep the conscience pure: thou canst not defile one without weakening the other. The godly person that is loose and careless in his holy walking will soon find his hope languishing. All sin disposeth the soul that tampers with it to trembling fears and shakings of heart."—*Gurnall*.

"One great and too common cause of distress is the secret maintaining some known sin: it puts out the eye of the soul, or dimmeth it and stupefies it, that it can neither see nor feel its own condition; but especially it provoketh God to withdraw Himself, His comforts, and the assistance of His Spirit."—*Baxter's Saints' Rest*.

"The stars which have least circuit are nearest the pole; and men whose earths are least entangled with the world are always nearest to God and to the assurance of His favour. Worldly Christians, remember this. You and the world must part, or else assurance and your souls will never meet."—*Thomas Brooks*.

20. "They are doubly miserable that have neither heaven nor earth, temporals nor eternals, made sure to them in changing times."—*Thomas Brooks*.

21. "None have assurance at all times. As in a walk that is shaded with trees and chequered with light and shadow, some tracks and paths in it are dark and others are sunshine. Such is usually the life of the most assured Christian."—*Bishop Hopkins*.

"It is very suspicious, that that person is a hypocrite that is always in the same frame, let him pretend it to be never so good."—*Traill*.

General Index

Scripture Index